THE ART OF STEALING TIME

LOUIS ANDRIESSEN
THE ART OF
STEALING TIME

Edited by
Mirjam Zegers

Translated by
Clare Yates

MUSIC
2002

Published by Arc Music
(an imprint of Arc Publications)
Nanholme Mill, Shaw Wood Road
Todmorden, Lancs OL14 6DA, UK

Design by Tony Ward
Printed at Antony Rowe Ltd
Eastbourne, East Sussex, UK

ISBN 1 900072 88 2

ACKNOWLEDGEMENTS

The publishers wish to thank:

Em. Querido's Uitgeverij BV, Amsterdam for granting permission
to publish Louis Andriessen's *Gestolen tijd: alle verhalen* in an
English edition, and for all the help that they have given Arc
Publications with this English edition;
Louis Andriessen for his enthusiasm for, and help with, this
project since its inception;
Mirjam Zegers for her unstinting work on every aspect of the
English edition, not least her scrupulous checking of the Eng-
lish text;
Clare Yates for her translation, without which there would be
no English edition;
MuziekGroep Nederland for their financial and editorial help
with the preparation of the English edition;
all those (as credited in the text) who have supplied illustrative
material and given permission for its inclusion;
Douglas Jarman for his checking of, and advice on, the English
text, and for other invaluable help;
Boosey & Hawkes music publishers.

The editor, Mirjam Zegers, wishes to thank Bas Andriessen,
Caecilla Andriessen, Christine Elkhuizen, Ike Huber, Ben van
Nugteren, Mark van Platen, Dick Staats, Saskia Törnqvist,
Maja Trochimczyk and Suzan Zegers for their technical, practi-
cal, moral, aesthetic, linguistic and musicological support during
the preparation of the original Dutch edition.

Contents

Foreword

In this book, Louis Andriessen speaks about his own work and everything which is directly, indirectly, and not at all, relevant to it. In the first half of the book he talks about his childhood memories, his likes and dislikes in literature and film, colleagues he admires and ensembles he has set up. The second half comprises interviews and lectures on his own work: from *De Staat* [*The Republic*], the piece with which he overturned the musical landscape in the Netherlands twenty-five years ago, up to and including his most recent opera which he created with Peter Greenaway, *Writing to Vermeer*.

The idea of keeping a record of his talks about his own work originated in Nijmegen, when Louis Andriessen held a professorial chair there in 1997. Because he talks informally rather than reading prepared texts, the only way of achieving this was to make recordings and then transcribe them. It goes without saying that, in making these transcriptions, a lot has been rearranged to do justice to the content while retaining, at least to some extent, their original form.

Mirjam Zegers

Translator's Preface

Translating *The Art of Stealing Time* has been an informative and rewarding experience. Louis Andriessen has a unique personal style and his wide-ranging and sometimes oblique references have posed a number of interesting challenges.

I would like to thank Diana Kloss, Annie Woodward, Christopher Yates and David Young for their help, and many other friends for providing vital snippets of information. In particular, I would like to thank Angela Jarman for her support, patience and enthusiasm.

Clare Yates
London, August 2002

Introduction

Music, for Andriessen is not so abstract that it can be distanced from the time and place of its creation. On the contrary. He links his own music very emphatically to the world around him. In it we hear references to music from all social strata and musical genres. Although he works at the very top of his house on the Keizersgracht in Amsterdam, his work is not in the least 'garret' music.

The concept of 'timeless' music pre-supposes an eternal value and a quality independent of time and social condition. For Andriessen, this is a 'bourgeois' if not a romantic thought. He argues that if timeless music does not exist, then 'datedness' in music can no longer be regarded a disadvantage, but rather an inevitable characteristic.

The texts which have been collected here are very much products of their time.

After a short biographical chapter, there follows a selection of older, mostly previously published, texts written by Andriessen on diverse subjects. They have been lifted from their own time, in some cases with a certain degree of reluctance on the part of the author. In them, Andriessen touches on subjects which have remained important to him throughout his life. To create a polished version of them, adapted to the present day, was not only not feasible but fundamentally impossible. Time cannot be recovered and one thing is certain: the texts would nevertheless remain products of their time.

The second half of the book consists of spoken material. As lecturer in composition at the Royal Conservatoire in The Hague, Andriessen regularly speaks about his work. In addition, in the eighties and nineties he was a guest at the universities of Yale and Princeton (amongst others) and at numerous festivals and composition courses.

An academic approach is foreign to him. As a holder of a professorial chair in Nijmegen, he declined to deliver his inaugural speech. He is a peripatetic: the first thing he does when he is going to speak is to go for a little walk. The chair which has been placed ready for him is turned round or pushed aside, the microphone switched off and he starts his little chat, apparently nonchalant.

The style of delivery he has adopted he once called a causerie, defined

by the Van Dale Dutch dictionary (1984) as "a short treatment of a scientific or arts subject etc., written or spoken in pleasant, amusing form, for a
lay audience". The actual meaning is 'chit-chat', which has doubtless contributed to the fact that, in general, the 'causeur' is not rated very highly as
far as his knowledge of affairs is concerned. He can speak well, but the
actual subject is immaterial.

There is a difference, however, with texts collected here. Andriessen's
erudition, an old-fashioned word here used somewhat hesitantly, ranges
from the music, painting, collages, books and films he likes, to the use of
microphones by jazz singers, the history of Amsterdam and the best way to
consume Italian 'Alchermes' liqueur. He has, of course, a very specific
knowledge of his own work.

Matters which he chooses to talk about sometimes appear to be very
far removed from the subject in hand. By means of anecdotes, sketches of
what went before, elaborations on details and sometimes serious reflections, Andriessen describes his sources, his way of working and his aesthetic. In contrast to the many obscure intellectual explanations which
have surrounded art in previous decades, his manner of speaking is provocative, if not polemic. He can trace the pre-history of a piece of his back
to the moment when as a child, his father counted his toes (and they never
added up to ten). With all this, he creates a pleasant illusion of simplicity.
Life doesn't seem nearly so complicated as you thought. But his music also
looks deceptively simple on paper. The Russians have a word for this delicate simplification: *uproshcheniye*. Removing one letter removes every subtlety: *oproshcheniye* just means simplification.[1]

With all his fleet-footedness, Andriessen avoids disclosing his recipes
and elegantly draws a veil over the fact he doesn't fully understand the
underlying mystery (ultimately the only thing of importance). One thing
he does know: if the truth is to be found anywhere, it will not necessarily be
hiding in the depths. It often lurks just below the surface.

'COMPONERE'

After he had been composing for years, Andriessen looked up the word
'componere' in his Latin dictionary. In a draft letter to Stravinsky written
in 1968 which he never completed, he wrote out its various meanings. He
underlined the words he judged to be especially appropriate (these are
indicated by italics):[2]

---

[1] Richard Taruskin introduced these words into the Stravinsky literature. In the article 'Oe-
muziek' (*Vrij Nederland*, 17 May 1997) Elmer Schönberger translated it into Dutch. He concludes that "the simplicity of *uproshcheniye* is, to refinement and complexity, what the simple
solution after the equals sign is to the complicated mathematical sum before the equals sign".
[2] From Dr. H. H. Mullinckrodt, *Latin-Dutch Dictionary*. The numbering follows the manuscript,
which more or less agrees with the dictionary.

1. *to pool [everything]*
2. *to draw together*
3. *to determine*
4. to agree on
5. *to sort things out*
6. to set down
8. *to add*
9. *to adopt an attitude*
10. to set in folds
11. *to dissemble*
12 to lay one's head down
13. to settle down
14. to keep
15. *to put in touch with*
16. *to confront*

With these definitions in mind, the present book can be viewed as an extension of Andriessen's compositional œuvre. Old and new ideas are juxtaposed and preserved. He brings us into contact with his friends in music, literature and the visual arts and adopts an attitude that challenges past and prevailing views.

Stolen time

Just as the painter appropriates a colour, so the composer steals time at will. In exchange for the theft, time takes a form, stolen time becomes fixed time. Since, at the beginning of the twentieth century, the futurists declared all kinds of noise to be music, and Cage, in his piece *4'33"*[3] composed silence, the passing of time is the only thing which all music has in common. Timeless music does not exist.

Mostly, composing is a time-consuming activity. Compositions which have taken less time to compose than the duration of the works themselves, are very rare and strongly depend on repetitions. A Scottish composer, John Maxwell Geddes, wrote a work which lasts for one hundred years, as long as someone somewhere in the world knocks two stones together on the appointed days. When Louis Andriessen and Greetje Bijma appear together, they have just as much time to think up the music as the duration of their improvisation. They don't only surprise the public, but themselves too. Andriessen still improvises a lot at the piano when he composes, but some minutes in his work have taken months to compose.

[3] The piece *4'33"* for piano by John Cage consists of 4 minutes and 33 seconds of silence.

Andriessen often mentions time in the titles of his works. With *Contra Tempus*, he looks at the past, in *Anachronie*, he stacks past, present and future on top of one another. *De Tijd* [*Time*] is a moment of eternity in sound (so timeless music does exist). *Facing Death* brings a metaphysical haste to the music, while in *De Snelheid* [*Velocity*] slowness overcomes speed.

'Stolen time' (the title of the book in its original Dutch edition) is the literal translation of 'tempo rubato'. Andriessen could have thought up this title himself, had it not been 'stolen' from the book *Stolen Time*, Richard Hudson's discussion of the history of rubato.[4]

The indication 'rubato' in a score indicates that the music should not be played rigorously within a bar, but with a certain freedom. The Italian 'rubare' means 'to steal / to rob', but also 'to withdraw (time) / to be deceptive'. Tempo rubato is a very elastic concept.

In Baroque music, rubato means that one semiquaver lasts slightly longer than the others. If a musician holds one note slightly longer, then he gives back the time this takes by making the remaining notes of the beat correspondingly shorter. So the theft is immediately cancelled out (and perpetrated afresh in the next beat). The bass line continues, the pulse is not interrupted, the musical lapse of time is objectified.

In Romanticism, rubato is expanded to such an extent that time is no longer 'made good'. Timing and tempo are extremely subjective, depending on the performing musicians.

In Baroque music, musical time was merely *lent*; in the nineteenth century time was actually *stolen*.

In 1981, when he was thinking about the concept of rubato, everything fell into place for Andriessen. During an interview he shouted:

> I now understand why I am so against Romantic music – because it is one continual, composed- out rubato!
>   What is nice about Classicism is that the concept is very rigid but you perform *à l'improviste*. This dialectic is interesting. What is happening in Romanticism? Formalisation of these things. That is boring. A Mahler symphony is about composed rubato."[5]

At various points, Mahler describes tempo changes and rests very precisely – in words and even by metronome marks – but then builds in flexibility by adding the words 'Zeit lassen' ['allow time'], an indication which applies to everyone in the orchestra, including the basses. Chopin composed rubati without really tampering with the underlying pulse of the chosen bar. Andriessen recognises these composed rubati as elements of Classicism.[6] What disturbs him about Mahler is that he does not keep to

[4] Richard Hudson, *Stolen Time, The History of Tempo Rubato* (Oxford: OUP, Clarendon Paperbacks, 1997, first impression 1994).
[5] Renske Koning and Kasper Jansen, interview with Ton Koopman and Louis Andriessen, special edition of NRC *Handelsblad* on the occasion of the Holland Festival, 19 May 1981.
[6] See the lecture on *The Last Day*, pp. 267 ff.

the limitations imposed on him by musical time. Mahler steals *real* time.

Andriessen loves to steal from other composers but time, *real* time, he never steals. The Art of Stealing Time in his œuvre is in this book.

DIALECTIC AND UNISON

It is not only the 'described' dialectic which Andriessen finds interesting, but every dialectic. For preference, he gives compliments in a combination of extremes: warmth and distance, formalism and vulgarity, or simply fast and slow. He likes to place opposites next to each other, or preferably on top of each other, in order to give his thoughts on a subject room.

And so, in the film and the first opera which he created with Peter Greenaway, he didn't choose to write accessible or inaccessible music, but made accessibility the subject. In so doing his playground is, at the same time, marked out and opened up. For large works, he makes a formal diagram which he will subsequently undermine when he thinks it necessary. By placing concepts opposite each other, he seeks to 'problematicise' them and let them work on each other. He finds good questions far more interesting than good answers.

To the philosopher Karin Melis, he wrote: "It is not my job to list all the points; *you* have to do that. I have to make beautiful pieces with splendid, crackling, electrifying antitheses."[7]

The ultimate example of a convergence of extremes emerges from his Catholic childhood in Utrecht, where he came to know someone who was both Man and God, and as such was celebrated in unison chant.

By the end of the sixties / beginning of the seventies Andriessen had a thorough grasp of Marxist philosophy, springing from the dialectic of Hegel. The revolution was announced in unison militant songs.

Andriessen's great interest in unison can perhaps be viewed as the counterpart to dialectic itself. Even this counterpart does not remain untouched. With evident enjoyment, he and Elmer Schönberger wrote about 'The Utopian Unison' in *The Apollonian Clockwork*, their book on Stravinsky.[8]

Andriessen is especially interested in the many ways in which a failed unison can be exploited, such as when one orchestra sits on the heels of the other at the end of *De Staat* [*The Republic*], or the children in the opera about Vermeer sing wrong notes full of conviction (because they know that they are the right ones).

---

[7] See Part 2, 'Romantic Irony', p. 73.
[8] Louis Andriessen and Elmer Schönberger, *Het apollinisch uurwerk* [*The Apollonian clockwork*](Amsterdam: De Bezige Bij, 1983).

Irony

In his text on the setting up of De Volharding,[9] Andriessen describes the group's repertoire from its inception. The reason he found Stravinsky's *Tango* so appropriate for De Volharding is a good example of his dialectical way of thinking: it is "a *critique* of the prevailing fashion for South American tangos in the forties but at the same time a part of it". For Andriessen it was about "this critical attitude which springs from involvement with what you criticise".

What he understands by irony has more to do with this form of involvement than with the freedom to say what you actually mean. Andriessen appreciated much in the ideas of the early Romantics, which infused the word 'irony' with new life. For them, irony was not a figure of speech but a philosophy of life which gave expression to their deeply melancholic understanding of the divisions in the world and the finite nature of life. Romantic humour emanates from this tragic outlook and is in essence very serious.

The Romantics were attacked by Hegel in particular because of their irony which he found too uncommitted. And even today, irony is attacked from various quarters as an empty shell, from the protection of which one can shirk all responsibility. But irony has been in disrepute since Socrates. He was condemned to death for alleged unbelief and his moral corruption of youth through his unsettling questions. That his lifestyle was no frivolous game he confirmed by passively accepting the judgment against him, although he could have easily got away with it.

Shortly after Socrates lived Theophrastus, who succeeded Aristotle as head of the Peripatetic School. He described the εἰρωνικός ['ironician'] in his *Character Sketches*. This 'ironician' is less complex than Socrates, the Romantics and Andriessen. For Theophrastus this ironician was just a dissembler.

'Componere': [...] 9. *adopt an attitude*; 10. to set in folds; 11. *to dissemble* [...]

It is remarkable that irony and composition, two things close to Andriessen's heart, therefore appear to have been related to each other for centuries, albeit in a much concealed and superficial manner. And outside his music too, he manages to sow confusion and to harvest order.

Overview

The texts collected here are organised into five parts, each of which begins with a short introduction. The sources of the texts are given at the

[9] See Part 4, p. 128.

head of each one.

The 'Biographical notes' begin with a walk through Utrecht, the town of Andriessen's birth. The period from 1950-1970 is in the form of a scrapbook, in which the composer gives a commentary on photographs in his personal archive.

The 'Aesthetic and Chinese observations' begin with Andriessen's first article for the periodical *De Gids*, in 1966, on the double meanings in quotation compositions. The final article in this part was written in 1998 and consists of a section of a letter on romantic irony. The fact that this closes the circle implies more unity than there is.

The titles of the other parts, 'Composers', 'Ensembles and commitment' and 'Own work' speak for themselves.

PART 1

BIOGRAPHICAL NOTES

Part I
Biographical notes

The walk through Utrecht actually describes two walks in 1998. The first was undertaken especially for this book by Louis Andriessen and Mirjam Zegers. The second, which set off in the opposite direction, was in the company of Han Reiziger, at the time the presenter of the TV programme Reiziger in muziek. *He was also programmer for the Netherlands Music Days and had chosen Utrecht as the theme. The recordings of these walks were broadcast by the NPS on Radio 4 as part of the Netherlands Music Days in the interval of a live broadcast. The recordings about the composer's photographs were made at his house.*

Louis Andriessen has lived on the Keizersgracht in Amsterdam for more than thirty-five years. Because he always likes to find the shortest way, he now knows all the short cuts and alleys and especially the lay-out of the different districts within the idiosyncratic circular form of the centre.

His attempts to fathom the hidden order of the city have been rewarded on several occasions with the suggestion of a still more hidden order. Thus, a stolen passport was immediately retrieved by a friend who found it in the street and the photograph below also found its way back

Collection Louis Andriessen. Photo: Rena Sholtens

to him. To the casual passer-by who took it, it was just a photograph of an anonymous rower. But the photographer turned out to be a friend of a friend of Andriessen's, who gave him the photo.

Andriessen: "The photo is a true record of the fact that, for years, I rowed every day in a rowing boat through the canals and across the Amstel. Later, it became a boat with an outboard motor. The advantage of this is that you can go further. That little boat was stolen and then returned – without the motor, it's true. So I put a note on the boat facing the canal: 'Thanks for returning it.'"

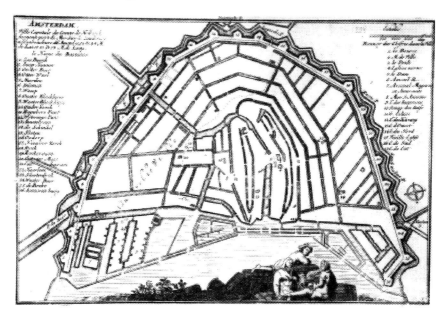

Map of Amsterdam at the end of the seventeenth century.
From the collection in the Gemeentearchief [Municipal Archives], Amsterdam

When he was fifty-nine, he realised that the map in the form of a circle matched the description of the sunken city Atlantis, the ideal city, in one of Plato's dialogues. The striking similarity was described in the magazine *Raster* by Boudewijn Bakker,[10] who speculated on the influence of Classical ideas on the master builders and governors of Amsterdam in the seventeenth century. An important source at that time was Plato's *Critias*, in which this student of Socrates describes Atlantis as a round city with a diameter of nearly two kilometres. A citadel on an island was surrounded by three concentric canals and two ring-shaped islands divided by con-

---

[10] Boudewijn Bakker, 'Het geometrisch ideaal en de Amsterdamse grachtengordel' ['The geometric ideal and Amsterdam's ring of canals'], *Raster* no. 81 (1998), pp. 15-29.

necting canals.

Whether the Amsterdammers consciously referred back to Atlantis or whether any similarities were coincidental, Andriessen's beloved city 'is about' another city, just as all music that in his view matters is about other music.

One of his favourite authors, Paul Auster, once let one of his characters (also called Paul Auster) get lost in Amsterdam.[11] In the circles, he discerned a less flattering model:

> For three days it rained, and for three days he walked around in circles. (…)
> It occurred to him that perhaps he was wandering in the circles of hell, that the city had been designed as a model of the underworld, based on some Classical representation of that place.

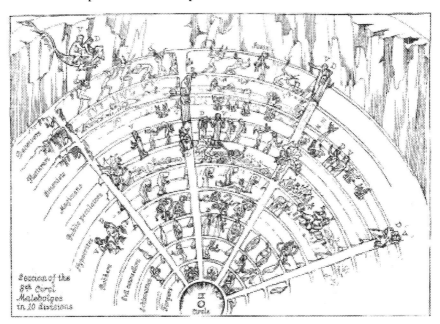

Map of hell, as described by Dante in *The Divine Comedy*.
Illustration: Phoebe Anna Traquair

To Andriessen, parts of Amsterdam are also references to another place close to him, both in time and distance: Utrecht, with tree-lined canals and beautiful façades. In both cities you find a stillness which is emphasised by bells and carillons. For the first ten years of his life, Andriessen lived in Utrecht, in the Herenstraat.

Utrecht is 'home' – the rich, Catholic tradition, the *esprit* that his family brought with them from Haarlem before his birth, and all the music which

---

[11] Paul Auster, *The Invention of Solitude* (1982), (New York: Penguin Books, 1988), pp. 85-86.

Andriessen got to know at home. Echoes of this can still be heard in his music. Just as he characterises Rimsky-Korsakov as a sort of proto-Stravinsky, so is Utrecht, with everything he heard there, a sort of proto-'Amsterdam'. The music which he wrote in Amsterdam is sometimes miles and miles removed from the aesthetics of his youth, but at the same time it is inconceivable without this background.

In autumn 1998, Louis Andriessen recollected his early life during a walk through the city of his birth. This walk was followed by an afternoon looking at photographs from the period 1950 to 1970.

1939-1951 Utrecht

"The nice thing about the canals in Utrecht is that sometimes there aren't any quays. The houses are built directly on the water, like these here on the Oudegracht, and so it really resembles Venice."

Coloured drawing by Peter Vos, 1999

[in front of Oudegracht 183[bis]:]

"My friend Peter Vos lived in this house. He was absolutely the best footballer in the whole of Utrecht and later he also became a very good artist. He was captain of the football club. I've carefully kept more than sixty letters from Peter from this time.

He was four years older than me, and so we never sat next to each other in class. His father (Fuchs, that's what he was known as) was the editorial secretary for *De Gemeenschap*, a progressive-Catholic artists' magazine in Utrecht. My father took a hand in it when he came to live in Utrecht, which, however, was not until 1934. I was not born then but all my brothers and sisters were."

"Now we are crossing the Lange Nieuwstraat. The second house along was the Conservatoire and the music school of which my father became the director. The church which you see there is the cathedral church, as it was called, the Catharijnekerk. At first, he was director-organist, later just the organist. Every Sunday there was High Mass for which he played the organ. The whole family often went to High Mass, but I certainly also remember the said masses. On Saturday nights he also played for Vespers which, in May, were sung every evening.

During high masses, a large choir of forty men and boys used to sing – usually a beautiful high mass by Palestrina or Perosi, a Puccini-type Italian composer, a bit like César Franck. The women's parts (sopranos and altos) were sung by boys. Every week my father came home shattered from a half-hour rehearsal with those terribly noisy children. He did like them but he found it difficult to keep control because he was a dear, gentle man. He could not understand their broad Utrecht dialect. So it wasn't easy rehearsing a great mass.

A choir like that consisted of the butcher and the baker, the shoemaker and the greengrocer. They rehearsed weekly and then complained that it was too difficult. The good thing about the boys was that they didn't know whether it was difficult or not. They just did what the director said – he sang it to them, and they copied him.

The church was an important part of his income. During the war, when we were financially very badly off because my father wasn't a member of the Kultuurkamer, he wrote a letter to the bishop saying that he needed assistance. He got it too – it would have been about six hundred guilders, not much more. Hardly anyone could imagine it these days."

[in front of the Catharijnekerk]
"There is a little picture of my father in the church but I'm afraid we can't go in. I was there every Sunday. The women and men sat separately, the women on the left, the men on the right. It's not like that now. If people go to church at all, they sit together.

I was brought up with Catholicism, day in, day out, and it becomes an inextricable part of you. It is the basis of your spiritual nourishment, as is the music, the Gregorian and the new Catholic church music and what my father wrote and played himself. He liberated church music from what he called German Romantic sentimentality. His music is dignified, French, to an extent more modal and also chromatic. He was a francophile and a great devotee of unaccompanied Gregorian chant; for him, that was the most beautiful thing of all.

In the thirties, Pijper[†] became important to him since he lived in Utrecht and before that it was Diepenbrock[††] who was his guru. He used to talk in depth to Diepenbrock in Amsterdam about French culture because Diepenbrock, apart from being a Wagnerian, was also French oriented."

Hendrik and Louis Andriessen on the Nieuwegracht, around 1943.
Collection Louis Andriessen

"We are now walking through the Ham*bur*gerstraat, as they say in Utrecht, not the *Ham*burgerstraat. You have to imagine that then it was about as busy as it is now, because Utrecht has a very progressive anti-car policy.

The Guldemond girls lived here; they were the first girls I played with. Guldemond was a huckster, I think. We are now crossing the Nieuwegracht, which, as you can see, is fantastically beautiful and where the same horse-chestnut tree is still standing – I used to collect the conkers when I was seven. The Herengracht is on the far side. I was born there.

The furniture maker Kuik lived around the corner. In his shop window, there was a sign written in broad Utrecht dialect. Incidentally, Kuik was the father of the writer and artist Dirkje Kuik.

I spent the first five years of my life at number 5, that grey house. I have been inside once since and actually nothing has changed.

[†] Willem Pijper (1894-1947) was a Dutch composer.
[††] Alphons Diepenbrock (1862-1921) was a Dutch composer.

Further down the street lived Wouter Paap', the founder and the then editor-in-chief of *Mens en Melodie*. He was a Roman Catholic too – younger than my father. We had a joke at home that went like this: Wouter Paap, not *even* the best composer in the Herenstraat (because, of course, my father lived in the Herenstraat too). The attic room was my room. There were three sisters and two brothers in the house, all a lot older than me.

At the back on the left was a stone kitchen. During the war, we had a bicycle wheel and one of the lads cycled on it when we needed electricity. That was the power supply. I imagine that bread was baked using it, but there was also a very ancient stove which was stoked up with anything

With his parents in the yard behind Herenstraat 5, around 1946.
Collection Louis Andriessen

combustible, including books by German philosophers. My father always said: 'The Germans dig deep, but find nothing.' "

"My father of course spent every day either at the Conservatoire or at a choir rehearsal, but upstairs in the sitting room he had his desk and a grand piano. He would sit up there in the evenings and on Sundays, composing.

But above all, I remember the organ playing in the church. In addition, there was a lot of piano-duet playing on the grand piano, by sisters and brothers and my mother. There was no record player. We did have a radio but it was always off. I can't remember much about that radio, except the adventures I had listening to music in the company of my father, music such as *The Sorcerer's Apprentice* by Dukas. You went to concerts because a live performance was the only thing that counted. It was only when one of my father's pieces was broadcast that we all gathered around the radio, as though we were at a concert. That's the opposite of what is usual today; now the radio is on the whole day long and no one listens to it. I still believe that an upbringing like ours ensures that you listen seriously to the musical message of a piece."

"At home, there was constant music-making. My eldest sister, Hiek, sang and could play the piano, Leen played the piano and also the flute very well, and they had friends who played other instruments. Cilia was still young, about fifteen. Jur spent the entire day playing the piano. Nico played piano and cello nicely. Their repertoire must have been educational, including *sinterklaas* songs [sung by children on 5 December, St. Nicholas' Eve] and Christmas carols. At that time, Cilia was already singing songs by the French singer Charles Trenet. I remember that very well.

From left to right: Louis, Nico and Jurriaan Andriessen. "Both my brothers have since died within a year of each other. The jacket I am wearing I guess is from 1968. This could well have been on the occasion of my father's seventy-fifth birthday, in 1967." Collection Louis Andriessen

Philip Loots was played too – *sinterklaas* songs and piano duet accompaniments to which children could invent nice dances. My father admired this man, but he has been completely forgotten.

With the 'Vermeulen girls'. Collection Louis Andriessen

I also remember the pieces from *La Nursery* by Inghelbrecht, a French composer who arranged children's songs for piano duet, and also piano quartets by Mozart and Beethoven. As soon as I could play, I was dragged to the piano to play simple piano duets. I well remember pieces by André Caplet, *Un tas de petites choses* in which the treble is very easy and the bass very difficult – and very beautiful. Such things are unforgettable; they have, after all, made me what I am. I still remember the transition when I no longer played the upper parts of the Caplet but the more difficult lower parts. I was about sixteen at the time – it was still before I went to the Conservatoire. I lived with my sister in Bilthoven for three months to prepare for the entrance exam and I had lessons from Annie van Os. In Bilthoven I

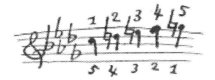

The fingering for the upper part, from Caplet's *Pour les enfants bien sages: un tas de petites choses (piano 4 mains) d'andré caplet*, premier cahier, Durand et Cie

was in love with the Vermeulen girls. Some of them could play the piano quite well. They weren't that good and could only play the easy, upper part of the Caplet. So I had to go and sit on the left – you just got on with it."

[opposite the house in the Herenstraat:]

"The friars lived here. I still don't really know what they were. They had not been ordained as priests but they used to wear black robes. The only time I ever went into that little monastery was when I was about six. I had to do a test to see if I could skip the first class at school. The friar who supervised the test was evidently a teacher. I remember two things about that test: I had to read a piece from the paper and also say how many cents there were on the table. I couldn't tell at a single glance and so I told the friar. No, no, he said, you just have to count them. I'd learnt to count from my brothers ages before and I still remember that there were thirteen. Later on, I made up for that missed year: I had to repeat the first year at grammar school.

It was wartime until I was six. The streets are now paved with stones but during the war blocks of wood were used. In the winter of starvation [1944 / 5], people took that wood from the streets to stoke up their stoves because there was no fuel. After a while, all the streets in Utrecht were just sand."

"I must tell you the story about Guusje Heck. Heck was a tobacconist and his son Guusje was one of my playmates. One day we were playing boats in the bath with all our violins – and we had quite a few in our house. We wanted to stuff the cello into the bath too but it was too big. My mother exclaimed: 'I can understand Guusje doing that, but you! You know what violins are.' Later, there was Guusje Heck's mother standing at the door, saying indignantly: 'Guusje certainly *does* know what violins are.'"

"Shall we just walk to the bridge? One evening, at about half past eight when it was already dark, I was on this bridge with my two brothers and my future brother-in-law. They all ate at home with us; what food we had fed ten people. We were going to the bridge to put rubbish in the canal. That's what you did in those days because rubbish was no longer collected. Suddenly, I heard a German soldier put his hands on the boys' shoulders and say: 'Sie sind verhaftet.' ['You are under arrest.'] There was *Arbeitseinsatz* [forced labour] and when you were seventeen, you were eligible for military service. I remember that both my brothers ran away very fast. I raced home and apparently I shouted (although I can't remember doing it, but so the story goes): 'The Krauts have taken the boys!' My sister nearly fainted, because her boyfriend was involved. It all turned out all right. They went on a very long detour of the city and recognised our whistle, whereupon they came back home when the coast was clear. At home there were two cupboards with double doors, so when there was a house search they knew where they had to go. There were as many as three men in the house eligible for military service, including the future son-in-law.

We are still on the Nieuwegracht. This is where the doctor lived who delivered me, if I can put it like that. I remember that I once sat on Bruno R****'s little sledge. Odd that you still know what a lad like that was called. I can't have been much more than three. We'll turn down this passageway; this is the Catharijneconvent, an old convent. I was sitting on the sledge which was being pushed by Bruno R**** and I asked him, wonderingly: 'What actually are enemies?' And Bruno said: 'The English.' I remember thinking: there's something not right with that answer. That's why I can remember the story. Indeed later, his family turned out to be NSB'ers." [members of the Nationaal Socialistische Beweging – the Dutch National Socialist movement.]

"On the right you see the back of the Cathedral. Of that church, only the presbytery and the towers are left. The rest collapsed in the seventeenth century after a hurricane and it was never rebuilt. The ruins have lain there for 150 years. When you are walking round it, you think that you are crossing a square but in fact you are walking through a church which isn't there any more.

Beautiful, isn't it? Such a deathly quiet street in the middle of the city, as if it is not real at all. I've suddenly remembered that, as a boy, on precisely this spot, I once leant into the wind for at least ten seconds or so.

I should say that the Cathedral is a Protestant church, and as a little Catholic boy you didn't go there."

[The carillon sounds.]

"What you have just heard is the carillon of the Cathedral towers, because we are standing in the cloister garden where the monks used to walk around praying and contemplating (you hope) although perhaps they were thinking about much more superficial things than we imagine. Carmiggelt[†] somewhere describes a nun in a train in Italy. She had such a pious little face but he suspected that in the nunnery she had much more contact with the mop than with the prayer book."

[More tunes from the carillon.]

"I think that must be a performance, because it's two thirty-seven. I find it difficult to talk through the bells. As you can imagine, this is an ideal place to listen to carillon concerts on summer evenings.

One of my most important memories, which I can't speak about with dry eyes, is when the bells were re-hung at the time of the liberation. I was nearly six and my father brought me here. The bells were hidden from the

---

[†] Simon Carmiggelt (1913-1987) was a Dutch author and well-known columnist.

Germans, because they would have made cannons out of them. So we hadn't heard them at all during the war. One afternoon, the Canadians came driving up the Biltstraat with tanks and cars and the following day the bells were in place again. The whole family, I think, went to the Cathedral square. It was swarming with people. My father held me by the hand. The sound of the bells was absolutely unforgettable, fantastic – just like my father's organ playing. I stood listening to the first sounds from those bells with tears in my eyes. I suspect also that I was so moved because my father was.

During the war he had been away from home for six months because the Germans held him prisoner in Haaren en Sint-Michielsgestel. When he came back I did not know straight away who he was. I was three at the time;[12] I simply recall that I saw him as a strange, but terrifically nice and kind man."

"Apart from the carillon, there's a group of tolling bells including a very big one called Sylvester, I think. It was only re-hung later as it had to be repaired. When you strike it, you hear nothing for a while. And then gradually – BWOOO – something tremendous happens. I think that my music has something to do with this. It struck me once that all the melodies in *De Materie* [*Matter*] run parallel with chords. And my harmonic preferences have to do with bells, too."

1951-1954 The Hague, secondary school
"This is the back garden of the house in The Hague – I think I was twelve or thirteen when I was here. It would not surprise me if Jur had brought back that cowboy hat from America, after he had been studying there for two years. In any case, at that time, he brought me back as a present something else unusual : probably the first blue jeans in Holland. I used to boast that these things were only imported into the Netherlands for the first time six months later."

"Much of the music which became important to me later I first became familiar with in The Hague. Puberty is a defining time in your development of knowledge and taste. After you are sixteen your fundamental characteristics don't change any more.

When I was at secondary school I often stayed with my cousin Wim Witteman in Haarlem. Initially, I had to repeat the first year of grammar school, but in the third year I had to take the entrance exam for the Conservatoire. Wim was my bosom friend. He played the piano very well and later became teacher of theory at the Conservatoire in Utrecht. We played an awful lot and improvised, both free improvisation and boogie

---

[12] Hendrik Andriessen was released on 18 December 1942.

'Nothing could be better than to have a cowboy hat.' With these words, Stravinsky says thank you for the cowboy hat which was given to him by the Texas Cowboys and Texas University on the occasion of his visit to Austin, Texas.[13]
Collection Louis Andreissen

woogie. I was composing at that time too: *Improvisations* for piano duet, a two-movement piece. It must have been similar to our free improvisations. But we also played symphonies by Bruckner, Tchaikovsky and Brahms. Wim was pretty much German Romantic oriented, more than me, even then. But we also knew inside-out everything we could lay our hands on by Bartók, Prokofiev and Stravinsky. It was not suitable for piano duet but we did have LPs. We listened to a huge amount of stuff together.

We already rated Frank Martin very highly at that time, for example, Ravel too, of course. Martin is an old love of mine – I can't say no to it. It is extremely good, at the very least, beautiful music. These days I find it a bit too beautiful."

"At home, our musical education was taken care of in the first instance by my mother who was a professional pianist. She had done very well in her final examination (at which she played Beethoven's Fourth Piano Concerto), but at that time was already in love with my father. She once told me: 'I saw him sitting in the room and I said to myself: I am going to make that man happy.' This was not a sensible decision with regard to a career as a pianist. You can't do everything at the same time.

One day, the teacher's assistant in the sixth class of primary school in

[13] From the film *Igor Stravinsky: composer* by János Darvas, Metropolitan 2001, in collaboration with Swiss and Swedish television.

The Hague came to me with a poem for the celebration of the teacher's sixtieth birthday. He was called Van der Post and he was the head teacher too. Could my father compose some music for it so that the children could sing it? My father thought the text was terrible: 'Joost van den Vondel [a famous Netherlands poet], zat niet in een gondel.' ['Joost van den Vondel was not sitting in a gondola']. Pretty soon afterwards (actually after one day's dawdling on my father's part), my mother said: 'Oh, Hen, just give it to me.' And so my mother composed the song. She was better at this than my father. I can even recall, with a bit of effort, the first line of the music.

   She taught me the piano and also how to study, and that is crucial. It was not until I was thirteen, in The Hague, that my father took over and began to help me with composition. My sister taught me as well.

   I began to write seriously when I was about eleven. Later, when my father became ill, around 1955 I think, Jur took over. I certainly cycled over to Jur regularly for a year and a half to talk about music. Those lessons were far and away the best I ever had. They dealt principally with practical things, how you solve technical problems. Jur was thirteen years older than me, so thirty at the time; I was about fifteen. If I am a good teacher, then I think it is due to those lessons with Jur. In the work of young composers, you see a lot of self-importance in the notation. 'Interesting' things are often

Qua vormgeving is Louis Andriessens *Souvenirs d'enfance* beslist de bijzonderste uitgave die in deze krant besproken wordt. De jeugdherinneringen zijn namelijk op losse bladen afgedrukt en in een doos verpakt. Een collectie muziek, teksten, ready-mades én een prijsvraag. Op blz. 2 meer over dit hoogst merkwaardige doosboek.

"As regards presentation, Louis Andriessen's *Souvenirs d'enfance* is certainly the most unusual publication to be discussed in this newspaper. The childhood memories were printed on loose sheets and packed in a box. A collection of music, texts, ready-mades and a competition. More details of this most remarkable box-book on page 2."

Souvenirs d'enfance appeared in 1966

nonsense. The music they compose can often be notated in a much more practical and efficient way, but that doesn't look as interesting."

1954-1962 The Hague, Conservatoire: Piano, Composition, Theory
" 'The gentlemen want to give you a trial,' my father said when he, as director of the Conservatoire in The Hague, came to tell me that I was accepted as a student."

At the Conservatoire in The Hague, Andriessen first studied with his father. and then, from 1956 to 1962, with Kees van Baaren. Here, he met Reinbert de Leeuw, Misha Mengelberg, Peter Schat and Jan van Vlijmen. The first thing they organised together was the celebration of Van Baaren's fiftieth birthday, on 22 October 1956. See also 1966-1969.

1956 *Sonate* for flute and piano
The earliest work to appear on the list of works.

1957 Hans van Sweeden
From: *Weekprogramma Randstad Holland Amsterdam*, 10-20 March 1966, page 17. Leo Hoost, 'Composer of the final hour: Louis Andriessen':

Leo Hoost: *In heaven's name, how can someone, to whom everything after Bartók is a closed book, open his mind to something so completely different as the music of Louis Andriessen?*
"Even I had difficulty, way back then, in understanding the new music until, in 1957, the young Amsterdam composer Hans van Sweeden played me some of his own work… and immediately it was as if a new world had opened up for me."

1958 *Séries* for two pianos
One of the first twelve-note compositions in the Netherlands.

1959 *Nocturnen* for soprano and chamber orchestra

1962-1963 Milan, studying with Luciano Berio
"I went to study with Luciano Berio because I felt most at home with his music: at the time of the twelve-note avant-garde, he went for the most musical and the most festive. *Allelujah* II can be compared with *Gruppen* by Stockhausen and *Poésie pour pouvoir* by Boulez.
We did a whole lot of different things, in particular talking a lot and playing cards an awful lot. Berio taught me a thing or two about percussion. At that time, I often played piano accompaniment for Cathy Berberian, to whom he was still married. For me, that was very important practical experience. Later, I performed with her."

Departing for Milan, from The Hague, with his girlfriend (and future wife),
Jeanette Yanikian and his parents, 1962. Collection Louis Andriessen

1962-1965 Foreign correspondent for *de Volkskrant*

For a few years, Andriessen was foreign correspondent for de Volkskrant.
*In that capacity, he published, amongst other things, a report on his visit to
Darmstadt in 1963, when Boulez, Stockhausen, Berio and Pousseur were all
there. The article on Darmstadt can be found on p. 114. Other articles published
in* de Volkskrant *have been listed in the Bibliography on p. 334.*

1964 Amsterdam, *Ittrospezione* III (Concept 1) for two pianos and ensemble

1964-1965 Berlin, studying with Luciano Berio

"I lived in Milan for a year and after that, in Berlin for a year, with a lot
of travelling to and fro on an American grant Berio had obtained to enable
him to live in Berlin. He could take a few students with him. A lot of
money was being pumped into the city, especially by the Americans (allegedly the Ford Foundation, but it was, I believe, controlled by the CIA)
in order to make it a model of fantastic Western capitalism. The most
important aim was to make the East Germans green with envy.

The only nice thing about Berlin was the cinema. There was a very
good cinema where I saw the entire repertoire of the German avant-garde,
including Robert Wiene, who also made *The Cabinet of Dr. Caligari*. To my
surprise I saw those same oblique camera angles and designs in the film *The New
Math(s)* by Hal Hartley, the first result of my collaboration with him in 2000."

"I also met some nice people in Berlin. W. H. Auden even showed up at Berio's house once; he was the librettist for Stravinsky's *The Rake's Progress*, a very imposing man. Frederic Rzewski stayed there, Vinko Globokar and Yugi Takahashi, all of them via the Ford Foundation.

I was there just before the great student uprisings. In 1965, the first student teach-in took place in Berkeley and in 1966 all hell broke loose everywhere. In the Netherlands there was 'Provo' and in Berlin there was sds, the revolutionary student movement. In Japan, you had that famous hooligan student movement, Zengakuren, who rampaged through the streets masked and armed. We ran, but they rampaged with spears and lances – astonishing."

From 1965 Amsterdam

"The weather was always cold and dismal in Berlin and we had always had a soft spot for Amsterdam.

It wasn't long before we were looking for a house in Amsterdam but for a time we kept on a little room in Berlin in the house of an aunt of an acquaintance of ours, so we could collect our scholarship once a month. Outrageous. Later, we took a little attic with two studies on the Overtoom in Amsterdam. There is still a chest in Berlin full of clothes and castanets which we never collected. In Amsterdam we constantly had calls from Berlin from the director: 'You've got to come now, otherwise your grant will be stopped.'"

1965 Reinbert de Leeuw, Peter Schat, Lodewijk de Boer

"When we arrived in Amsterdam, Peter Schat was working with Lodewijk de Boer on *Labyrint*, a revolutionary multi-media opera for the Holland Festival of 1966. I still remember how I arrived in Amsterdam in a confused state. I hung out a lot with Peter Schat, who could put up a good argument and use language very well (much better than I could in those days), and also with Reinbert de Leeuw, very intelligent, who never talked nonsense for the sake of it and never said unpleasant things about other people. It's always worth paying attention to people like this because you can learn a lot from them.

Lodewijk de Boer, one of my first friends in Amsterdam, turned up one day with some Frank Zappa LPs. At last, someone who used the jazz elements we liked, and even pop, in an intelligent way! No one – especially the average pop enthusiast – had heard of him. Elvis Presley and The Beatles were very 'in', but we didn't actually rate their music. You didn't listen to it. We found Zappa amazingly good. He knew a lot about country and western, rock 'n' roll and Varèse (whom he has often named as a great model) and in his music you can hear that he had really listened to Bartók, Stravinsky and other modern classical composers. He was a virtuoso guitar player and could think up good musical ideas.

There are also a whole lot of things about Zappa which I couldn't care

Louis Andriessen and Jeanette Yanikian on the Keizersgracht, 1969
Photo: Steye Raviez

less about, such as his need to be provocative and his literary side. What interested me were the odd quick figurations which he had written out and harmonised. They were played astonishingly well by the other musicians on keyboards or wind instruments.

Later on, he became a symbol of the 'de-hierarchising' of music through his use of both vulgar and highly developed musical material in his compositions, to put it officially."

1966 Andriessen conducts *Ittrospezione III* (Concept II)
Sunday 13 March: Andriessen conducts the Concertgebouw Orchestra playing his piece *Ittrospezione III*, during the second 'Experimental Concert' in the series 'Aktuele Muziek'.

1966 *Souvenirs d'enfance* for piano

1966-1969 Action for Bruno Maderna
In 1966, the five students [Louis Andriessen, Reinbert de Leeuw, Misha Mengelberg, Peter Schat and Jan van Vlijmen] of Kees van Baaren (along with many others) tried to engineer the appointment of Bruno Maderna, who was

really at home with the twentieth-century repertoire, as joint conductor of the Concertgebouw Orchestra, alongside Bernard Haitink.[14] *The upshot of this was the Notenkrakersactie in 1969. Dissatisfied with the way in which their suggestions were (not) answered by the Concertgebouw Orchestra, the students and their supporters disrupted a concert by massed clicking with frog clickers as soon as the conductor raised his baton.*

In the same year, the five composers wrote the opera Reconstructie *with the librettists Harry Mulisch and Hugo Claus.*

1966-1968 Contributor to the periodical *De Gids*

Alternating with Reinbert de Leeuw, Louis Andriessen took care of the 'Muziekkroniek' for De Gids. *Most of these articles have been included in the chapters headed 'Aesthetic and Chinese Observations' and 'Composers' (see also the Bibliography). Reinbert de Leeuw collected his articles for* De Gids *in* Muzikale Anarchie *(De Bezige Bij, 1973).*

1967 *Anachronie* I

1968 *Contra Tempus* for wind ensemble, percussion and improvising ensemble

1968 Political activist experimental concert
See 'Ensembles and Commitment'.

1969 *Reconstructie*, opera

"Writing an opera like this with a collective doesn't actually work. I think that it did ultimately succeed because we totally agreed about what was artistically under discussion. Even more important, we had the same political views. Everyone, not just us, but everyone who had some brain, was against the Vietnam War. The quantity of bombs and rubbish thrown down on Vietnam was approximately twice the total number of bombs used in the Second World War. That has all been forgotten. Much later the Americans retreated because they lost the war in Vietnam. They have never offered an apology. Nothing. Nil. Vietnam is still on its last legs; the minefields are still there. Hugo Claus called *Reconstructie* a morality play. We did indeed make a strong political judgement which I still stand by, from the heart.

Even with such a common motive, it is very difficult to write an opera providing a whole evening's entertainment with five composers and two writers. Someone came up with the idea of going to a monastery to work.

---

[14] The discussion is recorded in a *Gids* pamphlet, with the correspondence, articles and letters sent in on the whole Bruno Maderna affair.

The *Reconstructie* team in front of the monastery in Diepenveen. From front to back:
Misha Mengelberg, Hugo Claus, Harry Mulisch, Peter Schat, Reinbert de Leeuw,
Jan van Vlijmen and Louis Andriessen. Photo: J. H. Rutgers

That was a very good move. On two occasions, we spent quite some time
in Diepenveen in Overijssel; the first time it was a week. We spent the
whole day working, from reasonably early in the morning to late at night,
on the libretto in the first instance, with ideas as to how it would all fit
together. Evidently, photographs were taken of us, a rabble of artists, in the
monastery. In this photo we are posing like an Italian pop orchestra in one
of the better night-clubs. I don't believe this aesthetic exists any more –
the better night-club doesn't, and you don't get that sort of Italian pop
orchestra any more, so you always have to explain such photos."

"From a musical point of view, it had been important, with hindsight,
that the entire ensemble divided into four groups, each with its own conductor. We could thus compose four different tempi at the same time.
There was a fifth group: the electronics. *Reconstructie* was very advanced in
its use of not only tape but also live electronics to transform the sound.
The institution STEIM, which we set up, played an important role. Later,
live electronics became part of the essential equipment, but in those days
they had to be built from scratch.
It was also important that we did not start with a symphony orchestra.
We didn't have horns or bassoons and only had very few strings, so that we
couldn't achieve the saturated sound of a symphony orchestra. We didn't

"Luciano and Cathy weren't together any more but they both came to *Reconstructie* on the same evening. I experienced their dramatic divorce at fairly close quarters. I remember, for example, Cathy's telephone calls to California where Berio was at the time, full of intercontinental silences lasting minutes at a time."
Louis Andriessen with Cathy Berberian and Luciano Berio after a performance of *Reconstructie*. Photo: Maria Austria, Maria Austria Institute, Amsterdam

want to anyway.

The 'de-hierarchising' of the musical material in the opera was, at that time, a big step. You had the so-called modern music (which the layman calls 'plinkety-plonk music') but also pop songs and a liberal sprinkling of Mozart quotations. We did not quote Mozart literally but we wrote in his style because the allegory of American imperialism was translated into an interpretation of Mozart's *Don Giovanni*.

The score was also interesting because of its use of different types of voices. We had a large chorus and a speaking chorus-type avant-garde theatre group, Annemarie Prins' Theatre Terzijde, who spent the whole time bawling. Ramses Shaffy sang and also Yoka Berretty, a cabaret singer. Then there were the jazz improvisers, Willem Breuker and Han Bennink, who 'blew the whole lot down' continually. All in all, you could certainly call it a revolutionary approach."

"The six or seven performances were totally sold out a week in advance. Carré [a theatre in Amsterdam] was chock full.

During the preparations, it came to the ears of a journalist from *De Telegraaf* that American imperialism was being criticised and communism exalted with government funds. This stirred up a riot and resulted in hundreds of letters saying it was scandalous that taxpayers' money was being spent on this. Happily, at the time, we had a very liberal Minister for Culture, Marga Klompé. She reacted to it in a very sensible way."

1969 *Anachronie* II Musique d'ameublement for oboe and orchestra

1969 November: Notenkrakersactie

1970 First inclusive concert

1971 *Volkslied*
A unison melody, in which the *Wilhelmus* [Dutch national anthem] is slowly transformed into *The International*.

1972 *De Volharding* [*Perseverance*] for wind ensemble
See Part 4 'Ensembles and Commitment'

1976 *Hoketus* for two groups of five instruments

1972-1976 *De Staat* [*The Republic*] for four women's voices and large ensemble

1976-1980 Music theatre with the theatre group Baal

1976 *Mattheus Passie* [*Matthew Passion*]

1977 *Orpheus*

1980 *George Sand*
"Baal was one of the most important anarchistic theatre groups to originate in the Netherlands in the seventies. Het Werkteater has probably been in existence for longer and also has a longer record of service. However, Baal was very rigorous. Its absurd performance style was developed by the artistic director, Leonard Frank, but also emanated from the prevailing view that things had to be unrealistic and non-psychological. The group was named after Bertolt Brecht's first play, not one of his most clear-cut political works. Baal was an anarchistic boy who had always been a bad lot and did all sorts of things which you definitely shouldn't do. It is a very good play. A characteristic of the Baal theatre group was that music – often live music – always played an important part. There were a lot of songs, and there was tootling and dancing. Brecht saw songs as a form of alienation, ensuring that you,the spectator, learn something but don't allow

Baal performing *Mattheus Passie*. From left to right: Hans Dagelet, Diane Lensink, Elja Pelgrom, Kitty Courbois, Trudy de Jong. Photo: Hans Verhoeven

yourself to be carried away by psychological events. Willem Breuker worked with Leonard Frank and Baal early on, composing and also playing.

One day, Leonard came up to me and asked: can't we write an alternative Matthew Passion? I seized upon the idea enthusiastically. Then, as I continued to do later, I assembled my own small orchestra – for each new performance it was a totally different little ensemble depending on what was required. We generally had enough money for six musicians or so.

With Baal I later worked a lot with Lodewijk de Boer, but *Mattheus Passie* was directed by Leonard Frank. Together, we set out on the hunt for the ideal librettist. At that time, Louis Ferron had just made his mark with some very idiosyncratic books on Germany and the war (I still think that *Gekkenschemer* [*Twilight of the Mad*], *Het stierenoffer* [*Sacrifical Bull*] and *De Keisnijder van Fichtenwald* [*The Stone-cutter of Fichtenwald*] are masterly).

The songs were to be sung by actors and actresses, so I always needed to know in advance what they could cope with technically. I found the limitations of non-classically trained singers to be an advantage and I still prefer to see singing actors than acting singers. Singing actors don't reproduce the clichés inherent in 'proper' singing which I really don't like in classical music. Rather, they often intone extremely cleanly, in a refined way, even slightly sharp, all of which projects very well. The text projects better too.

Everything is simply sung in Dutch. I have learnt a lot from composing in my own language (I always did think that the odd custom among Netherlands composers of having to use French or English was faint-hearted). Just: 'Ik hou van je' – none of that 'I love you.' "

"Lodewijk de Boer started out as a viola player in the Concertgebouw Orchestra but in the sixties developed into a playwright and director. For Baal, we collaborated on *Orpheus* and *George Sand* – Mia Meijer wrote the libretto for this last piece. Later, we worked with the theatre group De Appel on *Doctor Nero*. With hindsight, I believe that the pieces for Baal (there are four of them) have been crucial in defining my insight into theatre music.

De Staat and *Mausoleum* are also theatre pieces, operas. While I was writing *De Tijd*, I once described it (in Schoenberg's words) as an 'accompaniment to a film scene'. For the world premiere of *De Tijd*, I brought in Paul Gallis, a famous set designer for, amongst others, Baal. He thought up beautiful things, such as an enormous pendulum that swept the stage.

1978 *Symfonie voor losse snaren* [*Symphony for open strings*] for twelve solo string players
   See Part 4 'Ensembles and Commitment'

With Mia Meijer and Lodewijk de Boer, 1980. Photo: Hans Verhoeven

1979 *Mausoleum* for two high baritones and large ensemble

1980 Erik Satie, *Messe des Pauvres* [*Mass for the Poor*], arrangement for mixed chorus and ensemble
   See Part 3 'Composers'

1980-1981 *De Tijd* [*Time*] for female chorus and large ensemble

1983 Louis Andriessen / Elmer Schönberger, *Het apollinisch uurwerk. Over Stravinsky* [*The Apollonian Clockwork. On Stravinsky*] Amsterdam, De Bezige Bij, 1983.

1983-1984 *De Snelheid* [*Velocity*] for large ensemble

1984 *Doctor Nero*

1984-1985 *De Stijl* [*The Style*] (*De Materie* part 3) for four women's voices, speaker and large ensemble

1986 *Dubbelspoor* [*Double Track*] for piano, harpsichord, glockenspiel and celesta

1987 *De Materie* [*Matter*] (part 1) for tenor, eight voices and large ensemble

Collection Louis Andriessen

"Berio had bought this little house in the north of Italy, overlooking the Mediterranean in the distance. It was there that he sat writing *Passaggio*, which received its premiere when I was studying with him. We went there every year on holiday – Reinbert would arrive on a little scooter. Later in the sixties Berio wanted to sell the house because he had to buy one in America; he'd got a job at Mills College. So we thought: do we know anyone who could buy that little house? Jeanette subsequently pressurised Frans Breuggen into buying it, so we had years more pleasure out of it. In the photograph, you see Reinbert, Jeanette and I grubbing about by the terrace door."

1988 *Hadewijch* (*De Materie* part 2) for tenor, eight voices and large ensemble

1988 *De Materie* (part 4) for actress, eight voices and large ensemble

1990 *Facing Death* for four string players (amplified)

1991 M *is for Man, Music, Mozart* for female jazz singer and ensemble

1991 *Hout* for tenor saxophone, marimba, guitar and piano

1994 *Rosa (a Horse Drama)* music theatre

Louis and Jeanette on the IJsselmeer, some time in the nineties.
Collection Louis Andriessen

1996-1997 *The Last Day* (part 1 of the *Trilogy of the Last Day*) for four men's voices, a child's voice and large ensemble

1996 *Tao* (part 2 of the *Trilogy of the Last Day*) for solo piano, four women's voices and ensemble

1997 *Dancing on the Bones* (part 3 of the *Trilogy of the Last Day*) for children's voices and ensemble

1997-1999 *Writing to Vermeer*, opera

2000 *The New Math(s)* for voice, flauto traverso, violin, marimba and CD

2000 *Feli-citazione* for solo piano

2000 *Inanna's Descent* for female voice and small ensemble

2000 *Boodschappenlijsjte van een gifmengster* [*Shopping List of a Poisoner*] for a singer who also writes

2000 *What Shall I Buy You, Son?* for voice and piano

2001 *De vleugels van de herinnering* for voice and piano

2002 *Fanfare, to start with* for six groups of horns

2002 *Garden of Eros* for string quartet

2002 *Klokken voor Haarlem* for two keyboards and two percussion

2002 *La Passione* for solo voice, solo violin and ensemble

2002 *Very Sharp Trumpet Sonata* for solo trumpet

PART 2

AESTHETIC AND CHINESE OBSERVATIONS

Part 2
Aesthetic and Chinese
observations

The five articles which follow have a common thread: Andriessen gives his opinion on some non-musical subjects.

From 1966 to 1968 he wrote for the Dutch periodical *De Gids*. In his very first piece he wrote on a subject which has been an important element in his music ever since: the role of quotations and the fine line between 'camp', kitsch and 'styleless-ness' which results from the unlimited combining of styles. 'Campness', that is to say raving about something which flies in the face of good taste, has its origins in visual art and was still a new phenomenon in the music of the sixties. Andriessen also examines the ideological differences between the quotation as a mark of respect, the quotation as parody and all that lies between.

At the same time he wrote 'quotation' compositions such as *Souvenirs d'enfance* (a collection of piano pieces, text and quiz in collaboration with J. Bernlef) and *Anachronie* I and II. These pieces should be regarded as his personal summary of the musical world which surrounded him. At that time, the quotation was one of the many experimental forms with which Andriessen was occupied. He wrote 'graphic' scores, aleatoric music and awoke the anger of the critics with a piece for 'pinkeltreintjes', little model trains with flashing lights which ran on a special track made of variable pitch sleepers.

These experiments, and particularly the 'quotation' music and American repetitive music to which he was introduced a little later, offered him alternatives to serialism, since when it has been impossible to imagine his work without quotations from existing music.

In a letter to the Dutch writer Louis Ferron which he wrote in 1976 at the request of *Vrij Nederland*'s Book Supplement, the subject of style and style quotation appears again, but this time from a literary standpoint.

In 1976 Andriessen travelled to China and published an account in *Muziek & Dans*.

Andriessen: "Is it necessary in 2001 to justify one's leanings towards Maoism? No. Socialist ideas have my great support and that won't change before my death. Do you, for example, hear anyone saying what a great statesman Tito was any more? And yet he succeeded in keeping that bunch of people together for fifty years without too much oppression. I think back to that journey to China with the greatest of pleasure. Chinese traditional music is amazing."

Anna Maria Pierangeli. Photo: Kolibri Verlag, Minden

In 1995, on the occasion of the centenary of the cinema, *De Filmkrant* invited Andriessen to introduce a 'forgotten masterpiece' to the public; Paulien Terreehorst was asked to interview him.

His personal film history begins with the American westerns of his youth (which were later to have an extensive influence on his opera *Rosa*) but by the early fifties, cowboys had severe competition from female film stars.

Andriessen: "The first film star I was in love with as a boy was Anna Maria Pierangeli. Later she was joined by French film stars. In the first instance I think of Françoise Arnoul who was considered to be an extraordinarily erotic creature. Later on I, along with many other boys of course, fell in love with Brigitte Bardot. At the time I was about twenty. I still remember sitting watching *Une Parisienne*. The film begins with Bardot driving along the Champs Elysées in a red open-top sports car with very loud be-bop playing, scat vocals sung by Christiane Legrand and André Hodier's big band. I found it so amazingly fantastic that I fell off my seat and ended up in the aisle. That just about sums up my career as a film fan. Later on my interests became rather more profound, although how profound remains to be seen. From my eighteenth year I had a great liking for experimental film. Actually that is the only thing I still find really good. In 1964 I went to the experimental film festival in Knokke. It was repeated later, and again, I was there.

In Berlin I saw a lot of avant-garde films. There wasn't a lot else to do there – it was a boring city and an anti-communist stronghold. In Amsterdam in the sixties you kept up with all the Fellinis – Jean-Luc Godard was very important too. He actually belonged to the *Nouvelle Vague* [*New Wave*] but he was much more rigid than the others, far less accessible."

Andriessen's forgotten masterpiece was the book *Achter de Spiegel* [*Behind the Mirror*] by Anton Haakman. Choreographer Beppie Blankert incorporated ideas from this book into his realisation of *Dubbelspoor* [*Double Track*] (1986) for which Andriessen wrote the music.

To conclude the 'aesthetic observations', Andriessen explains in a letter to Karin Melis what captivates him about early nineteenth-century Romantic irony.

Mendelssohn, fizzy drinks and the avant-garde

De Gids, 1966[†]

From 1966 to 1969 Louis Andriessen wrote for De Gids. *Alternating with Reinbert de Leeuw, he looked after the 'music chronicle'. In addition to the four Gids articles which have been included in this book, another article was published on the piece* Contra Tempus. *Reinbert de Leeuw published his collected articles in* Muzikale Anarchie, *Amsterdam, De Bezige Bij, 1973.*

In recent times, a phenomenon has occurred in modern music which is comparable with pop art. By pop art I mean paintings by Rauschenberg, Jim Dine, Lichtenstein and kindred spirits – paintings which contain fragments of objects or depictions not usually encountered in paintings, preferably utensils or depictions of utensils, household objects, fizzy drinks, washing-up liquid, children's toys and clothes. By removing commonplace objects from their environment and isolating them, they are destined to have, as often as not, a comical or poetic effect. The emphasis on the commonplace as commonplace, the magnification of clichés to oversized clichés or the duplication of utensils (Rauschenberg, Lichtenstein and Arman respectively) are all different aspects of pop art. If the phrase 'every cliché is thrown in' was met with strong disapproval a few years ago, these days it is more a recommendation.

This is saying a lot. I personally believe that we are dealing with a socialization of art on a scale unequalled in history. Of course, the first place this phenomenon makes its appearance is in the 'B'-arts – in film: in the film world's great veneration of Hollywood productions which were, until recently, judged to be extremely tasteless; in clothing; in typography; in the brilliant comeback of the rather 'twee' Jugendstil (also seen in the adverts). 'Styleless-ness' has its place not only in painting but in music too – and I am not talking of beat music which is erroneously called pop music. In music, 'styleless-ness' has different causes and, moreover, *more* causes than in painting. In the first place, the use of ideas from another musical world is very old in music. Most of the masses by Netherlanders (Dufay, Ockeghem) were based on popular folk melodies. Even in Romanticism, the use of folk melodies had not entirely fallen into disuse. In music we speak of quotations and hardly ever of plagiarism; even literal

[†] *De Gids*, 1966 / 10.

copies of Vivaldi concertos by Bach, published under Bach's own name, were tolerated and, because of the inadequate communications with Italy, actually applauded. And in Italy itself, a violin concerto by Padre Martini was indistinguishable from a violin concerto by Marcello was indistinguishable from a violin concerto by Corelli was indistinguishable from a violin concerto by Geminiani. Bach's sons lifted bits of their father's fugues to use as intermezzi, probably because they thought he wasn't appreciated enough (they were considerably more famous in their day than – at that time – the not-yet-so-old Bach). In the Romantic era quoting naturally diminished, as did everything else except artistic narcissism.

If I say that 'styleless-ness' (that is to say the simultaneous use of fragments originating from different musical schools of thought) is once again making an appearance in music, that wouldn't be entirely accurate, because the examples from history which I have just discussed differ substantially from what has been happening since 1950. In former times, fragments were interchangeable because there *was* only one style, because everything had the same style, everything belonged to everyone; whereas now it is a case of there being no universal style. The norm is the lack of norm or, better still, each piece has its own norm, demands its own norm. I cannot name any musical rule which forbids me to use a melody by Brahms in a composition if the piece can stand it and can also do justice to Brahms' melody. And there, I believe, lies the difference between using quotations now and formerly. In earlier times, a quotation fitted in because it had the same style – and today a melody by Brahms fits in a piece of mine because my piece doesn't have a style. The Brahms quotation is Brahms and is no invention of Andriessen's. (Naturally time will show that I am wrong. But because I have to compose the pieces, I need to be right and know that I am 'on the right track' – Stockhausen – because revolutionaries are always right.)

It is difficult to say when the first quotation was used in classical music.

Initially the phenomenon of quoting originated in aleatoric music which gives more freedom to the performer. Today there is more freedom for the composer. Aleatoric music has its origins in the strictly serial 'plinkety-plonk music' which is now definitely old hat. Furthermore (and I am convinced of this), painting has had a direct influence on 'graphic' scores too; action painting existed earlier than aleatoric music. Scores are now being created which are collages of other scores, preference naturally being given to stereotypes such as *Songs without Words*, of which more later. I would call this phenomenon a kind of democratisation: there is no idolising of individuals, nor any subjectivity, and in that sense society, or rather the awareness of society, has had influence. Those are the main features.

The first 'quotation' piece that I became familiar with was a piano piece by Kurt Schwertsik, played in Darmstadt in 1959, which consisted of the score of Lizst's *Liebesträume* completely cut up – literally. That was an example of 'styleless' music.

Votre Faust (1960) by writer Michel Butor and composer Henri Pousseur, known everywhere in professional circles but not yet performed is, for the most part, comprised of quotations in both text and music. In this particular case, the idea came from Butor who, having landed a contract to write a work for the theatre, wrote a piece which largely consisted of different Faust texts. Pousseur adapted his music to this process – more on this later too.

'Quotation' music was the first 'styleless-ness' phenomenon, comparable with the first photograph of Kennedy in a painting by Rauschenberg. A so-called 'ready-made' work is something completely different; since Duchamp's bicycle wheel is a creation of Duchamp's, it represents Duchamp's style. One of Liszt's *Liebesträume*, whether cut up or not, does not represent Kurt Schwertsik's style or personality in any way at all. It is nothing other than itself: a *Liebestraum* by Liszt which has been cut up.

And so we come to the word 'camp'. Originally, 'camp' came from New York's fashion scene and was used to indicate the wearing of an intrinsically dreadful piece of clothing by someone who was usually superlatively dressed. Subsequently 'camp' came to mean the placing of an intrinsically hideous piece of furniture (a Jugendstil lamp, a gigantic plush chair) in a very fashionable room. Thus 'camp' meant something tasteless having style because it was tasteless. This applied mostly to objects from the twenties and thirties. Later still, the term 'camp' broadened in meaning to encompass a conception of style which I have named 'styleless-ness'.

'Camp' meant listening to music which everyone rightly agreed was bad. It is not always clear precisely which music is camp. Doris Day is camp, Marlene Dietrich is not; Liszt's *Liebesträume* are camp, Chopin is not. Schwertsik would have made an irredeemable mistake had he made a collage of Chopin's Fourth Ballade.

Salon music is naturally very camp. Misha Mengelberg used a *Song without Words* by Mendelssohn for his *Viobum*; he cut it up, messed it about, turned it upside down, added notes etc. For the sake of clarity, I should say that Mengelberg's *Viobum* is *not* camp but Mendelssohn's *is*. (In American usage, this distinction is watered down – the *application* of camp is called camp too – and thus the force of the word is greatly reduced). A somewhat older example of how people used to work with quotations might help here. The *Piet Hein-rapsodie* by Peter Van Anrooy is certainly not a forerunner of 'styleless' music. When he chose the song 'De Zilvervloot', Van Anrooy did not laugh at it but found it to be a pleasant little song on which to write pleasant variations – thus a piece with style. It is obvious that there is a double meaning: the plush chair is not only ugly because it is ugly, it is not only beautiful because it is ugly, it is beautiful because it is beautiful. This is what I mean. Mengelberg does actually hear something in Mendelssohn's piece; as a consequence he (and Schwertsik too) did what Van Anrooy did; he also finds the plush chair is beautiful because it *is* beautiful. But only now is a double meaning appearing which is not present in the *Piet Hein-rapsodie*.

The camp aspect of the 'quotation' music is its use of second-rate music. It is an important part of the new wave in the avant-garde movement that I've been discussing here. A second aspect is composing in different styles and here we need to take a closer look at Pousseur's *Votre Faust*. Although it may appear to be, *Votre Faust* is not 'styleless' music. In order to compose his music and put it together, Pousseur devised a mathematical system (serial composer that he is) in which all chords, varying from chromatic note clusters to major triads, are allowed. The basis of the conventional twelve-note system was the avoidance of tonal harmonies which, of course, Pousseur needed if he wanted to quote pre-1900 music. The word 'styleless' is therefore not in Pousseur's vocabulary. He brought all styles together in his little mathematical book. He composed both a nineteenth-century violin study in G minor and a strict twelve-note fragment using the same system. Theoretically, this makes sense, but musically and practically it does not, by which I mean this: the music is not heard correctly because the nineteenth-century violin study came into being in a very different way – Pousseur is composing a different kind of piece and so the musical reasons for the violin study are emasculated.

Pousseur's system is, therefore, counter-productive. Much as he might wish to bring together all styles within his system, the very use of the system means that the violin study cannot be cited as an example. However, in so far as Pousseur used the system to compose fragments containing every gradation between diatonic and chromatic, without reference to a specific style or historical period, then it clearly does work. But all this is of little importance in this article since Pousseur's system is not an example of 'styleless-ness'. Appearances are against Pousseur. In *Votre Faust* we hear all sorts of music. His method of working is so closely allied to that of serial composers that his work should rather be called 'pan-serial' – the antithesis of 'styleless'.

A third type of 'quotation' music is the literal quotation of existing compositions (excluding 'camp' quotations for the sake of being camp). As yet, no rules have been made for this (in music, rules are always being made), and for the time being each piece demands its own rules. The reasons for incorporating literal quotations might be very varied. They might, in the first place be musical, but they might also be personal – a personal love of a musical fragment may persuade a composer to incorporate it in his own music. For him, that fragment is current music even if it was written in 1800. As soon as he sleeps around stylistically with that fragment, then he belongs in this article (for example, Van Baaren's *Musica per orchestra*); but whenever it is an unexpected joke or a literary idea, then he doesn't (for example, Frid's Double Violin Concerto in which the last movement of Bach's Double Concerto appears). Frid's piece is not 'styleless' because the composer prepares Bach's theme thoroughly with a very Bach-like so-called neo-Classical principal theme. But even so, I would still want to consider Van Baaren's piece a borderline case precisely because he sleeps around with that fragment. 'Polygamy' can also be described as 'styleless-ness', as regards the literal quotation of existing works. *Memoires*, a sophisticated electronic piece by Makoto Shinohara is 'polygamous'. The sounds in it range from the announcement 'coffee!' to beautiful abstract electronic sounds. Conversely, with *Telemusik*, Stockhausen wrote a conventional electronic work in which folklore from different countries is tastefully brought together.

Of these four last named compositions, two (Van Baaren and Shinohara) are examples of a new movement, but Frid and Stockhausen (extraordinary to find them together), are not.

But this distinction is erroneous. Frid and Stockhausen have nothing to do with each other, nor do Shinohara and Van Baaren – about as much as Mendelssohn has to do with fizzy drinks. But that is quite enough for an article on 'styleless-ness'.

Letter from a composer
to a writer

Vrij Nederland Book Supplement, 27 March 1976

Dear Louis Ferron,[15]

I'd like to take this opportunity to tell you how superb I find your books. After only a few pages of *Gekkenschemer* [*Twilight of the Mad*] I thought to myself: excellent writer! I must write to him and tell him how good I find this book and also one day try to explain why. Now, I may well say that, but personally I am not a writer. Writing is something different again from sitting in a pub talking – after three whiskies – about the combination of warmth and distance, quoting Brecht and dragging in Marquez. Writing in order to explain what you find good about something – and that applies perhaps even more to music – is a different kettle of fish. You should have seen Reinbert de Leeuw slaving away over his article for *De Gids*! He sweated blood but he succeeded in the end. See *Muzikale anarchie*.[16]

Socialising with writers doesn't help either. When I appealed to Harry Mulisch,[†] explaining that it required an immense effort on my part, he said that writing is never easy. Nevertheless, I know precisely which books I find excellent and which I don't. If we just restrict ourselves to the more recent literature of the Netherlands, quite simply I find it all bad.[17] Biesheuvel I could cope with, but I haven't read his third book. It isn't about anything. But I admit that he is very good at writing about it. I haven't read any Van het Reve since the letters from England,[††] and we don't have to waste any words on the rest of the 'kitchen sink'. And if a book is a result of long use of soft drugs, it makes me want to puke. But I must mention one name: Simon Carmiggelt[†††] is a great author, a virtuoso. He is the Chopin of the kitchen sink.

---

[15] In 1976 Louis Andriessen wrote *Mattheus Passie* with Louis Ferron (b. 1942) for the theatre group Baal. See 'Biographical notes' and also: Louis Andriessen 'A few observations on music theatre with reference to the *Matthew Passion*' in *Raster* 3, 1977 on music theatre, pp. 110-116.
[16] Reinbert de Leeuw, *Muzikale anarchie* (Amsterdam: De Bezige Bij, 1973).
[†] Harry Muslisch (b. 1927) is a Dutch author who reached a world-wide audience with *The Discovery of Heaven*, Penguin Books, 1998.
[17] People who have paid attention will understand that this refers to more recent literature *in 1976*.
[††] Reference to the book *Op weg naar het einde* [*On the way to the end*], 1963, by Gerard Reve (b. 1923).
[†††] See note on p. 29.

The most important reason I find your books so good is, at the same time, the most difficult to put into words: the aesthetic dialectic. You use the technique of writing to leave two options open. You carry the reader along only to trip him up. Your work is a combination of coldness and warmth, of involvement and distance. This is a question of style. Content is a different thing altogether. Nabokov is a master of this and so, in a different way, is Marquez . Irony is much too weak a word for it; it is grander than that, more the cosmic humour of Wammes Waggel.[†] Your style is dualistic too: you play with contrasts between the rational and the irrational. An example: in the middle of an exciting passage, an aunt is introduced who turns out to occupy a key position in the intrigue. Very exciting. In Nabokov's work, you find all of a sudden that the aunt married a rich Italian ship-owner seven years later, moved to America with him and died at a ripe old age from a persistent foot infection. Exit aunt. Written out of the book just like that. Masterly. That's the sort of thing you do too.

Wammes Waggel. From: Marten Toonder, *Als je begrijpt wat ik bedoel* [*If you see what I mean*], 'Het kukel' ['The Cookle'], Amsterdam, De Bezige Bij, 1967

But such things only work if you observe the dramatic conventions. And that is the second reason – connected to the first, by the way – I find your books so good. To alternate between the rational and the irrational you need literary conventions. These are 'style quotations' as it were: both distance and involvement are simultaneously real and not real, they are in inverted commas. Nothing is real, but at the same time everything is real, more real than the cup of coffee I am pouring out while reading.

The third point is the content. The great advantage your books have is that they are about something. Just because they are about something, such as the history of fascism, for example, or German late Romanticism, the style is functional; in order to describe history, you use the history of literature. I can't explain it any better than that.

This question of style is, strangely enough, a typically musical one. Not

[†] Wammes Wagel is a musical world spirit in the form of a quacking duck.

for nothing does music play an important part in your books, not forgetting the musicians. There is no occupation more mysterious than composing, the pushing of the combination of technique and nonsense to extremes. Since olden times, clowns have also been musicians; I don't need to tell you that Wammes Waggel has a lively interest in musical instruments. (In the Netherlands a piece has recently been composed which is rather like the form and content of your books, albeit a bit more 'civilized': *Abschied* [*Farewell*], a symphonic poem for large orchestra – all this in German, of course – by Reinbert de Leeuw. It is a farewell to German late Romanticism, and perhaps also to the institution of the 'symphony orchestra' – at least that is what he thought. But just after the premiere, Harry Mulisch said to Reinbert: "It is not an Abschied, it is a Willkommen!". The piece is an interpretation of German late Romanticism but at the same time a branch of it. It's a fantastic piece – you must hear it one day, a record is coming out.)

I can't tell you about everything. I don't want to name a pile of names (Arion, for example, very good; the writers I am friends with; Marten Toonder…). It mustn't become a supermarket – superficiality already reigns supreme. We'll discuss cultural policy another time.

Cordial greetings and much success.

In China, chromaticism is more rare than television

1982

In 1982, Louis Andriessen visited the Peoples' Republic of China. The Chinese Association for Friendship with Foreign Countries had invited a group of ten Netherlanders from the 'Culture and Media' sector for a three-week round trip, from 15 April to 6 May 1982. Louis Andriessen reported on this journey for the journal Muziek & Dans *(Muziek & Dans, June 1982, no. 4, pp. 9-11; July / August 1982, no. 6, pp. 19-21).*

BRIEF INTRODUCTION

Father P. de Chavagnac said it back in 1703: "You cannot convince the Chinese that something non-Chinese exists which merits some attention." As far as I can see, not much has changed in the last 300 years.

They have adopted some western things which are really useful, such as electricity and the petrol engine. But the junks in Hong Kong are steered with one paddle which also acts as a rudder, much more practical than our messing about in rowing boats. Squatting down in front of your door and smoking a little pipe – that is China. Chairs? Those are unwieldy things brought over by tall English colonialists because they couldn't get rid of their legs. The armchairs stand there nowadays complete with antimacassars, a little lost in rooms in which the Chinese only set foot when foreigners come to visit. Actually they get up at half-past five to do their tai chi and keep-fit exercises, hundreds of them at the same time. All of them doing exactly the same and yet all slightly different. When it gets dark they sleep. "The contempt that the Chinese have for all other nations is very great, even amongst ordinary people." The same Jesuit said this, and a little further on : "Even though they are far from reaching the perfection of art and science in Europe, one will never succeed in getting them to create things in the European way." [18] But Father P. de Chavagnac was a colonialist. He forgot, for convenience's sake, a few things: that in 200 B.C. slavery had already been abolished; that the Chinese had invented writing long before the Europeans; also gunpowder (to make fireworks, not weapons), paper and, by the sixth century, printing; that in 1000 A.D. Buddhism was already regarded as out of date; that none of their philosophies of life recog-

---

[18] *Lettres édifiantes et curieuses de Chine* [*Edifying and curious letters from China*]. Garnier-Flammarion, 1979.

nised a god or a hereafter, or a story of creation. No divine worship. The 'contempt' Father P. de Chavagnac spoke of now becomes a little more understandable.

One thing, however, is certain: when you speak of a country with such a history and which is so far away, generalisations are unavoidable. China is a very long way away. After three weeks there, the most you understand is that you don't understand anything at all. You are also totally illiterate. We mostly had four interpreters, two permanent ones and two which changed from city to city. These interpreters were extraordinarily important. Our two permanent interpreters were both called Wang. We didn't need to search long for nicknames because one was tall and the other was short. They became a permanent extension of our ears and our mouths, a sort of human *artifact* as it is called in *De Compositie van de Wereld*.[19] If Wang wasn't nearby, you had the understanding of a fourteen-year-old and the flexibility of a baby. I was standing in a shop in Shanghai where I wanted to (get someone to) phone for a taxi. The word taxi, pronounced in every possible way, was of no avail; only a little drawing of a car and a telephone produced a result. Now, *that* worked because Chinese is a language of pictures. I could write Chinese at once. (Here is one of numerous anecdotes: in old Chinese: the character for *man* is a sort of little figure with two little legs. The character for a *dead* man is the same little figure with a line through it.) Only a few Chinese speak English.

Immediately on our arrival in Peking (actually Beijing) we were shown into one of the fifties drawing rooms, where the *discussions* (last remaining vestige of the Cultural Revolution?[20]) on our basic programme were to be held. Opland (my room mate) and I had just succeeded in taking two water glasses half full of whisky in with us, but they were fairly quickly topped up with tea.

With hindsight, this misunderstanding seems to be very fundamental. Everywhere we went, the meeting began extremely formally: we were planted in armchairs, served with tea and had to listen to a welcoming speech followed by a 'brief introduction' to the institute at which we had just arrived. These 'brief introductions' remained with us ever since and the expression itself became the group's catch-phrase. It wasn't really a question of 'discussing'. But that didn't matter because usually we got our way. If we wanted another opera, that was immediately possible; if we

---

[19] Harry Mulisch, *De Compositie van de Wereld* (Amsterdam: De Bezige Bij, 1980).

[20] In general, the Cultural Revolution was regarded as a disaster for the country. That which perhaps in the beginning was a revolutionary movement soon led to anti-intellectualism and xenophobia. In the last few years, now that the last vestiges of the Cultural Revolution have been swept away, contact with Western culture has increased greatly.

wanted to laze around for half a day, that was fine too. The five members of the Youxie[21] in Peking were the last Chinese people to address each other as 'comrade'.

That same evening we watched television, this time with a glass of neat whisky. Lots of news, much more than in the Netherlands: well over an hour of national and international news, alternating with sports reports. One channel was broadcasting a Peking opera and there is an almost daily English lesson; the course is called *Follow Me*.

The imperial palace, the Forbidden City, is just as big as the centre of Hilversum but about a million times more beautiful. Having crossed two Places de la Concorde and having arrived in the room of Perfect Harmony at the very centre of the Forbidden City, the feeling that this is the centre of the world takes you by surprise. A bit further on, exactly at the golden section, is Tjangqingmen Gate, the entrance to the imperial quarters proper. Here, the serious atmosphere is all-pervading: only children are still running about. Having passed the women's quarters, we were taken still further into the innermost part – to the Emperor's open air theatre. The Emperor had his own opera company. The back wall of the stage is made of mirrors: the Emperor saw himself on the stage. Tea was served here too. But for the truth we had to go one room further: there, there is a little stage painted an unspeakable blue where the Emperor *himself* acted 'for his mother'.

Behind the Forbidden City there is an artificial hill. As the masses advanced, the last Emperor of the Ming dynasty retreated to this hill and hanged himself from a tree.

Peking. The cyclists are the real Maoists. They occupy more than half the road, do not give way to cars and don't use bike lights in the evening. There are 3.2 million of them in Peking. The Mao jackets are pretty and they come in many different colours, from bright blue through all sorts of shades of grey to black. No Chinese person looks the same as another. Most of the women wear trousers and medium heels. (Later on, in Canton, actually Guangzhou, in the south, it was totally different. You can't buy Mao jackets there any longer. The street scene is western, like Saigon or Jakarta.)

The first evening's official dinner with the Youxie proved to be representative of the importance accorded to Chinese gastronomic culture. The vice-chairman gave an extensive address on the subject, quoting Mao Ze Dong, who said "socialism should not be monotonous". Rather as if he was making excuses for the appearance of fourteen exquisite dishes on the table.

---

[21] 'Youxie': the Chinese Association for Friendship with Foreign Countries.

The famous Ming tombs wouldn't be out of place in the Amsterdam Municipal Museum. You see, there is nothing to see, just copies of the vases which had held the treasures. It looks like an installation. Opland photographed himself into the ground taking pictures of gigantic marble statues of people, philosophers and the animals which guard the approach. I will try not to include any more tourist attractions in this report. But the Forbidden City has had a sort of 'tablets of stone' function on this journey: the law of the great Kingdom, turned to stone and unchanged. Something to stop at and contemplate.

Scene from the Chinese play *Monkey subdues the White Bone Demon*

THE OPERA

On the way to the opera we passed Tian'anmen Square. It is the largest square in the world and gives access to the Forbidden City. A large portrait of Mao hangs at the entrance, one of the very few that we are still able to see in the China of today. Countless little flags in soft pop-art colours line the whole breadth of the square. These are in honour of Ceaucescu's [22] visit to China.

The building where opera is performed looks like a concrete sports hall. All the little plywood stools are occupied by Chinese people talking

[22] The then President of Romania.

animatedly. It will seldom be completely quiet during the performance.

Straight away it is clear that the opera is popular theatre. It always has been. Even at a performance of refined nineteenth-century Peking opera the hall is filled with 'workers and soldiers' these days.

An eight-man orchestra sits at the side. The line up changes. There are always four to five percussionists. The leader of the orchestra plays the *bangu*. This instrument sounds like a wood-block but it is actually a little drum; the top is covered in very thick hide, 5 cm are left open. The tempi are set on the *bangu*. In the introductions there are often soloistic accelerandi. The second percussionist plays the famous little gong; after it is struck, the pitch ascends immediately ('toing'). The third plays two hand-held cymbals. When the rhythm is regular, he plays the syncopation. The fourth plays a somewhat larger cymbal. The pitch descends ('tiiong'). A fifth plays wood-blocks and clappers.

The melodic instruments change from city to city. In every case there are one or more *pipas* (a vertical mandolin, played with a silver-coloured plectrum on each finger) and the *gaohu* (the two-stringed violin). In the Cantonese opera I saw a *zheng*, an instrument which is just about comparable to the Japanese *koto*. Now and then a *dizi*, a wooden transverse flute which sounds like an oboe in its lower register. Later it became clear that this is because one of the holes has been covered with very thin reed. I decide to buy one for Frans Breuggen.

The thing that struck me most of all about the Peking opera was the extremely artificial, Brechtian gestures. Each gesture has its own meaning; lots of acrobatics; many stylized sword fights. But sometimes the *gaohu*-player scratches his head with his instrument (later on, I understand that he is tuning it) and the stage hands are fiddling around during the performance. Sometimes a girl is looking on from the wings. In this way, the Chinese opera falls short of the rigid ritualism of the Noh theatre and the informality of the people round about is more reminiscent of a variety performance in the provinces.

There is a strong smell of urine. The music is dazzling. Always in unison, always pentatonic, in pure intervals.

Very occasionally two accidentals appear:

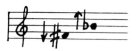

which are not tempered. The D is uncommon too, and therefore also sounds like an accidental.

Those moments in which someone takes his place (in an extremely slow and stylized way) on the top of a stool which is too high; or in which three characters glide from the middle of the stage imperceptibly slowly towards the wings, taking ten minutes to do it, make me think of Robert Wilson's *Deafman Glance* and *Einstein on the Beach*. There is a sudden general pause in the middle of an exciting fight in which everyone stands stock still. You imagine you are in an avant-garde performance in Amsterdam. The luxurious costumes, the headdresses. The singing is totally unnatural (but always more natural than our opera divas), with many small glissandi. The speech too is artificial and sounds like singing. All at once it strikes you that the 'glissando-ing' gongs fit in precisely with the vocal passages. The gongs are actually a type of singer. The text of all the sung passages is projected onto a screen – the Chinese cannot understand sung Chinese. This is because in spoken Chinese, the meaning of a word, in many cases, depends on the pitch of the syllables. A beautiful melody can turn the word 'table' into the word 'chair'.

I will never forget one stage set in a Cantonese opera. We are at court: ten characters in extravagant costumes stand motionless in a row for several minutes; the queen is allowed to sit. A diplomat sings a story. The king himself is wearing high white wooden shoes, a black beard, his face is painted black and white and he has a headdress with about twenty bright red feathers in the shape of a woollen billiard ball. And then suddenly he hits the table with a black piece of wood, at totally unexpected moments. Rage, but ritualised. You can't believe your eyes. The *bangu* plays:

You can't believe your ears either.

THE CONSERVATOIRES

The Peking Conservatoire is open again. This is worth mentioning because it was closed for some time during the Cultural Revolution, being the centre of decadent western influences. I can really understand that. Practically all the western music which I heard in the conservatoires was by Pablo de Sarasate. Fifty of the 250 students are studying traditional Chinese music only. Moreover, a second conservatoire has recently opened in Peking, exclusively for traditional music.

The little concerts conjured up for us by the directorate and performed by students alternated (in each conservatoire we visited) between western music and traditional music and sometimes there would be a singer who would sing first a Chinese song and then Mascagni.

The eighteen-year-old Wu Man played a brilliant *pipa* solo; we wanted to take her with us there and then so she could appear in the IJsbreker in Amsterdam. Everything makes it clear that they work a lot on their posture, and with traditional instruments it looks a lot more natural than in performances of an Italian opera aria, during which we were often treated to melodramatic wide-open arms on a final major chord. The *Chinese* modern music such as a duet, for example, for *gaohu* and *yangqin* (a sort of cymbalom) composed by the vice-principal is nothing more than a pentatonic melody in the upper voice and bad Chopin in the lower voice. Not until three weeks have passed do I begin to understand that I listen to it in the wrong way. The harmonisation of pentatonic music is not tonal but is a harmonic accompaniment unique to the pentatonic scale with triads, as sort of sub-partials. Instead of the dominant (in C) you hear:

because the B is missing in the pentatonic scale. Actually it remains in unison (rather like 'Le Cathédrale engloutie'[23]). But it doesn't improve the melody.

On the way to Shanghai we spent three days in Xi'an (formerly Sian) in the middle of the country and very important because of the archaeological excavations.

The first Emperor of the Qin Dynasty, Qin Shihuang, ensured that he was kept company in his mausoleum by life-size statues of all his men, plus horses, carts and weapons. At present, 450 of the 6000 have been dug up. The sight of these staring men is shocking. The entire burial mound covers 13 square kilometres and was discovered quite by chance in 1974 by a farmer. Qin Shihuang was alive in the third century B.C. At that time the Netherlands was a muddy swamp and no-one lived there – rightly so.

In Xi'an we heard a song recital. A strangely cosmopolitan programme complete with *Home on the Range* and *Song of the Flea*. The soprano goes strapless. As the accompanist leafs a few pages further on through the book looking for the next song, I get the feeling that the book was washed up onto the shore by accident. The idea that the Chinese have of western music can, to a certain extent, be compared with the idea that Ketelbey[24] had of Chinese music.

---

[23] Prelude by Debussy.
[24] Albert William Ketelbey (1875-1959), vaudeville theatre composer.

However, the following day we saw authentic Peking opera excerpts in a school-yard, brilliantly played and acted by children and an agit-prop group with a rather Volharding-like chorus, on the advantages of birth control. The actors accompanied themselves very hard on clappers. Four stone table-tennis tables stood in the playground.

Off to Shanghai. Rain, French plane trees along the boulevard, western architecture; the great Huangpu river, a tributary of the Yangtse, winds its way down the *Bund*, majestic nineteenth-century merchants' residences, reminiscent of Liverpool. More than eleven million inhabitants. Before the revolution (the word 'liberation' is used for everything which took place after 1949), this city had more slums than anywhere else in the world. Now there are no slums to be seen. I tell them a bit about what I have seen in the 'Free West', that is to say in the rough districts of Rio de Janeiro and Buenos Aires. But the Chinese nod patiently; they all already knew about it.

The conservatoire in Shanghai is older than the other conservatoires. It was founded in 1927. Of the 700 students, thirty percent study traditional Chinese music. There is a separate department for something – a bit creepy – which is called the class for national minorities. Fifty different nationalities (except the Han Chinese themselves) are crammed in together in order to preserve their cultures. I wonder what that will produce. There is a boarding department for gifted children of ten and over and there is – more from practical necessity than ideology, it seems – a workshop where instruments are made (harps, violins, *pipas, yangqins)* and also reconditioned (pianos). In a small room we listen to a record of a violin concerto about a girl and her lost love. Chinese music is nearly always for voice and if it is instrumental it nearly always represents something. In China I have heard a lot of butterflies fluttering on the *dizi*. The violin concerto was composed in 1959 and it is a collective piece. Actually it consists of melodies plus accompaniment. Many pentatonic arpeggios. Whether sentimental or joyfully frumpy, it is in 2/4 or 4/4. Bad Tchaikovsky but more breathless. I have never heard 3/4 time in China, let alone 5/4 or 7/4. The minority time signatures already toe the line.

The car horns in Shanghai are very interesting. The noise from the street provides – more or less – this musical picture (see above). Far beyond Varèse. If by chance it is quiet for a second, you hear approximately a thousand bicycle bells.

During a tea party in Shanghai I had a long conversation with Zhang Dunzhi, head of composition at the Conservatoire. He spoke extensively about how little China has felt the influence of western music, first through colonialism, thereafter through many wars and, since the liberation, through contact with the Soviets. "Which music was actually considered not to be decadent?" I asked. Bartók and Kodály. But now, after the Cultural Revolution, the study of Stravinsky, for example, is beginning. He had never heard of Ives, Varèse and Xenakis and when I talked about Takemitsu, we had real problems because the Japanese are called by other names in China.

"China is a land of song; they sing a lot in the country" and "no-one can act counter to the will of the masses". But at the same time Zhang Dunzhi voiced his concern about the influence of the music of Japanese TV commercials.

In the afternoon I had spoken about Peter Schat's Chinese opera *Monkey subdues the White Bone Demon*. He promised me he would listen to it (for both score and tape were available from the library of the Conservatoire) and he would look at the possibility of staging the work. It should be possible to get a harpsichord ('ancient piano' in Chinese) although the instrument wasn't actually in Shanghai.

In the Dance Academy I heard a beautiful chromatic piece by Glazunov. In China, chromaticism is more rare than television. And during a ballet, their singing as hard as glass, I heard a women's choir – singing something that sounded like Philip Glass too. It was, in fact, a piece that represented the sound of frogs eating leaves:

I noticed that there is a lot of waving to little birds in modern ballets. In Shanghai, in one of the many active Buddhist temples, I saw the largest temple-block I had ever seen – a cubic meter.

The last three days we spent in sub-tropical Canton. This time we heard Popper and Puccini in the Conservatoire. As requested, I played a little piece on the piano, having explained that I would be going to improvise. The word 'improvisation' was the only one that our interpreter couldn't immediately translate into Chinese. Later on in the afternoon, I heard a little bird singing outside:

Coincidence? Or do little Chinese birds always sing pentatonic? But I am sure that it was the same little bird that was tweeting as it was getting dark:[25]

A BRIEF CONCLUSION

Comparing China with the West is rather like comparing a bicycle with a table. Three hundred years of industrialisation and one hundred years of social democracy produce a completely different society than that of proud, agrarian China.

A comparison with a 'western', that is to say, non-communist country such as India is much more like it – over-population, difficult climatic conditions, little or no industry. And then you may conclude that in India people die like rats from hunger and illness. In China there is (almost) no hunger any more; medical help is, give or take a ten cent piece, free; I didn't see any beggars. Everyone has a roof over his head, water and electricity. These are the facts. There is compulsory education to fifteen. Children can read.

All the same, it seems as though Marxist-Leninism was adopted (by a country which adopts so little from the West) not only in order to achieve such material triumphs but also because it fits in with great Chinese traditions. Mao Ze Dong's mausoleum stands directly across from the Forbidden City as if he had been a last emperor, a last Mandarin. There are no social classes in China any more, but there is a strict hierarchy, for example as regards age: managers and assistant managers are never younger than fifty-five.

No Freud in China; no 'psychological' novels exist either – they have never existed (with a few exceptions). The Chinese are 'materialistic', they only venerate their ancestors. The Mao jackets are a continuation of the black jackets with braiding which farmers used to wear (and still do); they

[25] The beginning of *The Rite of Spring* by Igor Stravinsky.

are just more luxurious and more colourful. The jackets don't have anything to do with the 'uniformity in communist countries' which the 'Free West' goes on about. As we arrived in our hotel in Hong Kong, the porter carrying my case held out his hand and said 'thank you'. That was a shock. For three weeks we had lived in a society in which no-one had tripped over themselves to earn yet more money. In China, money doesn't come into it. It just doesn't exist.

You want to go back there immediately but at the same time you realize that you will never fathom it.

The forgotten masterpiece

Filmkrant, October 1995

On the occasion of the centenary of the cinema, each month in 1995, the Filmkrant
*asked a film enthusiast about his or her forgotten masterpiece. Paulien Terreehorst
interviewed Louis Andriessen about this.*

As far as I am concerned, the most under-rated masterpiece is not a
film, but a book about a film: *Achter de spiegel* [*Behind the Mirror*] by Anton
Haakman, a book that really should be reprinted.[26] In this book, Haakman
tells of a film that surely must be one of the most neglected in existence:
Emidio Greco's *Morel's Invention* (1974). This film is so under-rated that
not only has it never been shown in the Netherlands, you can't even *get* it
here. The film museum did try to obtain it at my request, but then they
referred me to the Italian Consulate. Of course, I hope that I'll see the film
one day, but I don't need to see it to know whether it's a masterpiece or
not; I *know* it is, for certain. *Morel's Invention* is about a man who is condemned to death, who escapes and eventually ends up on an island. There
he sees people walking around in a splendid uninhabited castle, he hears
them talking to each other and sees them walking in the gardens. But after
a while he realises that these people are not real at all. They are all images
projected by an inventor called Morel. He has been creating three-dimen-
sional images.

One of the things that I find makes art good is when it shows us underlying reservations. And I think that this film does that. I dislike realism in
film intensely. The more realistic it becomes, the greater the chance that it
will seem real, whereas I like to be continually aware that something is not
real. I much prefer emphasis on ambiguity and paradox rather than natu-
ralism. And that is why I only like films which create a certain distance.
For me, *Morel's Invention* is the ideal subject for a film because you suspect
that something else – other than what you think the film is about – is going
on. The real film is not the film which portrays reality, but the one which
lets you see how complicated the world is. Let me summarise thus: a film
about a woman who has a frightful illness and a small child in a wheelchair

---

[26] The publishers Bezige Bij took this to heart. In 1996, the book was reprinted with this
sentence on the back cover. But because this reprint can't be obtained any more either, this
exhortation is once again timely.

is wasted on me. If you have to identify with suffering, I'm out of there.

Another amusing scene in Anton Haakman's book happens when he is on holiday in Italy with his small daughter. They are sitting on a hill and all at once an enormous Roman army appears in the distance. It is only some time later that they realise they are on a film-shoot. I don't mind if Anton thought that up. Such hyper-realism may work the other way round but the point is: this is the way to deal with reality.

Greenaway attracts me for these reasons too. It is not for nothing that I did an opera with him later on. I already liked his films very much. The thing I find so good about him is the strange combination of formalism with passion and carnality. Very many people seem to think that these are the antithesis of one another.

His first film *The Draughtsman's Contract* is, I think, his best because he creates a tremendous distance by using a historical point of departure. As far as *The Belly of an Architect* is concerned, any fool can see that there is always something standing in the middle, such as a pillar or an obelisk. This is a rigid approach which must be taken literally and I find it more interesting than the fact that a man has stomach cancer – which is the last thing I am concerned about because I don't want to identify with characters in a film. I already found *Bambi* sentimental at the age of ten. I don't let myself get carried away by films. I let myself get carried away by someone who loves me. By a real person.

Romantic irony

From a letter to Karin Melis[†], 25 April 1998

My thinking on Romanticism emanates in the first instance from the study of the music of Bach's son Carl Philipp Emanuel. He wrote pieces (from 1760) in which contrasting thoughts are not only expressed in sound, but also (generally, roughly half way through) are confronted with each other and thereby changed. Such a section was later called the 'development' and is the central section of sonata (or compound binary) form, which consists of an exposition, a development and a recapitulation.

This confrontation in the development section, the 'structural development' thinking, coincides with the development of dialectics. Schlegel is the first to use the word 'irony' again (it was a Greek concept). He elaborates on Fichte (and Kant). Fichte was concerned with the contrast between the 'I' and what surrounds the 'I'. Schlegel goes further: "The world is paradoxical and only an ambivalent attitude can comprehend the contradictory whole." That is Dramatic Irony. The universal irony of existence is expressed by the *one* absolute certainty: that of death, through the unpredictability of life and through the chain of cause and effect. Hegel adopts the phrase and talks of *tragic* irony. Rightly so. He condemns it, moreover. The perception that everything not only has its antithesis but carries the antithesis within itself is ironic. Schlegel calls this Chaos, but also ascribes to it light-footed, and especially amoral, qualities. With Nietzsche, it is worse still: *total* irony. Nietzsche says: "Art is more valuable than Truth." You can deal with people like them.

This lofty detachment (as you correctly observe) is of course Romantic through and through, and also idealistic, but above all, aesthetic – artistic, if you like. That's why it reveals itself best in art.

Shakespeare is one of the great examples. Things, but people too, are never just what they seem to be; they are always something else. (Beethoven read Shakespeare in Schlegel's[††] translation.) I was very impressed by a stage adaptation of five plays about women by Ibsen. They are all heroines, but bitches, too.

Schlegel said somewhere: "Mit der Ironie ist durchaus nicht zu scherzen." ["You can't mess around with irony at all."] The acceptance of the non-

---

[†] Karin Melis is a philosopher.
[††] A reference to August Wilhelm Schlegel, brother of the philosopher Friedrich Schlegel.

permanence of the world. That is ironic. But it is certainly insight. And actually a liberation.

In general, it is only the early Romanticism which interests me: after 1830 things become subjective and sentimental. It's about Poe, that sort of guy.

The musical world around 1790 is already completely bureaucratised: the Classicism of Haydn and Mozart. Romanticism begins with Schubert and Chopin – around 1830, anyhow. Chopin is ironic through and through because he is, in essence, desperate. The 'late Romanticism' in music interests me little.

It is not my job to list all the points; *you* have to do that. From these splendid, crackling, electrifying antitheses, I have to make beautiful pieces which can console people, and at the same time intensify the mystery.

PART 3

COMPOSERS

Part 3

Composers

In this part, a number of texts by Louis Andriessen discussing other composers are brought together. It covers articles which originally appeared in *de Volkskrant*, *De Gids* and *Tirade* with, in addition, an interview and a lecture.[27]

The first article dates from almost forty years ago. If you order the articles according to the dates they first appeared, then the order would be: Visit to Darmstadt, Machaut, Gesualdo, Stravinsky, Wagner, Satie, Composer of Genius. From this there is not much to be discerned about any developments in Andriessen's preferences, simply because this small selection is too limited to reflect his formidably generous heart.

The chronological order, which of course can be followed by the reader, does reflect a clear sense of Andriessen's spoken and written style between the ages of 24 and 57.

However, we have chosen an order which follows the year of birth of the composers under discussion. The result of this is that, in ending with the article on Darmstadt, we arrive in the same time zone as Andriessen – then, at any rate. And thus the article forms a suitable prelude to the following part which mostly covers the sixties and seventies.

In 1963, Andriessen visited the International Summer School for New Music in Darmstadt, allegedly as correspondent for *de Volkskrant*. In the then Mecca for new music, Pierre Boulez, Karlheinz Stockhausen, Henri Pousseur and Luciano Berio were the special guests that year. The Andriessen article does have some curiosity value, especially as he was to distance himself pretty quickly from the Darmstadt aesthetics.

Andriessen: "That press card was enormously useful: I could get into concerts free everywhere and I wrote a piece now and then. Now that I've read that article again, I really have to laugh at the solemn self-importance of a twenty-four-year-old.

Two things in particular have remained with me from that Darmstadt visit: meeting Terry Riley, at that time still a jazz soprano saxophonist; and lying stretched out on a moving 2cv belonging to Danish fluxus artist Eric Andersen. We unravelled toilet paper over a field belonging to Kranichstein

---

[27] The Bibliography on p. 334 lists other articles by Louis Andriessen that are not included here.

castle. I still remember a German lady sticking her head out of a window in the administration building and roaring at me: 'Herr Andriessen! One cannot do this here!'. That was actually my most important experience in Darmstadt."

Beginning with 'Mendelssohn, fizzy drinks and the avant-garde' (see Part 2, p. 52) Andriessen alternated with Reinbert de Leeuw to provide a 'musical chronicle' for *De Gids*.

The articles he wrote for *De Gids* on Machaut, Gesualdo and Stravinsky's *Perséphone* have been included here. The most important aspect of these articles is their topicality. Andriessen compares the individuality of Machaut to that of Stravinsky. He places Gesualdo alongside Wagner (as far as harmony is concerned) and Stockhausen ('moment form'). He regards both Machaut and Gesualdo as early examples of avant-garde artists.

At the same time, at the end of the sixties, Louis Andriessen formed a plan to write a book about Igor Stravinsky. The *Gids* articles should be regarded as the first drafts for that book, which he ultimately wrote with the composer and musicologist Elmer Schönberger and which was published in 1983 under the title *The Apollonian Clockwork. On Stravinsky*.

In the uncompleted letter to Stravinsky, which has already been briefly mentioned in the Introduction, he wrote: "Since '67, I have been writing a music chronicle for a Dutch periodical about those composers who belong to your re-written musical history: Gesualdo, Pergolesi, Webern etc. I chose them *because* they belong to your musical history; thus an article on Machaut turns out to be an article about Stravinsky."

Wagner comes up again in an interview with Paulien Terreehorst during the 1981 Holland Festival. In that year, Louis Andriessen was the featured composer and commentator. There were many of his works on the programme, including the premiere of *De Tijd*. The article on Wagner came into being as a result of a visit to a performance of *Parsifal*.

This is followed by an article on the other extreme – Satie's *Messe des Pauvres*. This appeared in 1987 in an issue of the literary periodical *Tirade* which was completely devoted to the recently-deceased poet and biologist Dick Hillenius.[28]

Andriessen: "Dick Hillenius was a leading publicist in the sixties. He wrote a lot for the *Hollands Maandblad*. Here he was known as a music-lover and was famous for his 'Schiller' shirts – white shirts with wide collars, wide open over the lapel of his jacket. He appeared regularly at concerts. Furthermore, he was a friend of my friends, Bernlef and Schippers.

---

[28] Dick Hillenius (1927-1987) also published collections with good titles such as *Against vegetarianism* (1961), *The Romantic Mechanism* (1969) and *What can we learn from Rich People?* (1986).

Dick was a great Satie fan and regarded him as one of the five greatest composers. I believe that he, like me, was one of the 'scorers' for a performance of *Vexations* by Reinbert de Leeuw, which was to consist of 840 repetitions of the same little piece. The performance came to a premature end because the cafe owner closed the joint."

In Paradiso, Amsterdam, Andriessen spoke on 'Composer of Genius' at the invitation of the K. L. Poll Foundation for Education, Art and Science. Together with Elmer Schönberger, he opened a series of lectures on Genius, which the Foundation organised in 1996.

Guillaume de Machaut
and the *Messe de Nostre Dame*
De Gids, 1968[†]

Objective historiography does not exist. For each person who studies a particular aspect of history, the significance of known facts differs greatly. Thus there is no absolute value which can be ascribed to historical facts. This applies to music history too. Music history is made by composers and theorists, never by musicologists or critics.

The *Grand Larousse* of 1872 describes Guillaume de Machaut as a composer "d'un interêt purement historique", whose works "fourmillent de fautes d'harmonie".[29] Nowadays he is regarded as the greatest composer of the fourteenth century, whose *Messe de Nostre Dame* shows so many parallels with Stravinsky's Mass that Stravinsky stated in 1959: "I heard Machaut's Mass for the first time a year after mine was composed", a revealing pronouncement, about Machaut as well as Stravinsky. Machaut's 'fautes d'harmonie' were not the last thing which gave me cause to study his *Messe de Nostre Dame*.

We can trace the year of Machaut's birth to a 1335 decree by Pope Benedict XII, in which it is stated that Machaut had been John of Bohemia's secretary for about twelve years. He was born in Northern France around 1300, in the area around Reims – there is a village there which bears the name Machault-en-Champagne. The archbishop of Reims must have recommended the young Machaut to John of Bohemia. This notorious thug (I mean John of Bohemia) was accompanied on his many campaigns by Machaut. And although a travellers' diary does not exist, Machaut refers in different poems to the countries he visited in the company of John of Bohemia. A strange, but perhaps significant, sign in terms of Machaut's character is that as John's campaigns became less successful, so Machaut said less about him. In 1330, through John of Bohemia's intervention, Machaut became a canon in Verdun. Later, an appointment followed in Arras, also through the intervention of his master and finally, in 1335, Benedict XII appointed him to the office of canon at Notre Dame cathedral in Reims, where he was to remain until his death in about 1377.

The canons were obliged to live in a sort of monastery close to the

---

[†] *De Gids*, 1968 / 1, pp. 53-57.
[29] "teem with harmonic mistakes".

cathedral reserved for them and were only permitted to leave the town for three days each month. There were lay canons (like Machaut) too, mainly singers, who were responsible for the music for the services. However, Machaut remained (albeit with ever increasing intervals) in John of Bohemia's employ, so that the year 1337 found him in Lithuania. Clearly, as a canon, Machaut had special privileges. This is understandable when one considers that, at the time of his appointment, he was known (over the borders too) not only as a famous composer but also as a celebrated poet. It is difficult to fathom why Machaut, at the age of barely fifty-five and following a decade of adventure, more or less buried himself in Reims. (In any case it is certain that he chose to do this himself: it was John of Bohemia who urged Benedict to give Machaut that position.) In those days, Reims was France's second city, certainly culturally. Being a canon in Reims provided financial security, protection from the plague, a house, servants, a great cathedral with experienced singers and an abundance of time for Machaut to compose freely. It so happens that, apart from his Mass, his works are worldly: twenty-three motets and some hundred songs. In his poems too, love is always being mentioned, but never God.

Furthermore, his talent was rewarded with extra privileges; in 1362 he undertook a long journey through France with his then lover, the poetess Peronne d'Armentières ("qui n'avait que quinze à vingt ans"). Machaut's collection of his three-year correspondence with her in verse exists under the name *Le Voir-Dit* ('le vrai dit').[30] Peronne was perhaps Machaut's last lover (he was then in his sixties); she was certainly not the first. In one of his *Rondeaux* he names, in the form of an anagram, the names of ten women he is said to have loved. One of Machaut's other pastimes was the hunt; he was interested above all in hare hunting. Twice he complained that he did not have a horse. But this little bit of 'royalism' is not typical of Machaut; he was not of noble birth and preferred "franchise et po d'avoir que grant richesse et servitude avoir".[31]

A pronouncement such as this is unthinkable from the mouth of Philippe de Vitry, aristocrat and bishop of Meaux, the great music theorist and contemporary of Machaut. Vitry, who was the theorist of Machaut's music, wrote his *Ars Nova* in 1330. This book was revolutionary to such an extent that, ever since its appearance, the music from the previous century has been known as Ars Antiqua (Vitry calls it Ars Vetus). Both terms have remained with us until today. We would be wise to look more closely at Vitry's book.

In the first instance, the Ars Nova was, for contemporaries, a purely technical affair. The word 'ars' meant not so much art as skill, technique.

---

[30] 'the true history', 'the true story'.
[31] "freedom and poverty rather than great wealth and slavery".

With his Ars Nova, Philippe de Vitry introduced various new things, of which I shall mention two.

In the first place he put perfect and imperfect mensuration on a par. In the centuries before Vitry, music theory only recognised perfect mensuration; the imperfect mensuration which began to appear in practice was called 'tempus imperfectum'. The fact that, in the Middle Ages, triple time was called 'tempus perfectum' can be explained by theology: the number 3 refers to the Holy Trinity.

In the second place, Vitry invented signs for smaller note values than the ones which were known hitherto.

The reasons for Vitry's systemisation had an obvious cause: the development of polyphony. Whenever several singers and instrumentalists sing different notes at the same time, a generally-applicable notation is necessary for the smooth running of the composition. Vitry had his predecessors too, as polyphony had already been developing for several centuries. However, Vitry's determining of imperfect mensuration proved to be definitive when you consider that the binary system (also known as 'numerical notation – 2/4, 3/4, 3/2, 2/2 time etc.) on which today's musical notation is based, developed from it; in this system the denominator is always two or a multiple of two.

Vitry's *Ars Nova* was the effective answer to a pastoral missive from Pope John XXII on polyphony, written in 1322. This unspeakably conservative decree is worthy of being quoted here at length. In an introduction, John writes about the singers' sweet tones as they receive God into their hearts and sing Gregorian melodies recognisably and in the right way. He then goes on to say:

> But some followers of the new style have the aim of continually adding new notes to the old (which they don't want to sing) whilst they measure the duration of the notes precisely; the hymns are sung in semibreves and minims[32] and counted by means of these note values. Some polyphonic composers interrupt the melodies with hoquets,[33] make them slippery ('lubricant') with discantus and triplum voices[34] and sometimes add motetus voices in the vernacular; so much so that they do not do justice to their source (an Antiphon or a Gradual) they do not know on which one they are basing their music; they do not know the church modes, they do not distinguish between them, they even confuse them, since the rises and falls of a correctly and properly performed song, where the church modes are properly recognisable, are obscured by the large numbers of other notes.
>
> They run on and do not rest; they make the ears drunk ('inebriant') and do not bring them to rest. They act out what they are singing with gestures. Because of all this, the required piety is nowhere to be seen and a condemnable

[32] the smallest note values.
[33] each note of a melody is sung in turn by one of the voices.
[34] added, agile upper voices.

cheerfulness takes its place. [...] In saying this, we do not in any way want to prevent the use, especially on feast days [...] of some harmonies, namely octaves, fourths and fifths, which observe the original melody, based on Gregorian song in its original form.

Less than four years later the same pope was to interfere in Germany where Master Eckhart made the believers drunk with mysterious and paradoxical statements: "Thus if I say: 'God is good', that is not true. I am good, but God is not good. If I say in addition: 'God is wise', that is not true – I am wiser than Him. If I say furthermore 'God is a being', that is not true! He is a being above being and a supernatural denial." Vitry, himself a bishop and academic, was doubtless familiar with Eckhart's work.

These forerunners of the Renaissance, as extreme as the Dadaists, formed the fourteenth-century avant-garde.

Machaut himself was a practitioner, poet and composer, not an academic ("Si qu'on croire sans doubter Que ce sont miracles apertes Que Musique fait. C'est voir, certes" [35]), even though he says he studied 'les arts libéraux' and 'l'arquemie' (alchemy). His music had great influence throughout France and later in England over a period of about one hundred years. Until the beginning of the fifteenth century, his scores were copied diligently in large quantities and his body of work was often collected together in one manuscript. At the end of the thirteen hundreds, a group of composers who came together at the luxurious court of the popes of Avignon developed Machaut's inventions to their furthest consequences. They acquired the name 'mannerists', chiefly because of their cryptic scores in two colours with many new symbols. The music of these composers (Mattheus de Perusio, Solage, De Caserta) sounds, as a consequence of the sophisticated notation, rhythmically very flexible and extraordinarily advanced, in terms of both harmony and melody. Three different time signatures at the same time and use of quintuplets was not exceptional. In the manuscript from which we know of this school (Chantilly) we also find a motet by Andrieu, called *La Mort de Machaut, le noble rhétorique*. (This is, moreover, the only work by this composer that we know.)

If Vitry was the Schoenberg of the fourteenth century, then Machaut was the Stravinsky of that century. Neither Stravinsky nor Machaut shrank from breaking new ground and using obsolete forms. Like Stravinsky, Machaut led a normal life and it was his music that was revolutionary. The fact that Machaut's *Messe de Nostre Dame* is similar to Stravinsky's Mass is due to technical reasons too. In both masses, the Credo is written in the so-called conductus style. The conductus style (same rhythm and same text in all voices) was already obsolete in Machaut's time.

---

[35] "So that one must believe, without doubt, that it is intelligent miracles which are created by Music. That is true, certainly."

Beginning of Stravinsky *Mass* (1948) Agnus Dei

Beginning of Machaut *Messe de Nostre Dame* (c 1350) Agnus Dei

The musical material in both masses is not tonal, but diatonic. With Machaut, we speak of pre-tonality, and with Stravinsky of pan-diatonicism. Machaut's four-voice polyphony is the last which is really linear because the harmony comes into existence via the part writing. The result of this is that almost every conceivable diatonic chord can appear. The rules governing the combining of four-part chords and doubled triads are very difficult to establish in Machaut's work because for every rule you can point to an exception. If you use a bit of musicological imagination you could thus call Machaut's Mass pan-diatonic too. This not only applies to the movements in the conductus style (Gloria and Credo) but also to the remaining movements which are in the Ars Nova style. These are, contrary to the Gloria and the Credo, not so much conceived in four parts but in two plus two parts. The cause of this lies in the fact that the composer's starting point was a given tenor melody, originating from Gregorian music. This tenor part is elaborated along strict mathematical lines and determines the length of the whole work. This technique is isorhythmic, so called because the tenor has a fixed repeated rhythm. A second part is added to the tenor voice, harmonically and rhythmically a complement to the tenor voice and having the same range; this is called the 'contratenor'. These two lower parts have a steady tempo and were probably instrumental.

Differing greatly from these lower parts are the two upper parts (the already mentioned triplum and motetus, high men's or boys' voices), which are more mobile, in a different register and have melodically little to do with the lower parts. Yet the two upper parts, just as the lower parts, complement each other melodically and rhythmically.

The melodic complement has its origins in the hoquet mentioned above. Each note of the melody is sung by one of the voices in turn. When the note to be changed is held up to the start of a new note, and thus over to the entry of the other voice, one can talk of a 'bound' hoquet. This is common in Machaut's work and here Machaut writes, in effect, the first syncopated passage: all notes of the line come on the off-beat. When the two upper parts complement each other rhythmically, one of the two voices is, to a large extent, syncopated. Harmonically, and in contrast to the lower parts, the upper parts seldom complement each other because they were conceived in a linear way. The number of dissonant harmonies in the upper parts is thus much greater, so great that even as regards the isorhythmic movements of the Mass (Kyrie, Sanctus etc.) one could talk of pan-diatonicism. Despite the technical differences between the movements, the Mass is a compositional unity through these harmonic means, not to mention the many melodic formulae which are common to all the movements.

This 'Romantic' element in Machaut's Mass is not an important element of this work, and neither are the moments where we could speak of 'word painting', such as the most dissonant combination on the word 'Crucifixus' and slowing down on 'ex Maria virgine'. Machaut's Mass is an example of pure abstract musical thinking and it also has this in common with Stravinsky's Mass. (Word painting is a very personal affair; it can never be universal, is nearly always at the expense of the musical significance and thus quickly becomes obsolete.)

The harmonic similarity between the masses of Machaut and Stravinsky are evident. But on closer inspection, there is an important difference: Stravinsky's Mass is, give or take a few moments, conceived vertically and Machaut's horizontally. Machaut's is melodically superior by far to Stravinsky's. Just by means of this vertical writing, Stravinsky acknowledges his solidarity with Russian Orthodox church music which is more rigid, more static and heavier than the Gregorian Romanesque style. This applies equally to another of Stravinsky's choral works, *Symphony of Psalms*, the last part of which was originally written on an old-Slavic text (the *Gospodi pomiluy*), the liturgical language of the Russian church.

Precisely because Stravinsky, a member of the Russian Orthodox church, chose this style, Machaut's famous pronouncement: "Qui de sentiment ne fait, son dit et son chant contrefait" [36] is applicable to him too. Sentiment can be the motor of composition but never the intended aim. And that is what Stravinsky is trying to say with the oft-quoted sentence: "Je considère la musique, par son essence, impuissante à *exprimer* quoi que ce soit: un

---

[36] "He who does not create with feeling distorts his story and his song" or "fakes his story and his song".

sentiment, une attitude… et cetera".[37] Sentiment can be the cause – and it is, too – of Stravinsky's choice of style, but not the aim, and not the means to expressiveness. And with that we come to the already-stated, most important, point of similarity between the two works, whereby we leap over six centuries: both compositions are ideal examples of abstract musical thought.

---

[37] "I consider music, by definition, incapable of expressing something: a feeling, an attitude… etc."

Carlo Gesualdo di Venosa

De Gids, 1968[†]

On 26 October 1590, Carlo Gesualdo, Prince of Venosa, Duke of Caggiano, Marquis of Laino, Rotondo and S. Stefano, murders his wife Donna Maria d'Avalos and her lover Fabrizio Carafa, Duke of Andria and Count of Ruovo, as he surprises them, *in flagrante delicto*, in Donna Maria's bed. He flees to his country estate, thus evading the vengeance of the Avalos and the Carafas, and then murders his newborn second child, whose paternity he now doubts. Criminal proceedings are not brought against him.

Carlo Gesualdo learnt to play the lute early on. Following other royal houses, his father Fabrizio founded an academy where regular gatherings of musicians, composers and poets, which were to be imitated by Hooft and his *Muiderkring*,[††] made music and sang together.

> Not only did the prince love music but in addition he surrounded himself, at his own expense, with many excellent singers, musicians and composers, so that I often think that if this nobleman had lived in ancient Greece – where someone who could not make music was regarded as ignorant (and proof of that can be found in the story of the philosopher Themistocles, who was very embarrassed and ashamed when, during a banquet, it transpired that he was not in a position to play an instrument), no matter how great his knowledge of other things was – a statue would be erected for him, not of marble but of purest gold. (Scipione Cerreto in *Della prattica Musica*).

Fabrizio's court had great prestige and could compete with the Medicis and the Estes. The young Carlo was musically very talented but, as a consequence of his poor health, was not a worthy descendent of the combative Gesualdos (Luigi, who rebelled against King Ferrante II and was stripped of his rights, and another, who fought Ladislaus, King of Naples and, unarmed, threw him from his horse).

After various short and brutal wars, the principality of Naples was returned to the house of Gesualdo by agreement between France and Spain, and Venosa was added in 1546. Carlo devoted himself entirely to music as

---

[†] *De Gids*, 1968 / 4, pp. 256-261.
[††] Pieter Cornelisz Hooft (1581-1647), politician and poet, was the central figure of the *Muiderkring*. Hooft had an extensive and interesting circle of friends; his closest friends, including poets, artists and musicians, who were often guests at the Muiderslot, have been known as the *Muiderkring* since the nineteenth century.

his older brother Luigi was the heir.

Of all the far-reaching events in his life, the early death of his older brother was certainly the most unfortunate. The difficulties began from that moment on. Obliged, as heir, to provide descendants, he marries in 1586 his charming, yet frivolous, cousin Donna Maria d'Avalos, just twenty-one years old, and yet at that age already with two unhappy marriages behind her. "The marriage appears to have been extremely happy for some three or four years – which seems about as long as Donna Maria could endure one husband " [38] and she gives him a son, Don Emmanuele.

Thin, weak and probably asthmatic, Gesualdo cannot prevent Donna Maria from forming a relationship with Duke Fabrizio Carafa. A chronicle from the time portrays him as a charming, handsome young prince, "graceful as an Adonis" and courtly in manner and appearance. Their relationship quickly becomes public – and public opinion is always on the side of the young lovers (read Boccaccio) – and Carlo decides to intervene. He announces that he is going hunting, waits till nightfall and climbs, along with three armed servants, up the stairs to Donna Maria's quarters.

A servant girl finds the two strangled corpses covered with blood and stabbed in different places. The 'scandal' chronicles all take the victims' side, mainly because of the fact that Gesualdo did not commit the act single-handed, but made use of a 'maraut esclave' (according to the biographer Brantôme).[39] In addition, the lovers had received a priestly warning of Carlo's vengeance, so that the chronicles go on at length about the decision of the lovers to face death together.

Four years later, Gesualdo goes to the court of Ferrara and lives there for two years with a household of one hundred and fifty people in the company of Duke Alfonso d'Este. The sojourn in Ferrara was very important for Gesualdo in many respects. In the first place, he married one of the Estes in 1594, Donna Eleonora. Furthermore, it was clear his father's academy was merely a pale reflection of the leading court of Ferrara which, one could say, had taken over the function of the Medicis in Florence. The really important late Renaissance poets, Ariosto, Tasso, Guarini, were in Ferrara, not to mention the brilliant composers who worked at this court.

In 1596 Gesualdo returns to Naples. His health is declining sharply. Everyone complains about his intolerant nature, which can probably be ascribed to the fact that he suffers from chronic constipation (for which he seeks relief by means of flagellation); he tyrannises his servants; Donna Eleonora manages to divorce him and he spends his last years with his deceased son's wife, the German princess Polisena von Fuerstenberg, with-

---

[38] The biographical notes are from Cecil Gray, an exceptionally witty and creative musicologist, who, in the twenties, was the first to figure out the whole murder case on the spot in Italy.
[39] In Brantôme, *Lives of the Galant Ladies*, ed. Ludovic Lalanne (Paris: 1864). See Cecil Gray and Philip Heseltine, *Carlo Gesualdo, Musician and Murderer* (London: 1926).

out lawful issue, composing madrigals until he dies in 1613. "So it pleased God to destroy, both in earthly possessions and in honour, a royal house descended from the old Norman kings" (*Rovine di Case Napolitane del suo tempo*, 1632).

The unsavoury life of this Neapolitan prince would not need to be told had he not been the greatest madrigal composer and, what's more, one of the most personable musical spirits in musical history. He was, in addition to being very proficient, a highly virtuosic composer who had mastered all the techniques of his time and furthermore added new ones.

Just as the other musical forms in the fifteenth and sixteenth centuries, the madrigal was developed by the 'oltremontani', as the Netherlands and Flemish people living in Italy were known. The madrigal, originating around 1540 as an alternative to the popular frottola, developed into a very sophisticated vocal form which was mostly practised in the academies. They were five- or six-part compositions without instrumental accompaniment, alternating between homophonic and polyphonic, setting short verses (madrigals) by contemporaries or by poets from the past who were popular at the time, such as Petrarch. Words were 'painted' as far as possible in the compositions. The atmosphere of the poem determined this in the first instance, but even for certain words musical equivalents were sought, such as quick imitations of 'fuggire' (to flee), gradual losses of tempo on 'ritenere' ('to detain') and rests on 'respiro' ('breath'). This technique of word-painting led to the manneristic 'eye music': two white notes on 'le tue occhi' ('your eyes'), the notes E-F on 'mi fa' ('make me') and a series of black notes on 'oscuro' ('dark, obscure'), 'notte' ('night'), and on 'diavolo' ('devil'). The important madrigal composer Marenzio even 'coloured' the notes if a colour appeared in the text. (One still encounters 'eye music' one hundred and fifty years later in Bach's music, in his sacred works, especially in the *St. Matthew Passion*.) 'Eye music' is the extreme form of word-painting where the intended effect cannot really be heard, but can be read or seen.

Galileo's father, Vincenzo Galilei, lashed out at the exaggerated use of word-painting, especially by Marenzio, in his *Dialogo della musica antica e della moderna* from 1581. "They have ready-made patterns for all words: for screaming, laughing, roaring, raging, deceit, heavy chains, rugged mountains, steep cliffs, harsh beauty." Word-painting was a striving towards the greatest possible expressiveness in the madrigal. Musical expression was subordinate to the text. This need for dramatic expression was to lead to the beginnings of a new art form in which the musical material, compared with Gesualdo's madrigal art, would become impoverished: the 'stile rappresentativo', the opera, the beginning of tonality; the singing of long, dramatic recitatives, accompanied by instruments playing simple triads. Hocke shows this rightly in his *Manierismus II*: "In the art of composition, the stronger emphasis placed on the musical qualities of speech may have led to an emphasis on monody at the expense of polyphony and to the melodramatic recitative, the manneristic precursor of the Baroque opera."

Gesualdo soon extricated himself from Marenzio's mannerism. He regarded musical expression as superior to the text to such a degree that he wrote the text for his later madrigals himself. He retained the stylistic qualities of the madrigal, the sonnet-like *volte face* as regards mood in the last lines, the frequent use of oxymorons ("O dolorosa gioia" – "O painful joy"), the conciseness. "I die of my illness, and he who could give me life, oh, he will kill me and will not want to help me. O grievous fate, he who has given me life, gives me death" (*Moro, lasso, al mio duolo*).

Gesualdo completely ignores the musical simplicity of monody (dramatic monologues with simple instrumental accompaniment). Just one aspect of the musical developments in his time interests him: chromaticism. His last two volumes of madrigals from 1611 can be said to be extremely chromatic. There are chord progressions in there which are not used again until the high Romantics (Wagner, Franck).

For a long time it was assumed that Gesualdo's work was a curiosity falling outside history, produced by a sickly amateur shut off from the world. Gesualdo's extreme harmony, however, can be explained very well if we take into account the following things. In the first place he had, by reason of his birth alone, not a single social obligation and could therefore allow himself to compose freely, without making any concessions to patron or public. The fact that he wrote almost exclusively choral works and was not, unlike his great contemporary Monteverdi, active in all musical areas, is no proof of amateurism. Think about Chopin who only composed for the piano.

The idea that Gesualdo, out of a random desire to experiment, wrote down unprecedented chord progressions that he could not even hear himself is just as untrue when one sees with what microscopic precision he notates sharps and flats. In the second place, by choosing to write for *a capella* voices, Gesualdo proves that he is deliberately aiming for sophisticated harmonic combinations, because the instruments in his time were tuned in mean temperament and thus had great harmonic limitations. Madrigal form was the terrain for harmonic exploration *par excellence* because, compared with sixteenth-century instruments, the human voice had the greatest range of harmonic possibilities. We must remember that, in Gesualdo's time, a C sharp was not the same note as a D flat. This difference, which is difficult for a lot of us to hear, was taken for granted by Gesualdo's court singers. Gesualdo composed using those sorts of differences.

The demand for smaller intervals, directly linked to expressiveness, grew from the beginning of the sixteenth century. The first important initiator of chromaticism was again an 'oltremontano', Willaert, choir master of San Marco. Among his students was the theorist Vincentino who, perhaps at Willaert's instigation, immersed himself in tuning problems. As the number of small intervals, and thereby modulations, increased (tonality had yet to be invented), the problem of instrumental accompaniment became greater. And so Vincentino created an 'archicembalo' (a harpsichord-like instrument) with an infinite number of strings on which all modes could be played on all notes of the scale. This unmanageable instrument was developed in Ferrara where Vincentino had worked and where Gesualdo became acquainted with it. In due course, the problem of enharmonic equivalents, namely the question of whether a flattened D could be equivalent to a sharpened C, was encountered. In Gesualdo's time this point had not yet been reached. The invention of the so-called equal temperament tuning (the division of the string-length proportion 1:2 in twelve equal parts) would not take place for another hundred years.

It is often assumed that Gesualdo's chromaticism was influenced by Vincentino's 'archicembalo'. That is highly improbable and is, moreover, of little importance. All theorists and composers of note in the sixteenth century immersed themselves in chromaticism. Vincentino's harpsichord was one of the many technical results. The fact that Vincentino was attracted to the court of Ferrara is one of the proofs that chromaticism and related tuning and intonation problems were current (Robert Craft calls Ferrara the 'Darmstadt' of the sixteenth century). In 1548, Zarlino built a chromatic harpsichord with the octave divided into thirty-six notes. 'Oltremontano' Cipriano de Rore, Vincentino's successor in Ferrara, wrote a choral work in two different modes at the same time.

As far as chromaticism was concerned, Gesualdo was well-informed and, if one looks at the technical activities of his contemporaries, his use of it is easily explained. Gesualdo's most extreme employment of chromaticism is of a purely musical nature. It is incorrect to assume that it originated from an excessive need for literary expression or self-pity. It is obvious that one would come to that conclusion if one thinks about his personal life, about the literary expressiveness which is attributed to chromaticism and about the prevalence of word painting. But as far as Gesualdo was concerned, the text served the music, as is demonstrated by the following: the fact that Gesualdo, in his last volumes, renounced word painting entirely; that 'eye music' itself rarely appears; and, above all, that he did not use, for example, Tasso's great works such as *Gerusalemme liberata* – Tasso, his friend, who had written at least forty texts for him – but wrote his texts himself. It is exactly the need for subjective literary expressiveness that caused monody to come into existence, opera, the Lamenti, and all musical avant-garde forms in which Gesualdo did not immerse himself. It is for purely musical reasons that he chose madrigal form. The human voice is capable of extraordinarily precise pitch discrimination. I do not want to deny that literary subjectivism: "morse, il mio duolo, morire, ti mordero ancor io" is an important aspect of Gesualdo's madrigal art; it is, however, more a driving-force, more a cause of the finished work, than a *quality* of the work.

It goes without saying that this extreme chromaticism is particularly appealing in our time. One may compare it with the late-Romantic chromaticism of Wagner, for example. Such a comparison is understandable and not completely incorrect. Gesualdo's madrigals are not tonal, if one refers to the kind of music where tonal functions operate as 'tonal'. Whenever one wants to analyse madrigals harmonically, it is easiest to start with modes and triads on different notes of the scale. It then transpires that combinations of triads which have a common third are preferred to triads which have a common fifth (and tonal functions were to be built later on these triads). These so-called relationships of thirds are indeed found in Wagner, especially in *Parsifal*. But this is not a principal characteristic of Wagner's chromaticism, which is always conceived as tonal with his relationships of thirds an extension of tonality. This is not the case with Gesualdo. Gesualdo's chord combinations, unlike Wagner's, do not function tonally. They are very condensed and always of very short length; there are 'moments' of chromatic extension, without consequences for the further musical course of the piece. It is precisely this 'moment' technique which is typically twentieth-century.

With the changing of musical content at the beginning of the twentieth century, form changed too. The only Classical form which remained preserved in atonal music was the form that was least bound to the dynamic of the tonal functions: variation form. This can loosely be compared to moment form. It is not the dynamic development which is of prime importance, but the closed, rounded structure (in the classics, one already finds in each variation unity of rhythm and timbre), autonomous in relation to a different structure. The external dynamic of the tonal functions is replaced by the internal dynamic within the closed variation form.

The first theorist of the moment form is Karlheinz Stockhausen. The term 'moment' is not a quantitative indication in terms of duration or length but

> each formal unit in a particular composition, recognisable by means of a personal and distinctive characteristic." "In terms of form, a moment can be a shape (individual), a structure (dividual) or a mixture of the two; and in terms of time, it can be a 'Zustand' [state] (static) or a 'Prozeß [process] (dynamic) or a combination of the two."

These definitions apply far more to the pre-tonal music of Gesualdo than to the classics. A chromatic fragment in Gesualdo's work, always in a slow tempo, never appears in a quick modal imitation and is thus a "formal unit recognisable by means of a distinctive characteristic". It is exactly this contrast of static-dynamic that links it to the work of Stockhausen and his contemporaries. The chromatic moments in Gesualdo's work are static in relation to the quick modal imitations, but in themselves they are dynamic.

This feature actually applies to Stockhausen's work too. One seldom meets absolutely static fragments and at the moment when a 'Zustand' (static) is combined with a 'Prozeß' (dynamic), this will be heard in practice as a 'Prozeß' and not as a combination of the two. Thus it is better to interpret the words 'static' and 'dynamic' in Stockhausen's definition as gradual extremes rather than contrasts.

In 1954, the year in which Stravinsky puts together his first twelve-note series, he begins his study of Gesualdo's works. This is not coincidence. Webern's twelve-note chromaticism is just as static. Webern, especially, used variation form as moment form. Returning to Wagner, we can – except for this difference in form (Wagner's chromaticism is, by reason of the tonal functions, externally dynamic) – also establish a difference in content. In general, Webern used as his starting point melodic intervals from which the harmony would be formed, whilst in Wagner's music the melody is always led by the harmony. Stravinsky says of Gesualdo: "Gesualdo's music must be approached through the art of his part-writing. His harmonic system was discovered and perfected through the inventions of part-writing." That is again a way in which Gesualdo's chromaticism differs from that of Wagner and corresponds to that of Webern.

In 1957, after three years of doubt as to how to appropriate them, Stravinsky begins to complete three *Sacrae Cantiones* by Gesualdo, of which two parts are missing. He is not aiming for a historically correct reconstruction and even avoids the most obvious solutions. In 1960 the *Monumentum pro Gesualdo di Venosa* appears – three madrigals scored by Stravinsky. "The music could not simply be 'written out for instruments', of course, but it had to be imagined anew." The first madrigal was changed fairly drastically. Repeated notes in a quick tempo are dropped, many repetitions are added, there are octave transpositions, and even a complete fragment has been transposed. The other two madrigals follow the original fairly literally, except for unison doubling and doubling at the octave. At the beginning of the third madrigal (*Beltà poi che t'assenti* – see the example below), two orchestral groups alternate in a melody ten times, a sort of 'farben' ['colour'] instrumentation, which sounds very authentic because of the floating intonation, but at the same time sounds very twentieth-century because of the changing timbres. Such dialectic is very characteristic of Stravinsky's work. "It was a backward look, of course, – but it was a look in the mirror too." This is what Stravinsky said of his ballet *Pulcinella*.

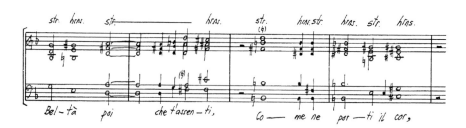

Beginning of *Beltà poi che t'assenti* by Gesualdo with Stravinsky's instrumentation above it. (Str. = strings, hrns. = horns.)

' "No Wagner, thanks!" is too easy'
Paulien Terreehorst: conversations with Louis Andriessen

NRC *Handelsblad*, 1981

In the Holland Festival of 1981, Louis Andriessen was the 'central composer and commentator'. Many of his works were on the programme, including the premiere of De Tijd. *At the festival, Paulien Terreehorst wrote down a few conversations with Louis Andriessen for the* NRC Handelsblad. *Five articles appeared, of which only the fourth is included in this book: 'Wie voltrekt het kunstwerk?' ['Who computes the work of art?'] (17 June 1981), 'De rol van de clown' ['The role of the clown'] (19 June 1981), 'Het belang van onechtheid' ['The importance of artificiality'] (22 June 1981), ' "Wagner-niet" is gemakzuchtig' [as above] (24 June 1981) and 'De noodzaak van destructie' ['The inevitability of destruction'] (26 June 1981).*

PT: *So what happened to you during* Parsifal?
LA: It has a lot to do with my father. We have already established that he was pro-French and anti-German. The consequence of that was that he condemned German late Romanticism, and Wagner was the ugliest and the most 'Kraut' German that you could imagine. Luckily, I agreed pretty soon. So I had never, although I'm now forty-two, heard a Wagner opera in its entirety. Yes, I had heard a few bars, and I had known for a long time that *Tristan* was revolutionary. You didn't need to tell me that Wagner was a great composer. But it was better not to have a lot to do with him. And so I was sitting in the opera as a novice. It really got to me in the second half of the first act during Amfortas' aria. The passion of that music had an awful lot to do with the passion in my father's music. Up to and including the chords. Certain chords which, for me, are inextricably bound up with the music of my father, often appear in those passages.

But worse: much better and much more pronounced. That is something which my father dared not pursue, yet could have learnt from that man. Wagner ensures that his music is never boring and that something odd is always happening. I think that this happens less in the other operas. *Parsifal* is fairly late too, 1882; a new world is beginning.

Give me an example of what happened then?
It has something to do with one of my preoccupations in the last few years: the apotheotic. Wagner often succeeds in making you feel that you are nearly there. For example, we are at the end of this improbably gripping scene, then he turns round at the door and says a bit more, keeps

going with this for a long time and, when it's nearly over, something else happens. For a long time, the subject of the music is the postponement of the ending and so you are continually in a satisfied, euphoric state. Precisely what all Wagnerians are saying all the time. This happened to me.

What does that tell you?
You can't actually come to a conclusion – you just gradually begin to understand that. Perhaps that has something to do with the fact that I have said the same thing so often in all these interviews. Anyway, it tells me that I'm becoming wiser and can rid myself of certain viewpoints. "No Wagner, thanks" is far too easy a way of thinking. That's what I have learnt from *Parsifal*. As far as I'm concerned, it suits me fine that I like it now. Real Wagnerians find *Parsifal* his least successful opera, so I haven't become a Wagnerian. That's not the way it is. […] It all sounds amazingly good – why shouldn't we like it? People such as Elmer Schönberger like Mahler too. It doesn't mean that you should like French culture any less.

But as I see it, that's only possible when you have adopted a radical standpoint like yours. Imagine you had liked Wagner when you were twenty-three. You might have drowned in it. You yourself are distanced from it now, it is not just a question of distance and restrained passion in the music.
That is so.

Messe des Pauvres by Satie

Tirade, 1987[†]

The last time I encountered Dick Hillenius was in January '87 in a shop selling household goods in the Utrechtsestraat. Doubtless I was on a trivial errand. Just as at our previous encounter, he said (Dick *always* said something nice) that he had found my orchestration of Satie's *Messe des Pauvres* [*Mass for the Poor*] really beautiful; he was referring to the performance in Paradiso[††] in 1981 under the direction of Reinbert de Leeuw. I promised I would make a tape of it for him on my return from America. But the return journey was on 9 May, and I was thus too late.[†††]

At the concert in question, he had walked up to me to compliment me and, after a charming joint silence, he slowly shook his head and complained about Satie's popularity. Until the sixties, Satie was a closely-guarded treasure for music lovers, a sort of secret love which you managed to share with a small group of insiders. I agreed with him, but we also agreed that fashions never last long and that there really would come a time in which Satie would again be completely forgotten except, of course, by us and the other members of the secret society.

I remember Remco Campert having a similar thought but long before that, sometime at the beginning of the sixties. Remco Campert (on TV, in shot from the knees upwards) was giving an introductory talk on a film about Vladimir Nabokov. In the talk, he said he regretted that Nabokov had become so famous; that he had cherished Nabokov for a long time as one of his most-loved writers; that no-one had ever read anything by him (except of course *Lolita*); and that a love such as this had something to do with the writer's obscurity.

At least, I remember something like that and I found it a striking thought. You love certain things – books, compositions, paintings – as you would a lover. And a lover is yours alone – no one else's.

Satie's *Messe des Pauvres* is a work for organ and choir. It was published posthumously and was probably written in 1895 at the time he had his

[†] *Tirade*, July / August 1987, 31, pp. 363-365.
[††] Paradiso, an ex-church in Amsterdam, is now a hall used for pop and avant-garde concerts.
[†††] Dick Hillenius died on 4 May 1987 at the age of 59.

own church community: L'Eglise Métropolitaine d'Art de Jésus Conducteur.[†]

The piece sounds like left-overs of Chabrier and Franck, some surviving chromatic chords from French late Romanticism, few in number but continually repeated in a Gregorian-like rhythm. The choir doesn't quite seem to belong, and after the second movement it stops completely. When all is said and done, it *is* a mass for the poor.

The bareness, the rhythmic limitations and the reticence made the work a historical precursor to the conceptual art of the seventies. I didn't know the work even though I had a pro-French upbringing. There was no record of it in the Netherlands but again a writer, Henk Bernlef, played me an American recording of it – after we had listened to practically everything by Lennie Tristano – and my heart stood still, I was so moved. This was also in the sixties.

In the past twenty years I have thought about that piece a lot; such love makes you want to steal the piece, to make it your own in one way or another. It was not until I had experimented with an ensemble of twelve string players whose strings were all tuned differently and who only played on open strings (that became the *Symphony for Open Strings*),[40] that for the first time I heard a way to orchestrate Satie's *Messe*. The open string sound is just as unfeeling and cold as Satie's rhythm and harmonic progression but the bowed string forms the basis of the Romantic string orchestra too. Because the notes of the melody are divided between different instruments, the notes also resemble single organ pipes; sometimes one is a bit out of tune, another sounds a bit late – like an organ in a rather poor church.

This open-string technique became the structural basis of the orchestration of *Messe des Pauvres*.

The use of the bass clarinet is a metaphor too; it is the last remaining pipe of an organ which is in pieces, the church meanwhile having been demolished. Satie himself had started composing the demolition.

Mass for the Poor. In the closing part a sort of melody appears, resembling a song which has been stripped of its words long ago. No other instrument could have projected the melody more strikingly than the accordion, French symbol of melancholy and wretchedness.

This arrangement was first performed by Reinbert de Leeuw and the Netherlands Chamber Orchestra on 26 September 1981 in the Hague. Two days later it was performed in Amsterdam, in Paradiso. Dick was there.

[†] Satie was its founder and only member.
[40] See Part 4 'About the Open Strings Project', p. 139.

Composer of genius

Amsterdam, 1996

In 1977, the K. L. Poll Foundation for Education, Art and Science organised a series of lectures about 'the genius', in Paradiso, Amsterdam. On Sunday 15 October 1996, Louis Andriessen and Elmer Schönberger opened the series with two lectures on 'the composer of genius'. Because of a strike, the text was not, as originally planned, published in the NRC *Handelsblad.*[†]

My father had the greatest contempt for people who read out a lecture. He said: "politicians do that", and that was more or less the worst term of abuse you could imagine. I have always taken these words very much to heart. When you are young, you stand there stuttering and lose the sentence half way through. And when you are over fifty – as I am now – you hope all that's over. But I can't guarantee it.

After a lot of consideration, I have decided to talk about one composer. During a little family dinner party on the occasion of the disbanding of the Hendrik Andriessen Committee which organised the celebration of my father's hundredth birthday, I told my older brother Jurriaan, also a composer, that I was preparing a lecture on a composer of genius. I let him guess which twentieth-century composer I was going to talk about. "Not Stravinsky," I added, because Jurriaan and I are tremendous Stravinsky fanatics. Furthermore, he knew that Elmer Schönberger and I have written a book on Stravinsky, and so that would be too obvious. "Actually there are only two geniuses", Jur said, "and they are Messiaen and Stravinsky." "No," I said, "You really do know it. Just think for a minute – you can have one more guess." Jur was still for a moment and then said: "Well then, Ravel, but you can't use the word genius for him. He is far more than that."

He was right. I want to talk about Ravel. The main reason for this is that I love his music with all my heart and soul. You think someone is a genius because you so love his music; genius has a magical quality which can't be described. It has *everything* to do with beauty, but that is a concept we haven't really grasped. In Ravel's case, it is probably a lot more complicated. Nevertheless, beauty is essential.

[†] Thanks are due to the K. L. Poll Foundation who made the text available for this book. Elmer Schönberger published his lecture in *De kunst van het kruitverschieten* [*The Art of shooting One's Bolt*], (Amsterdam: De Bezige Bij, 1998).

You have to have been brought up with a love for Ravel, hence the story about the family dinner. It's important that you have some insight into, and feeling for, the culture which surrounded him. We took it in with our mother's milk. It was clear to me early on that the transition from Romanticism to modernism was much larger in France than in Germany; Debussy and Ravel are miles away from Fauré, Franck, Chausson and Duparc. Schoenberg, on the other hand, is essentially a Romantic composer.

Hendrik Andriessen in Paris, 1927. Collection Louis Andriessen

It's not very trendy to talk about Ravel. He is certainly world famous and immortal – great works such as *Bolero* and *La Valse* are known by large numbers of people – but in my field, which from the sixties has been dominated by what we today call modernism,[41] Ravel wasn't actually *bon ton*. Debussy was the great innovator and Ravel was the boy who wrote those brilliant, fluent but slightly superficial pieces. Now that we have moved on a little from that modernism, we can also enjoy a few benefits of postmodernism. One of these, perhaps, is that it opens a little door in Ravel's direction once more. Anyway, I haven't really noticed that yet. Young

[41] Everything which springs from the avant-garde movement in the fifties, in which Boulez and Stockhausen played an important part.

composers are really still at a bit of a loss when it comes to him. "Yes, Ravel, yes… " they say.

I must, therefore, make a small plea in favour of Ravel, partly because his work – and with this I offer a partial definition of genius – is a singular combination of subtlety and naivety. Elmer Schönberger and I have talked about this a lot, amongst other things in connection with the book on Stravinsky. This description is very similar to a description of Goethe's about Haydn which Schönberger quotes in *The Apollonian Clockwork* about naivety and irony.[42] These are words which are extraordinarily important in describing highly exceptional beauty which comes into being spontaneously from nothing. This, of course, is very seldom the case. If you were to think: "Shame I am not a genius, pity it didn't come naturally" – don't worry about it, because it didn't come naturally to the geniuses either.

It is common knowledge that those pieces of Ravel's which sound very simple did not come into being easily. He had periods when he didn't get anything down on paper. He would just go into a cafe to talk to a few friends, but would then stand up without any reason, leave the cafe and go for long night walks through Paris beyond the city limits into the woods. He could be gone for days and nights on end. In such a case nowadays, you would seek psychiatric help pretty quickly.

So, composing isn't that easy. Take that very elegant, simple, slow part of the Piano Concerto It didn't come just like that. He struggled dreadfully, it didn't come to anything for a whole year and then suddenly – as he wrote to his friends – it went well.

Another piece, the *Rapsodie espagnole* is a virtuosic piece lasting about a quarter of an hour. He wrote it in a month. I really mustn't dwell on it. It can't be good if you can produce such a brilliant thing in a month, with so many small details. That must be a sort of lunacy. Sometimes Hugo Wolf would compose absolutely nothing for ages and then suddenly would write twenty songs in three days and three nights. The following day he would be collected – pills and the psychiatric hospital, nothing but trouble and misery.

This is actually more of an informal talk than a sermon. Ravel was an agnostic but he would have found it very bizarre that, on a Sunday morning in a church – Paradiso was a church originally – he was the subject instead of God.

PIANO CONCERTO (1929-1931)

Let us take a look at the slow movement of the Piano Concerto. It's only a couple of notes which make it a work of genius. It is virtually noth-

---

[42] "Anyway, what more could he exaggerate: temperament, sensitivity, spirit, humour, spontaneity, gentleness, power or the two ultimate characteristics of a genius: naivety and irony; he already possesses all this."

ing. The wonderful thing about it is that Ravel uses precisely the *right* notes and he manages to sustain the clarity of the attack. A second thought follows, then a third but, for all that, the story is continued from the beginning. The continuing of a story with very restricted means is specific to compositional refinement.

He composed the Piano Concerto in G shortly before he became ill. He was ill for seven years. Today we call it dementia praecox, a dementia which appears far too early. It must have been agony: all of a sudden he noticed that he could no longer write his own name and after that he lived for another seven years.

Ravel's music often refers to an existing genre, an existing musical language or dance form. This piano concerto is actually about jazz. At the time (1931), the first and the last movements were awfully hip: jazz was the newest of the new. Ravel had strongly fashionable features.

The slow movement begins with a very long piano solo. This beginning is about a lot of things, but definitely about three composers. I am going to try to let you hear in about one bar how the other composers would do it. Mozart, for example, in an Adagio:

It is also about Chopin. He was, and is, regarded as a composer of genius and, naturally, Ravel knew his music well. Chopin was almost a Frenchman and, at the time, was regarded as such. If he were the composer, a beautiful slow little bit of a piano concerto would be something like this:

It also resembles – and this is perhaps even more interesting – the work of a friend and contemporary of Ravel's, who at that time was not appreciated as much as he is now: Erik Satie. Chopin was the waltz composer *par excellence* in that part of Europe. Satie used these 3/4 bars too, but he did it this way:

The beginning of the second movement of the Ravel doesn't seem much, but it develops with an elegance which is at once very constrained and very refined. That is genius:

Something strange is happening and I want to draw your attention to it, because this is where an important part of Ravel's genius is hiding. You don't hear what is written. It has to do with counting. *All* music is about counting. When you hear that little waltz in a piano lesson, you soon think that this is what you are hearing:

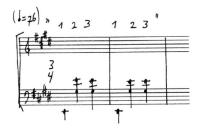

Do admit that that's how you would have counted it.

But that is not what is written at all. This is what is written and you can hear it in the melody:

It is certainly a waltz, but a very slow one, with the left hand twice as fast as a normal waltz accompaniment. This friction between the simplicity of the thought and how it is written down has a direct influence on the structure of the whole movement. You must listen to it. My father said in the past: "You can talk all you like, but at the end of the day, the only question you put to your student, your audience, your girlfriend, or whoever, is: do you hear it? do you hear it? do you hear how beautiful it is?"

Ravel has yet more surprises – odd, wrong notes and a strange rhythm:

After that elegant entry, the going gets a bit heavier (there *is* trouble and worry in the world but it's not, after all, that bad) and then that long passage for solo piano comes back. The orchestra comes in – a beautiful cor anglais plays the melody you have just heard – followed by the piano playing about with it in a Chopinesque way. Actually, it's not playing about at all; the piano has a wonderful counter-melody like an arabesque which your lover scrawls on your back.

If you've got good ears you will, of course, hear yet more specific, subtle flourishes and details which are all in keeping with something as perfect as this. Perhaps 'perfect' does apply to this musical thinking.

It is important that you listen to the whole movement. I can't, of course, explain everything but I will just single out a few things, for example Ravel's idea of letting the orchestra come in at a certain point after the long piano introduction. The orchestra does have to come in beautifully, and Ravel does it – it doesn't happen automatically – exactly right and unforgettably. Even if views change about what constitutes good music (I don't know in what way), there will always be someone who thinks: *this* is really good; the flute comes in with exactly the right note. Of course, you can spend a long time discussing whether it is precisely the right note and why. I wouldn't want to avoid that, but no one can convince me to the contrary. If you are in love with someone, you can't for the life of you imagine that everyone else isn't also in love with the same person.

GASPARD DE LA NUIT (1908)

Listening to works by the young Ravel teaches us another aspect of his genius which is that the quality of the first pieces does not actually differ so much from that of his later work. Worriers like Beethoven develop.

Ravel began to invent a few things, supposedly casually, especially in harmony. The early pieces have a curious perfection; furthermore, ambiguity, in the guise of refinement and naivety, is also present.

In 1908 Ravel composed a collection of three excellent piano pieces. At that time they were very modern and they helped to propel music history forward. I'd have to be technical to explain this properly, but it has to do with harmony and tonality. As I see it, in the period from 1900 to 1910, Ravel did more with this than Debussy. You can't turn on the television today without hearing, whenever two people are in bed together, or a cowboy is trudging through the desert, music nicked from Ravel's 1910 output. He invented it and that makes him a great composer. And he was very short; I have always found that strange. Stravinsky said of Schoenberg: "He was shorter than I am." Ravel proves that you *can* be a great composer all the same.

The three piano pieces from 1908 are together called *Gaspard de la Nuit*. Ravel couldn't play them himself, although he was a good pianist. Too difficult. The titles are taken from a small collection poems written in about 1830. Aloysius Bertrand, the poet, is now totally forgotten but it is interesting to note that his particular genre (prose poems one page long) later served as a model for people like Baudelaire. It even made him famous, but he pinched it. Anyway, geniuses do this all the time: steal a lot. They *do* do something with it, of course.

Stéphane Mallarmé had a high opinion of Bertrand. He was what you would call a sort of 'cult figure' today, because he had written that one small collection which no-one wanted to read, and then died young. He probably had TB, as befitted an unusually gifted young poet at that time. Edgar Allen Poe is also not unimportant in that company. But it all originates from the poet-composer E. T. A. Hoffmann. He wrote an opera about the subject of the first piano piece: *Undine*. Ondine, a woman who lives in the sea, seems to be the subject of an old German poem from the thirteenth or fourteenth century. In French Romanticism she became a favourite theme for beautiful works of art. She doesn't have a soul and is stunningly beautiful. If she marries a human being, she will acquire a soul. You are sitting pretty if you can find her. I knew her, apart from Ravel's piano piece, from a play by Jean Giraudoux, the brilliant French playwright; the play was staged by Shireen Strooker ten or fifteen years ago.

'Ondine' is the first part of *Gaspard de la Nuit*, Ravel's three-part suite for piano. The treatment of harmony produces a completely new sound which we now identify as impressionist – beautiful in a film about new sailing boats (I'm making it as trivial as possible). But someone did hear this sound for the first time in 1908 and wrote it down and it is, if you listen closely, very sophisticated. It is very difficult to play because the speed which is prescribed is very fast: semihemidemisemiquavers or hemidemisemiquavers if I am not mistaken. These are actually kept up through the whole piece, with a few exceptions – there must always be some. The strange thing is that although the piece is played very quickly it is a very slow piece. 'Très lent' is written above it. The quick playing happens within a slow tempo. 'Thinking' that tempo in the fast rhythm is fairly essential to the conception of the piece. The slow melody could be heard better if it were played on a flute or an oboe; the piano notes fade too quickly. Ravel is therefore writing something which is impossible. That is also what's amazing about this piece. Fundamental to it is the contrast between very fast and extremely slow and, as I've already said, it is also a wonderful combination of refinement and naivety.

['Ondine' is played]

My father probably would have found it a bit insipid playing a record during a lecture. He didn't think much of it. "Just ring someone who'll come and play it, or play it yourself." Of course, that would be a lot better, but in this case it would be a bit complicated because the piece is so terribly difficult. An orchestral piece would be even more difficult. But he was right and for that reason alone, the little surprise that we have devised for the end of this lecture is rather elegant.

MA MÈRE L'OYE (1908)

Ravel wrote *Ma mère l'Oye* for two children of friends. We are going to play it for you, after I have told you in three sentences what it is about.

The main features and serious observations which I have already made on the subject all apply to *Ma mère l'Oye*. The *ingénu* side especially is strongly present. It is 'child-like' which has nothing to do with 'childish'. *Ma mère l'Oye* is, of course, *Mother Goose*.

Ravel wrote five little pieces for piano duet for the Godebski children. Cipa Godebski was a rich Pole and his two children were called Mimie and Jean. Ravel visited them often and he liked being with them. He could tell fairy tales very well – just like Lewis Carroll – and he probably made them up on the spot too. The Godebskis are world famous in art history. Cipa's sister was Misia Sert, none other than the driving force behind Diaghilev. She made her mark on the Parisian artistic life of the time and is, amongst other things, immortal because Ravel dedicated *La Valse* to her. You should be so lucky, you'd be fine for the rest of your life – and long afterwards.

For *Ma mère l'Oye* Ravel chose five fairy tales from *Mother Goose* by Perrault. Usually, there are a few lines from the fairy tale at the beginning of each piece.

Elmer Schönberger and Louis Andriessen play Stravinsky's *Valse des fleurs* at the presentation of *The Apollonian Clockwork* in De IJsbreker, 1983. Photo: Jan van der Weerd

The first piece is a pavane for Sleeping Beauty in the forest.

The second piece is about Tom Thumb. You hear Tom Thumb walking in the woods, you also hear the bread crumbs falling. As you know, he can't find his way back because the birds have eaten up all the crumbs. You also briefly hear the little birds in the piece – you are spared no child-like cliché.

The third piece is about the Empress of the Pagodas, a Chinese princess. *Elle se déshabilla*: she undressed – I just thought it might be worth a mention. It is a beautiful bit of chinoiserie which was very fashionable in Paris at that time. You would have had some of those tasteless Japanese lacquered boxes on the table. Ravel is a typical example of someone who does not avoid that sort of kitsch. You hear the nice little Chinese scales (only black keys, you've certainly all heard that before). The piece is good, particularly because of the middle section with the wonderful Chinese gongs, which he combines – very often, for that matter – with the Chinese dance from the beginning of the piece when it recurs. The form is therefore A-B-A, and in the second A, there is also B. So it's a sort of C which comprises A and B.

Part four comprises 'Les entretiens de la Belle et de la Bête', a dialogue between Beauty and the Beast. You are of course familiar with this, from Cocteau's film, for example. The girl is a beautiful waltz *à la Satie*, almost a style quotation. Sure enough, the beast is a growling low left hand on the piano. Later Ravel scored this for double bassoon, a very large wooden, grumbling, funny instrument. And here, too, he produces a mannerism – he combines the theme of a waltz with a growling beast. 'Les entretiens' ['the conversations'] – the word says it all.

To conclude, you hear a beautiful apotheotic piece that in fact is also a dance, namely a sarabande – nearly all the pieces refer to dances. It is called 'Le jardin féerique', the magic garden.

I hope you can remember all this. If not, Ravel will remind you of what I've just said. The children for whom Ravel wrote it were seven and nine. Although they tried it in the family and for the neighbours, they never really dared to play it in public. And so we certainly won't do it any worse than those children, I think. Although…

[Elmer Schönberger and Louis Andriessen play *Ma mère l'Oye* by Maurice Ravel.]

Perséphone

De Gids, 1968[†]

Since Diaghilev's *Ballets russes*, no season in Paris passed without several premieres of musico-dramatic works of historical significance. In two decades, Gide, Valéry, Claudel, Bakst, Picasso, Léger, Braque, Cocteau, Debussy, Milhaud, Honegger, Satie, Ravel and many others produced several hundred premieres, tens of which became world-famous. Audiences and artists had a preference for ballet, a French theatre form from way back, which was influential particularly in French-oriented Tsarist Russia. Even before the revolution broke out, Russian émigrés such as Larionov, Nijinsky, Gontsjarova and Stravinsky turned up with Diaghilev in Paris where they gave considerable impetus to Parisian theatre life. Amongst them was actress, dancer, impresario and reciter Ida Rubinstein, a well-to-do and rather eccentric lady (at the age of eighteen she hired private trains to transport her from Moscow to St. Petersburg) who commissioned various artists to compose theatre pieces for her company. As early as 1910, she brought Debussy and d'Annunzio into contact with each other; they were to write the mystery play *Le Martyre de Saint Sébastien* together, the first in a series of flops which can be summarised as 'declamatoria'.

After Diaghilev, and with Dada as the most extreme form, one theatrical innovation after another was introduced. Dancers began to declaim, musicians appeared on stage, scenery moved, actors entered the auditorium, texts were in rhyme, extended musical sections blocked the dramatic action and the plot of a classical drama unfolded in tails and dinner jackets.

The distinctions between opera / oratorio / play became, for the most part, blurred. These shifts emanated principally from an increasing acceptance of music as part of stage production. Honegger wrote long sections of incidental music (which accompanied a considerable part of the action) for various plays by Claudel.

There is a connection here with the influence of ballet. Ballet music, originally written for orchestra, also expanded to include chorus and even vocal soloists as, for example, in the works of Ravel, de Falla and Stravinsky. These soloists were often brought into the *mise-en-scène*. It was not only the influence of the music which was of importance to the staging of a

[†]*De Gids*, 1968 / 5, pp. 329-332.

theatrical production, but also the influence of the composers themselves. *L'histoire du Soldat* was, in its entirety, one of Stravinsky's projects and was – with his line up of eight musicians, one dancer, a speaker and an actor – an example of the mixing of various theatrical forms. Alongside more or less traditional operas, composers wrote great narrative dramatic works which they called oratorios, or 'psaume dramatique', or 'declamatorium', or pro-fane cantatas, depending on the subject or the line-up. Sometimes the method of scenic production was completely undefined and two perform-ances could differ completely, each being visually unrecognisable from the other. And with that, the composer's word remained law: the sanctity of the score was, literally, enforced. This predisposition towards the music was characteristic of the time. With the emergence of film, the precedence of the aural as compared to the visual faded and with it, the quality of the music fell (nothing dates a film more easily than its score). Even now, new music is written for a new film about Oedipus, but for a new production of Stravinsky's *Oedipus Rex*, Stravinsky's score is the starting point. The same applies to ballet. New choreographies of *The Rite of Spring* are undertaken annually, but new music is never composed for Nijinsky's original choreog-raphy of the *Rite*.

The first big success of the new oratorios came with the performance of *Le Roi David* by Arthur Honegger in 1921. The piece was performed count-less times in Europe and beyond. Recitation does not play a large part in the work, choral speaking is absent. In addition to the religious aspect, the musical language (which was later to be called 'universal') determines the *succès d'estime*: "Le public parisien, qui s'entêtait jusque là à ne pas vouloir comprendre la musique moderne, eut alors la sensation d'en pénétrer les secrets."[43] Only in 1935 did Honegger really get going. Having written about twenty film scores, he was then commissioned by Ida Rubinstein to write *Jeanne d'Arc au Bûcher*: 'declamatorium', oratorio and opera for two speakers, vocal soloists, children's chorus, mixed chorus and big orchestra, on a text by Paul Claudel, the ambassador, "grande fresque où les procédés de la musique de fond pour le cinéma semblaient avoir aidé à l'élaboration du soutien sonore et au support choral…".[44] Religious nationalism is added to the religious content using French folk songs and children's songs: this and that 'shown' in eleven scenes. "Indeed 'shown', because the music is so evocative and flexible, so rich in expressive resources […] so vital, that one sees feelings and evocations expressed in this score passing by, almost

---

[43] "The Parisian audiences, which until that time had maintained that they did not want to understand modern music, got the feeling at that time that they had penetrated the mysteries." (Darius Milhaud in *Notes sans musique*).
[44] "a large fresco in which the techniques for the background music for the cinema seem to have contributed to the development of sound support and choral support… " (*ibid.*)

visually as though in a public procession" (Frank Onnen in *Excursies door de Franse muziek* [*Excursions through French Music*]). "It seems that Honegger with his *Jeanne d'Arc* has discovered the miracle of a musical language which grips everything and everyone" (R. N. Degens).[45]

It is natural to compare the reception of Honegger's work to that of the recent important works of Penderecki: *Pour les victims de Hiroshima* and his *Saint Luke Passion*. The fact that the critics forget that a 'gripping musical language' such as this is indeed precisely dependent on associations outside music, such as religiosity and the sorrow of war, is a sign of superficiality, which even though somewhat understandable, is very regrettable.

In *Jeanne d'Arc*, another new aspect came to the fore: the expressive and musical power of the text. "Si à l'exécution il se dégage quelque émotion, il n'est que juste d'en apporter la plus grande part à Claudel dont je n'ai fait que suivre les indications en mettant à son service mes connaissances techniques pour tenter de réaliser de mon mieux la musique qu'il avait lui-même créée",[46] said Honegger of *Jeanne d'Arc*.

In glaring contrast to the success of *Jeanne d'Arc* are the three performances which, a year previously, Stravinsky's *Perséphone* had to endure. *Perséphone*, like (almost) each work of Stravinsky's, responds to a given style and, at the same time, is the answer to that style. It is a kind of double investment: if the model is no longer current, the answer *is* current and vice versa. *Perséphone* is Stravinsky's answer to the French 'declamatorium' as it existed in the thirties. It was Ida Rubinstein who commissioned him to write a theatre piece on an older text by André Gide, and Gide rewrote the work in 1933-34 at Stravinsky's direction. If Gide had harboured some desires with regard to the stage presentation, producer Jacques Copeau and Stravinsky were in complete agreement on a static staging ("like a Holy Mass") without any changes of décor, so that Gide left the first meeting discouraged. When, at Ida Rubinstein's house, the music was played by Stravinsky, Gide only said: "Très curieux, très curieux", and appeared neither at rehearsals nor at performances. As early as 1914 he was no match for Stravinsky's authority when Stravinsky, in response to Gide's request for incidental music for an adaptation of Shakespeare's *Anthony and Cleopatra*, answered that if one wanted to work with Shakespeare one had to give Shakespeare a new image.

In Stravinsky's case, 'adapt' means 'metamorphose', but in such a mysterious way that both the model and the metamorphosis are present in

---

[45] R. N. Degens was at that time critic for the daily newspaper *Trouw*.

[46] "If, during the performance, some emotion is released, then it is only fair that it should be largely attributed to Claudel; I have done no more than follow his instructions and in so doing have put my technical knowledge at his disposal, in the best possible attempt to realise the music which he himself created."

their entirety and remain recognisable. *Perséphone* is an oratorio in the French style but it is, at the same time, a consecration of that style. In most of the reference books on Stravinsky, *Perséphone* is regarded as the 'female' counterpart of *Oedipus Rex*. The choruses are predominantly written for women's voices, a children's choir is added, and the melodies are softer and more flowing. But in comparing Stravinsky's works amongst themselves, one restricts oneself to Stravinsky's personal contribution (and then we are not talking about the completely obsolete notion of dividing into periods: the Russian, the neo-Classical, the American and the serial). One has to regard Stravinsky's way of working as the transforming of a model. The models do not occur chronologically but are widely spread over musical history. The children's chorus in *Perséphone* is the children's chorus from *Jeanne d'Arc*, irrespective of the fact that *Jeanne d'Arc* was written two years later (Stravinsky's models also lie in the future). The melodies are simple folk-like melodies from the Groupe des Six composers, also used by Honegger and a current aspect of composition at the time.

The recitation in *Perséphone* is conventional. The predominantly moaning recitation of Gide's text is accompanied by flutes and a string orchestra. Very unconventional, however, is the way that the French text is accentuated musically. This makes it one of the answers to the style. The main reason why Gide did not appreciate his music, says Stravinsky, was that "the musical accentuation of the text surprised and displeased him, though he had been warned in advance that I would stretch and stress and otherwise 'treat' French as I did Russian...". The difference in outlook between Honegger and Stravinsky is clear. Indeed, Stravinsky 'broke' words, used the wrong stresses and quick tempi, all in service of the music and not in order to interpret the text or to make it clearer. In so doing, he acted both against Honegger and the French tradition, in which the shifting of stresses in the music was very often used to give an extra dimension to the text – from Lully's time used by Gounod, Bizet, Debussy and, of late, very seductively by Michel Legrand in *Les Parapluies de Cherbourg*.[47]

Perséphone represented an investment in a musical style which at that time was no longer current, "a consummate farewell to French lyricism and especially to Gounod" (David Drew). Stravinsky's answer was not sufficiently rigorous (partly because of the conventional treatment of the speaking voice) to make the style relevant for today, and certainly not as rigorous as, for example, *Socrate* by Satie, although the work has had some influence on his surroundings. This 'French lyricism' continues to exist in a down-graded form in the French film music of Delerue, Legrand, Kosma and all the others; the first step was taken by the Groupe des Six (Auric,

---

[47] The film *Les Parapluies de Cherbourg* (director Jacques Demy) dates from 1964.

Honegger).

The most dated aspect of *Perséphone*, recitation, was certainly not the main reason for its limited success. In answer to Craft's question posed twenty-four years later: "How is your feeling now about the use of music as accompaniment to recitation?", Stravinsky replied: "Do not ask. Sins cannot be undone, only forgiven." Yet four years later, in both *A Sermon, a Narrative and a Prayer* and *The Flood*, Stravinsky again uses music as accompaniment to recitation, albeit more determined and precise than in *Perséphone*. In this way he is indicating that *Perséphone's* datedness lies not so much in the use of recitation as in the chosen style. *Pulcinella*, ninety per cent of which is music by Pergolesi, is more typical of Stravinsky than *Perséphone*, which does not contain a single literal quotation, except from his own sources.

Although French lyric drama, staged or not, was a characteristic trend in composition in Paris in the thirties, and was therefore an interesting investment project for Stravinsky, we may assume that he was not sufficiently committed to the style to make it relevant for that time and that *Perséphone* would probably never have been written without Ida Rubinstein's commission.

Three months after the premiere of *Perséphone*, Stravinsky received French citizenship.

Visit to Darmstadt

The musical avant-garde from all corners of the world at the feet of four masters. Will composing become an international craft?

August, 1963

This article is from De Volkskrant, *16 August 1963. From 1961 to 1965, Louis Andriessen occasionally wrote for* de Volkskrant. *His other pieces are included in the Bibliography on p. 334.*

The annual International Summer School for new music in Darmstadt is indisputably the centre of creative musical thinking in our time. And it has been since 1946. Immediately after the war, the Germans began to recover their losses caused by the Nazi prohibition on performing 'entartete Kunst' ['degenerate art']. Darmstadt is a clear example of this recovery. This year, Darmstadt was the only place in the world where you could find together the four most important composers of what we call the avant-garde movement and which is, without the slightest doubt, actually the most developed movement in western European music.

They were the Frenchman Pierre Boulez, the Belgian Henri Pousseur, the German Karlheinz Stockhausen and the Italian Luciano Berio. These four, who differ greatly in personality and outlook, all gave a course in Darmstadt this year. Pierre Boulez' course was called 'The necessity of an aesthetic orientation'; Pousseur's was 'Music, a craft?'; Luciano Berio's was 'Instrument and function' and Stockhausen's was 'Complex forms'. In addition, Stockhausen analysed his *Gruppen*.

FOLKLORE KICKS THE BUCKET

These courses were attended by composers from all four corners of the earth. Quite apart from visitors from nearly all western European countries, there were also Americans, Argentinians, Brazilians, Chileans, Japanese and Chinese. From this it can be seen that modern music is largely internationalised and that composing in a national tradition has given way to non-tonal thinking, introduced in 1900 in western Europe.

It is not easy to see whether this is transient; you could perhaps assume that it won't be – the present-day means of communication have made the world smaller. A contemporary music concert is no different in Chicago than it is in Paris or Tokyo. You can see this as a one-sided development. You can regret that typical folk-based music has reached the end of the road but the laws are made by those who are creative. Nature goes its own way. Last year I travelled through Morocco. The Moroccans pointed proudly to the westernised elements in their country: television and the emancipation of Moroccan women.

Whenever a typical national character exists, it will always show itself. As I have already said, nature goes its own way. And so, two months ago in Amsterdam, we heard an orchestral piece by the Japanese composer Yoritsune Matsudaira; it is inconceivable that this piece could have been written by a Dutchman.

Moreover, apart from their similar ideas, the course leaders in Darmstadt, with their four different nationalities, are not only very different in personality but also in national background. The German, Karlheinz Stockhausen, immediately divided his course participants into five groups; each had its own turn and was encouraged to do things for itself. With striking discipline and clear organisation he took them through an analysis of his *Gruppen*, focusing especially on the structural elements.

The Frenchman, Pierre Boulez, on the other hand, read out lectures on musical aesthetics written in exemplary French. Afterwards he gave a summary in German.

Henri Pousseur has used the last year to develop a new rational system for harmonic analysis. Numerical codes derived from overtones throw a new light on harmonies, especially as regards dissonant and consonant notes in a chord. The Italian magician of timbre Luciano Berio's way of thinking is somewhat opposed to this. In his analysis of his work *Circles* for voice, harp and two percussion groups, he clearly demonstrates his interest in phonetics, well-known to those who are familiar with his works. In this analysis he points to the 'auditive' connection between the human voice and the instruments, a very simple example of which is the exclamation "Tò!", likened to a stroke on the wood-block.

Not only phonetics but also linguistics are among Berio's personal hobbyhorses. And so the text of his opera *Passaggio*, performed recently in Milan, was written in five languages.

In addition to the four composition courses, there were also interpretation courses and, practically every evening, there was a concert of brand new compositions from all parts of the world. Of the interpretation courses, we should mention those of Heinz Rehfuss (song), Aloys and Alfons Kontarsky (piano) and Severino Gazzelloni (flute), these musicians all being among the performers in the concerts. These names represent the very highest level of the interpretation of modern music today. Let's also mention the cellist Siegfried Palm who gave an unforgettable performance of *Monologue* for solo cello by the Greek composer Nikos Mamangakis.

The fact that the four composers mentioned above were together was used to advantage by organising open forums and discussions with them. Especially worthy of note is Pierre Boulez's statement at one of these forums, namely that, because of the great attention given to Webern, Debussy is under-estimated as an avant-gardist. He added that he found Debussy's significance for modern music ultimately to be of greater importance than Webern's.

SCRAPING, SQUEAKING, TWANGING

In the ten concerts which were put on in these twelve days there were not many masterpieces. In this time of investigation, rapid development, intense international concentration and self-criticism, we are concerned less with masterpieces than with definitive links or musical ideas which open up new channels. This is a bold statement and the great personalities do not adhere to it; but it is fitting that a festival such as Darmstadt should distinguish itself from other festivals by playing experimental pieces and confronting current, unresolved problems rather than merely presenting comfortable concerts of brilliant products which have already secured their positions.

Many visitors found (as I did) that this year too little attention was paid to experimentation. In a way, there were too many 'masterpieces' on the programme, by which I mean works constructed as well as possible in a specified impersonal style. An exception to this was the String Quartet by Michael von Biel (born in 1937) which caused a tremendous stir. This string quartet was an anti-string quartet in which only scrapes, squeaks, taps, twangs, and grumbles were to be heard (within a wonderfully measured time-span), in which not a single note was sounded, and in which the bows never touched the instruments in a normal way.

This piece made a great impression because of its originality, conciseness and inventiveness. This way of occupying oneself so unashamedly with music is reminiscent of, for example, François Villon's way of living. Perhaps it is what we would call antisocial, but it is not in the least boring and it bubbles over with initiative. In music we would call it re-orientation. That is to say, in the case of van Biel's Quartet: "What actually is a string quartet ? I have four people at my disposal with wooden boxes of different dimensions with strings on them and sticks with horsehair. I can get them to make the sounds I want."

This last thought could have been Mozart's in parentheses. This way of thinking occupies a large place in current musical creative thinking. To be completely unfamiliar with the psychological and social associations which a string quartet presents, and to describe the objects exclusively as objects, has a lot to do, of course, with phenomenology. Not for nothing are phenomenological analyses of serial compositions only now being thought about and worked on. Not for nothing was this the year in which a lecture was given in Darmstadt by L. A. Hiller of Illinois University on information theory and music.

Of the compositions being performed, I'd also like to mention *Répons* for seven musicians by Henri Pousseur: literally a party game in which the seven musicians move through the musical structures like a game of halma and a big board on the side shows the audience the state of play.

This idea of Pousseur's is not as strange as it seems if you think that music-making has got everything to do with playing together. In this game of Pousseur's, however, the point of departure is more successful than the result, which many consider a drawback. And of course it's a drawback if you perform it as a composition in a concert. In my opinion, this especially interesting project of Pousseur's works better when you, as a musician, take part in it with friends in front of a small audience or no audience at all. At the end of the day it is better to play Snakes and Ladders than to watch it.

LAUGHING AND CRYING

The last evening was devoted to musical theatre. Before the interval we saw a staged performance of Luciano Berio's electronic work *Visages*, a continual chain of the most effective sounds the female voice can make, with quick, sometimes unnoticeable, transitions from exuberant laughter to hysterical crying and vice versa and ending in long, sonorous, radiant electronic passages. On the stage you only see a few people, among them two children and an old married couple – completely motionless – who are all looking at a woman sitting in the middle of the stage, totally immobile with her head in her lap. The production was by the composer.

After the interval we saw the musical theatre piece for speaker, singer, mime artist and three musicians, *Sur scène*, by the Argentinian composer, now living in Germany, Mauricio Kagel. The speaker, in a pitch that continually changes from falsetto to growling, talks the uttermost nonsense, first from his lectern and later shuffling among the instruments (such as piano and harpsichord) on the stage; the singer explores the walls with his hands, uttering a few notes now and then or interrupting the speaker; and the mime lives his own life with little Marcel Marceau-like tricks, except for some moments in which he is directly involved in the actions of the speaker or singer.

The three musicians have contact with each other or with the three moving characters; they exchange places or play a glockenspiel (which has been placed in the middle of the stage) together.

Each performer goes his own way and these ways sometimes coincide. The completely abstract expression of the players seems rather at odds with the conventional theatricality of the mime.

As is evident from these widely-differing productions (think about Stockhausen's *Originale*), the theatre plays a role in music which no one had expected. The movement of the musicians as a means of dramatic expression; the movement of the actors as an expression of time passing; the contact with one another; or the co-existence of as many different expressions as possible: these are a few aspects which at the moment are being explored by composers.

Neither on the music theatre, nor on the so-called 'neo-Dada' and 'happening' manifestations, has the last word been spoken.

PART 4

ENSEMBLES AND COMMITMENT

Part 4

Ensembles and commitment

"I may not be socially committed, but I do have something of a musical-social conscience," observed Louis Andriessen back in 1966 in the daily newspaper De Tijd.[48]

This is a striking pronouncement when compared with his activities in the years which followed. He contributed to the 'political-activist experimental' [PDE][†] concert, the Notenkrakersactie[††] and the opera Reconstructie: Don Giovanni which casts Che Guevara in the title role. Within ten years, he had set up De Volharding [Perseverance] and composed De Staat [The Republic –Plato].

In all of this, there is a great deal of identifiable 'musical-social conscience' and so, rightly, his position is well-known. Because of the famous and infamous actions which followed, this careful comment doesn't seem like him.

Maybe we ought to be surprised at being surprised. Andriessen himself often stresses that the sixties only really started with the protest movement against the Vietnam War in about 1966. Moreover, his commitment – whatever that word may mean – has always been, first and foremost, musical.

At the performance of De Staat during the opening of the Ars Musica festival in Brussels on 15 March 2001, Andriessen said in an interview: "According to Plato, you are already committed when you become aware of your own historical limitations in the choice of a musical theme. Commitment means to me that you make the gap between theory and practice, between what you think and what you do, as small as possible. I compose for musicians who like to play my music."

The four texts which follow deal, to a large extent, with ensembles which Andriessen himself founded. The first text is from the programme of the 'political-activist experimental' concert, for which musicians from different orchestras were brought together. Taken together, these texts offer

---

[48] Louis Andriessen, 19 February 1966.
[†] PDE – 'politiek-demonstatief experimenteel' ['political-activist experimental']
[††] The disruption of a concert by the Concertgebouw Orchestra, whose artistic policy the protesters regarded as conservative (see New Grove, volume 1, p. 637). See also p. 37.

The first political-activist experimental concert in Carré, 1968.
Photo: Ed van Elsken / Nederlands Fotoarchief

an insight into the artistic and political considerations which were important at the time. He always wrote the texts shortly after setting up the
ensembles. Only the piece on Hoketus is retrospective. It was written five
years later.

After the PDE concert in Carré [a theatre in Amsterdam] on 30 May
1968, everybody was very confused. There were anti-riot squads on the
alert because there were rumours that Carré was to be occupied. That had
never been the organisers' plan, but none-the-less, some visitors joined the
Revolution with alacrity. The theatre was in the possession of Zwolsman, a
speculator, and it was feared that this would mean the end of Carré. Peter
Schat could barely hold Jutte, the sculptor and well-known agitator at
council meetings, back from the stage and the timpani . The instruments,
which had been hired, had to be moved quickly to safety. Subsequently
the composers were reproached for being not sufficiently revolutionary.

Louis Andriessen and saxophone player Willem Breuker founded De
Volharding [Perseverance] orchestra, which started off with Andriessen's
piece *De Volharding*. After De Volharding, Andriessen collaborated closely
with groups of students from the Royal Conservatoire in The Hague. In
1977 he organised a project on string playing with one hand. The *Symfonie
voor losse snaren* [*Symphony for open strings*] resulted from this. The group
Hoketus and the piece of the same name had come into existence one
year earlier, as a criticism of the smooth sound of American repetitive
music. Less than ten years later, Hoketus disbanded.[49] In that period, the
group had played all over Europe.

Different musicians continued in smaller constellations: Peter van
Bergen, Patricio Wang, Huib Emmer and Gerard Bouwhuis carried on
with the group LOOS. Gerard Bouwhuis also formed the Het Pianoduo
with Cees van Zeeland. Diverse musicians modelled themselves on this
way of playing and working: the piano duo Post / Mulder; in Canada, the
group Sound Pressure Toronto; in Great Britain, the Steve Martland Band
and Icebreaker. This last ensemble was set up especially to play *Hoketus*
and Diderik Wagenaar's piece *Tam Tam* which he wrote for Hoketus.

In America too, Andriessen and Hoketus attracted attention. *Hoketus*
was performed at one of the first Bang On A Can festivals in New York by
an inter-continental group consisting of members of Hoketus, Icebreaker,
Californian E.A.R. Unit and Sound Pressure. Andriessen: "It was a marvellous performance which lasted a good fifty-five minutes. It only went a bit
wrong at letter E. This spot, where the continuous melody begins, is notorious. After a minute's trauma it landed on its feet again."

[49] Pay-Uun Hiu wrote a good article on the history of Hoketus under the title: 'De Haagse hik'
['The Hague hiccup']. In: Frits van der Waa, *De slag van Andriessen* [*The Beat of Andriessen*]
(Amsterdam: De Bezige Bij, 1993) pp. 72-88.

The symphony orchestra marching behind the music

1968

Taken from: Musical and political commentaries and analyses to a programme of a political-activist experimental concert with new Netherlands music in nineteen sixty eight (*written by a working group in collaboration with Konrad Boehmer*).

This evening [50] you will hear and see a revolutionary symphony orchestra, revolutionary in its line up and revolutionary in its foundation. Furthermore, it is the only one of its kind. The standard symphony orchestra originated in the court orchestras of the European royal houses, from small groups of string players and a changing line-up of wind players in Bach's time, to the colossal machines which throughout the world are in the service of a small minority of composers whose monopoly can be characterised by one concept: authority or, in musical terms, subjective or individualistic expression (with acknowledgement to Peter Schat).

You can read about the democratisation of music elsewhere in this booklet.[51] The comparison between social structure and the structure of a symphony orchestra is very tempting but I am too much of a composer to lay this in any detail at your feet. I shall restrict myself to a discussion of the symphony orchestra as musical machine.

Subsidised symphony orchestras each have at their disposal over one hundred musicians who specialise in the music of, let's say, 1780 to 1930. This is a period of a hundred and fifty years. This period in musical history is usually called the Romantic period. It was a period of evolution. In the first instance, great changes did not take place. Each composer worked on his own to evolve the most personal interpretation of a common language which was slowly extended by a few words until, by 1910, the lexicon was finished, because it was a limited language. The symphony orchestras are the interpreters of this language, of which the composers of today have a thorough command, but with which they have nothing to say.

---

[50] This concert was performed on Thursday 30 May in the Carré Theatre, Amsterdam, on Thursday 6 June in De Doelen in Rotterdam, on Sunday 9 June in the Circus Theatre in The Hague and on Friday 14 June in the Stadsschouwburg in Eindhoven.
[51] In the programme booklet, there are articles on musical and political subjects by Peter Schat, Misha Mengelberg and others.

The limitations of the symphony orchestra become more perceptible the longer they exist. Because of the specialisation in the music of the hundred and fifty year period mentioned above, the orchestra is neither technically nor mentally able to perform music composed in the five hundred years preceding this period, nor that composed (and being composed) in the fifty years following it. With the increased interest in non-tonal music, so has interest in pre-tonal music grown, both on the part of composers and music lovers.

The interest in tonal music remained, and still remains, albeit to a lesser extent. (Not all of Tchaikovsky's works are good – his symphonies perhaps – nor Beethoven's Ninth, nor the hollow virtuoso violin concertos by gifted violinists who also compose.) The task of the symphony orchestra becomes infeasible when you consider that each style demands its specialisation; the specialisation of such an orchestra in, for example, the Romantic repertoire is in itself very proper and necessary, but for whom? For which audience? Specialisation in music needs not only technical skill but, above all, needs musical 'commitment' to a style. Frans Breuggen[†] is not the best Baroque music performer because he plays historically correctly but because he hears more accurately what that music is about. For this reason he studied the Baroque and as a consequence plays historically correctly.

But who is committed to the Romantic repertoire? Who 'inhabits' this style? Even though two strategies exist which purport to have found solutions to these problems, – the so-called Heuwekemeijer plan and Ton de Leeuw's plan (the first of these maintains that orchestras should be expanded to such an extent that they can be divided into several specialised orchestras which can appear in various places simultaneously; the second refers to the formation of one orchestra which would only play new music – let us give preference this time to the recruitment of volunteers from several orchestras, who can, as necessary, form particular groupings with which modern composers can experiment. To do this, however, requires very detailed co-ordination between the different orchestral administrations.

It was not only irony which led Webern to call his opus 21 *Symphony*. But the piece was certainly not written for symphony orchestra. The first radical change in composing for orchestra was the soloistic treatment of all instruments, which Schoenberg perhaps began with his Chamber Symphony (1906), and also with that, the limitation of numbers.

An increasing number of composers were writing less and less for a string orchestra made up of forty adult men and women playing as one, or for woodwind and brass instruments played by fifty adult people and sound-

---

[†] Frans Breuggen was a recorder player in the sixties, and is now conductor of the Dutch Orchestra of the Eighteenth Century.

ing like one organ, but they were using an increasing range of soloistic capabilities.

Even in *Gruppen* by Stockhausen, which is written for three orchestras, all the parts are soloistic parts. Parallel to this ran an extension of the instrumentation, not only in the woodwind, but especially in the percussion. No orchestra could cope with buying the instruments necessary to perform new works, especially where percussion was concerned. New compositions for an orchestra – and by new, I also mean 'old' music which an orchestra doesn't know – obviously demand more rehearsal time than works which have already been played many times. And for this reason alone, it makes economic sense for orchestras to restrict themselves to the mainstream popular repertoire; because of the funding conditions, the number of concerts is so great that little time remains to rehearse new pieces. The number of premieres of new (and old) works is, in the case of all subsidised orchestras, a small percentage of their programming, and management argues that demand for 'mainstream repertoire' is high. But who demands the 'mainstream repertoire'? In the arts, just as in commercials, supply creates demand and not vice versa. If, by means of a mysterious bolt of lightning, only modern music were to be played and, as a great exception to this in accordance with the 'sandwich-technique', Mozart's Symphony in G minor were programmed between *Socrate* by Satie and *Momente* by Stockhausen, the auditoriums would be crammed full, far fuller than at present. The audience would be directly linked to what is happening on the stage because it is being confronted with a current language; also because Mozart's Symphony in G minor should be interpreted not as an evolution, but as a revolution in the history of the symphony.

This evening's concert is, to a certain extent, a realisation of the thoughts expressed above. It consists exclusively of premieres of new pieces. The fifty musicians or so involved (who now form the permanent core) have been drawn from six different orchestras. They are all specialists in modern music. Most of them are members of permanent ensembles: the Netherlands Wind Ensemble, with members from six different orchestras and a permanent core of about fifteen musician; the Percussion Group Amsterdam, comprising six percussionists, likewise from different orchestras, who have a large number of percussion instruments at their disposal; and finally, the Amsterdam String Quartet. Nearly all the rehearsals took place at night.

Tonight's band has been put together in an *ad hoc* way, a new sort of orchestra which has been formed according to the needs of the chosen scores.[52] The scores are not written for symphony orchestra, all parts are

---

[52] The programme: Louis Andriessen *Contra Tempus*, Misha Mengelberg *Hello Windyboys*, and Peter Schat *On Escalation*.

solo parts, there are only seven string players and the percussion is liberally expanded to include not only the instruments of the Percussion Group Amsterdam but also organ, clavinet, pianet, electric guitars, etc.

When I compare the programme which I just outlined with the actual content of the scores, it emerges that none of the three works is explicitly non-tonal. Even if Mozart is not represented at that concert, his language will certainly be spoken in each of the three pieces; there may not be an original thought expressed in that language, but there will certainly be quotations in this language.

When one sees the increasing interest in pre-tonal and non-tonal music, and the increased performance activity in both areas, the present symphony orchestra with its repertoire cannot be regarded other than as a historic monument of a glorious, feudal past. For as long as managements judge modern music according to the degree to which it suits the mainstream repertoire (and with that, they take the sting out of it) they ignore the most important characteristics of a composition: the exceptional and the dangerous. Between Satie and Stockhausen, Mozart too becomes a tremendous revolutionary again.

Brief history of De Volharding

1972

From Louis Andriessen's rough books, 1973.

	MUSIC	MUSIC POLITICS
Dec. 1965	Maderna action	
1967	the symphony orchestra *Anachronie I*	
1968	*Contra Tempus* against the symphony orchestra	PDE concert[53]
1969	*Reconstructie*	
Nov. 1969		Notenkrakersactie[†]
1970	*Spektakel I*	First inclusive concert
	Spektakel II with Willem Breuker	
1971	*Volkslied* (unisono)	

PERSONAL PRE-HISTORY

In 1967 I wrote a work for symphony orchestra: *Anachronie I*. The title already points to the fact that I found the symphony orchestra anachronistic. But because my background and upbringing had taught me to deal with that 'production machine' I wrote a piece for it; but I fragmented the various musical styles which the symphony orchestra has more or less mastered (Brahms to Peter Schat), and placed them opposite each other so that they were alienated from their own environment. Consequently they functioned as quotations: ("In the concert world, atonal music was replaced by a way of composing in which the melody recurred in the form of alienated style quotations taken from musical history." Harry Mulisch in 'The age of alienation' in *De toekomst van gisteren* [*The Future of Yesterday*]).

I noticed that, in practice, little came of this alienation because the whole piece was already alienated from the producers: the orchestral musicians. The piece was dumped on the musicians' music stands, they had to do what Sir said and after two rehearsals and one concert it disappeared in the cupboard. No one understood *what* he had played and *why*. And nobody gave a damn. I could hear (and see) *that* by the way they played. The

---

[†] See p. 37 / note on p. 121.
[53] PDE concert: political-activist experimental concert, 30 May 1968.

audience heard nothing at all.

In 1968 we[54] decided to organise a concert of our own music and we engaged the musicians ourselves. That was the 'political-activist experimental' concert in Carré, the evening when everyone thought that Carré would be occupied. The extreme right bourgeoisie chortled at the fact that we didn't 'succeed', but wouldn't they have been furious if we *had* occupied Carré?

In 1969, *Reconstructie* was composed and performed. Working on the subject matter of this opera gave me a fundamental insight into the social relationships in the world. There are people who possess things and obtain more by buying the work of other people. The differences between these two groups can be great (as in South America) or not so great (as in the Netherlands). Later I realised that, in *Reconstructie* too, the performing musicians sold their power to work in order to realise the piece. The working relationships between composers and performers did not differ from those in the symphony orchestras. The difference was that the musicians were invited and were 'happy to do it'.

It was not until the Notenkrakersactie that I understood clearly that my discomfort with the working relationships in a symphony orchestra had a political root. The Concertgebouw Orchestra really does have a social function: defending the interests of the ruling classes in the Netherlands, its audience. (Not only in the straight economic sense – tours in America and Japan have a favourable influence on trade relations with those countries – but also psychologically: the musicians have to be dressed as the ruling classes, they need to have the same opinions etc. etc.) This function conflicts with the questioning of music-making, putting music-making in inverted commas as, for example, in *Anachronie I*. Moreover, I detest that class of ladies and gentlemen who consume the music which affirms their self-satisfied social status. This is not so much due to the music itself as to the method of production.

In the Netherlands there were only a few musicians who played music which was really their own intellectual property, and was not either juvenile or reeking of money (like pop music): these were the Instant Composers Pool under the inspirational direction of Willem Breuker. The instinctively anti-bourgeois manner of their playing (anti-aesthetic as regards the sound, and without distinguishing between conception and production, as the name of the group indicates), had already attracted me for a long time. I wanted to work with musicians who would play nothing other than that which was, or would become, their (musical) property and who would call for work of high quality. Various members of the ICP were introduced to the well-established music with which I was familiar, such as avant-garde

---

[54] Reinbert de Leeuw, Peter Schat, Misha Mengelberg and I.

music and the more anti-aesthetic historical examples – Eisler, Varèse and Milhaud.

In 1970 I wrote *Spektakel*, a piece in which both sorts of musicians are confronted with each other: a production for the Nederlands Wind Ensemble, the Percussion Group Amsterdam and some free improvisers. It turned out that the piece was not equal to the psychological chasms which arose between the representatives of the different musical milieus. These psychological chasms originate without doubt from class distinctions.

For the second performance of *Spektakel* in the Holland Festival I unconditionally came down on the side of Willem Breuker who had written a new version. The Percussion Group Amsterdam disappeared from the piece and some free jazz freaks appeared in its place. "It was a total disruption of concert music. It was an insult to the Concertgebouw," wrote a certain G. Van Ravenzwaay in *De Zaanlander*. He was right. We No Longer Belonged.

Because we didn't actually want to leave classical music exclusively in the hands of the ladies and gentlemen, we organised 'inclusive' concerts: freely accessible supermarkets (though not as clean or well-ordered) where pop, jazz, avant-garde and Syntagma Musicum[55] came together. These concerts haven't produced a lot yet. For me there were no two ways about it: there were connections between these apparently different worlds, the most striking being authenticity. I would have been pleased to see the creation of musical productions which conformed less to their own milieu, which used more musical material than their own style permitted, but later I understood that this was anarchic idealism. *It turns out that musical material cannot be separated from the method of production*. The term 'method of production' is divisible into three phases:

1. The conception of a composer;
2. Confronting the performers with the idea;
3. Confronting the audience with the performance.

At the performance of *Anachronie I*, these three phases turned out to be so far removed from one another that the audience didn't understand the composer's idea at all. I saw that, in order to resolve this, we needed to work not only on better connections between performers and audience (like the inclusive concerts, phases 2-3) but also on the relationship between composer and performers (phases 1-2).

As far as phase 1 is concerned I was, in 1971, interested in 'unison, different instruments playing precisely the same thing at the same time. You will find early indications of this at the beginning of *Contra Tempus* (1968) and at the end of *De Schat van Scharlaken Rackham* [*The Treasure of*

---

[55] Syntagma Musicum, under the direction of Kees Otten, was at the time one of the best-known ensembles for ancient music.

Scarlet Rackham] (1970). I wrote a unison piece called *Volkslied*, in which the national anthem was gradually transformed into the international workers' song The International. This piece wanted to get rid of phase 3 – the piece was to be played, not listened to. Furthermore, the piece could be used to give the players some very elementary political instruction. As well as countless amateurs, three ICP members also took part in the first performance in De Doelen in Rotterdam. Practically all the members of symphony orchestras were conspicuous by their absence. In the speech which I gave on that occasion, I said amongst other things: "Even if music can't express anything anyway, or means nothing (and this last is incorrect), music is in any case a *reflection* of society."

And precisely because the piece had political content, I learned that:
(1) getting rid of phase 3 and
(2) writing for an arbitrary group of people
was far too easy and too free of obligations. A piece needs to operate in an *organising* way.

Furthermore, because I wanted to be directly involved in performance and could only play the piano, I began work on a unison piano concerto. The models which inspired me were not only the new American works by composers like Steve Reich and Terry Riley, but also Stravinsky's Piano Concerto, the Bach suites, *Eclat* by Boulez and Japanese gagaku, all of which have this element in common. I imagined a sound which would be difficult to categorise: is it jazz, is it avant-garde or is it something else?

Why must it be like jazz? Jazz is *the* folk music which is musically the most developed at the moment. Moreover, it has a musical quality which is common to all folk music and which is almost completely neglected by western art music, that is the 'physical' qualities of playing, in other words a player's staying power which becomes an issue if the duration of the playing is not established up front. *De Volharding* (my piece for wind / brass ensemble) is about this: continual repetitions of small musical motifs which are gradually transformed into other motifs, something which often occurs in improvised folk music, especially in Africa where jazz partially originates.

But it can only be like jazz if it's played by jazz musicians. I considered a line-up of three trumpets, three trombones and three saxes. Do you look for people for that line-up or do you tailor your line up to fit the people who want to be involved? I was not going to contribute more than a few indications of the style; the content of the piece needed to come into being in the rehearsals. I called upon Willem Breuker for help. After a few discussions (autumn 1971) we decided to engage a mixed group and start from the line-up which I had in my head and, to an extent, on paper. After much deliberation, we demanded of the jazz musicians that they should read music well, were versatile and not too individualistic. They were Theo Loevendie (alto sax), Herman de Wit (tenor sax) and Willem van Manen

Louis Andriessen plays the beginning of *De Volharding*;
behind him the flautist Dil Engelhardt

(trombone).

I knew Cees Klaver to be a good trumpeter and organiser of Alpho (the joint orchestral classes of the two professional training institutes in Amsterdam) and to be a cheeky sod who absolutely *never* did what he didn't want to. He said yes immediately. Cees brought a second trumpeter whom he knew from musicals with him: Arthur ten Bosch.

I myself asked John Floore (trumpet) and Frans van Luin (trombone), both from the Rotterdam Philharmonic Orchestra, with whom I had had various enjoyable meetings. Sytze Smit, a fellow combatant in the Notenkrakersactie, recommended Bernard Hunnekink (trombone) from the Kunstmaand Orchestra. We agreed to meet on 6 January in my attic.

THE REPERTOIRE[56]

1. *De Volharding* (1972) by Louis Andriessen
A composition of 16 pages (published by Donemus in 1972), the performance length of which is not fixed (15 - 40 minutes). The piece is an interpretation of techniques which Terry Riley developed in *In C* from avant-garde music on the one hand (Fluxus and anti-dynamic form) and jazz music on the other hand: continual repetition of simple melodic phrases.

During the first performance in Carré, the (packed) hall was in a flutter – a lot of cat-calls, shrieking and clapping. At the end, this turned into protracted and warm applause.[57]

2. *Volkslied* (1971) by Louis Andriessen
A unison composition, in which the melody of the *Wilhelmus* [the Dutch national anthem] is gradually transformed into the melody of The International.

3. *La Création du Monde* (1923) by Darius Milhaud, arranged for De Volharding's line up.
Milhaud's ballet about African creation myths caused a scandal at its premiere in 1923. The ballet-going public was shocked by the (at that time avant-garde) jazz music in the score. For us, the *Création* is the best historical example of a piece of music in which musical styles, linked to different social classes, were combined. Furthermore, we were in agreement that, because of this, the *Création* could never be played well: symphony orchestras can't play the jazz parts, and jazz orchestras do not have the whole set of instruments at their disposal.

4. *Tango* (1940) by Igor Stravinsky
Of Stravinsky's output, only *Tango* is actually suitable for De Volharding's

---

[56] In 1973.
[57] A recording of this concert on 12 May 1972 was released in 1997 by publishers Donemus as a special release with the journal *Key Notes*, on the occasion of the twenty-fifth anniversary of De Volharding.

musical politics (one may consider Stravinsky to be an example of someone who composes as a result of an existing compositional practice but not
for a new performance practice, the exception being *L'Histoire du Soldat*).
Tango is a critique of the prevailing fashion for South American tangos in
the forties, but at the same time a part of it. This critical attitude, which
springs from involvement with what you criticise, is the model for De
Volharding.

(For this reason, too, the first part of Peter Schat's *Het Vijfde Seizoen*
[*The Fifth Season*], originally written for De Volharding, was not suitable for
us. Apart from the fact that musically and technically it was not conceived
from within the group, the piece was not in a dialectical relationship with
its musical subject, in this case, pop music. The piece certainly 'said' something about pop music but it was not a part of it.)

5. *Solidariteitslied* [*Solidarity Song*] (1931) by Hanns Eisler
    Written for the film *Kühle Wampe* and the best socialist battle song from
Germany in the thirties. It was demonstrated in practice that the critical
attitude of De Volharding needed to be expressed musically, not only im-
plicitly, but also explicitly and politically. Alongside *Tango*, therefore, militant songs. But not only the two songs by Louis Andriessen from the political doctrine *De Maatregel* [*The Measure taken*] by Bertolt Brecht.

6. *Reeds sprak de wereld* [*Already the world spoke*]

7. *Stakingslied* [*Strike Song*]

8. *Bevrijdt het Zuiden* [*Fear the South*] by Huong Tong Peng
    Arranged by M. Mengelberg for De Volharding. Hymn of the National
Liberation Front of South Vietnam. Necessary choice of repertoire in the
current political climate, M.'s arrangement has a reference to *Russian* harmonies. The melody is a good example of a fusion of genres – the Chinese
pentatonic in western march rhythm.

9. *Vietnamlied* [*Vietnam Song*] music: Gilius van Bergeijk
    New Netherlands political song of high musical quality.

10. *Dat gebeurt in Vietnam* [*That happens in Vietnam*] music: Louis Andriessen,
text: Paul Binnerts.
    New singing techniques developed in *De Maatregel* are used here: an
agitated singing style with many repeated notes in quick quavers, frequently
in irregular rhythms, accompanied by harmonically complicated chords.
The development of this style could become important for agit-prop music theatre manifestations.

    At the moment the following are being composed and / or rehearsed:
11. *Het paard van Troje* [*The Trojan Horse*] by Willem Breuker
An instrumental piece, arranged for De Volharding (20 minutes).

The orchestra De Volharding on location, around 1972. Photo: Olivier Vrooland

12. A new piece by Willem Breuker, still untitled.
13. *On Jimmy Yancey* by Louis Andriessen. Jimmy Yancey is one of the first and most authentic boogie woogie pianists. The boogie woogie piano style is somewhat comparable with *De Volharding*: the continuing repetition of fixed rhythmic patterns. The piece will be a sequel to *De Volharding*.
14. A piece by Gilius Van Bergeijk (still untitled).
15. Arrangements of Georgian secular songs.
People who know Georgian music know about its qualities; an explanation for people who don't know it cannot be within the scope of this article.

THE IDEOLOGY

De Volharding tries, through practical performance, to make a contribution to what in theory is called 'the materialistic art theory'. In music, that signifies that De Volharding tries to uncover the relationships between conception of music (phase 1, the composer), production of music (phase 2, the performing musicians), and consumption of music (phase 3, the listeners) and to change them. In so doing, De Volharding starts from a critical attitude towards prevailing practices, in which existing relationships are affirmed. This critical attitude stems from a socially critical stance.

De Volharding tries, through its way of working, its repertoire and its way of playing, to reach other and new audiences, who could be more involved in the production and, because of this, would demand another sort of musical composition. De Volharding has the advantage that it starts from different musical techniques (which are connected to different social classes) because it has at its disposal classically-trained musicians and jazz musicians.

An advantage of working with De Volharding is that the musicians commit themselves completely to the repertoire and to the audience. We are always discussing both of these things.

The consequence of this is that De Volharding at a political meeting, for example, has a different function from other musicians who may appear.

De Volharding is building a repertoire which stems from the social commitment of the listeners and the members. Taking the audience's needs and tastes as a starting point, we need to develop and criticise them at the same time. De Volharding discusses whether it will actually play somewhere or not. (We have rejected many appearances offered to us, of which the most important was VARA's[†] last day.)

At the same time we rehearse the specific musical problems posed by the new repertoire (such as notation) weekly. A jazz musician plays certain notation in a certain musical context differently from a classical musician. The same applies to rhythm. In the *Création du Monde* there are many examples where the methods of playing become attuned to one another after many rehearsals. Also, sometimes, for example at the beginning of the fugue, the 'timing' is left to the musicians themselves. As far as that is concerned, we are still in the preliminary phase; the exploration is experimental. It does need to be said that De Volharding does not enjoy musical experimentation just for the sake of it. Musical exploration cannot be regarded as distinct from the functioning of the group in society (see 'Concerts').[58]

[†] VARA is a left-wing broadcasting institution.

[58] Under the heading 'Concerts' there is, in the notebook in which Louis Andriessen wrote this text, a list of the 21 appearances of De Volharding between 17 September and 19 June 1973, at political gatherings, schools, universities, clubs and community centres.

Hoketus in the Concertgebouw

October, 1981

From Louis Andriessen's rough books, October 1981

In April of this year, Elmer Schönberger wrote an article in *Vrij Nederland* on *Bint* by Cornelis de Bondt. He compares the piece with the closing bars of Stravinsky's *Les Noces* and *Requiem Canticles*. "*Bint* begins where Stravinsky – literally: in the postlude of *Requiem Canticles* – leaves off." [59]

The horrible, unbearably slow-to-get-going, yet unstoppable 'human machine' which is *Bint*, is indeed an example of a type of musical thinking which is grafted more onto Stravinsky than the Viennese School. It looks as though the rest of this century will be devoted to overcoming the differences between Stravinsky and Schoenberg. Or to put it more strongly: it could well be that the hegemony of German music, which Schoenberg predicted, is waning.

Composer Huib Emmer certainly utilises Schoenberg's chromatic harmonies, but uses them in montage forms which seem more likely to be derived from Stravinsky than from Schoenberg.

Cornelis de Bondt belongs to the young generation of composers who regard twelve-note music as the final radical consequence of Wagner's Romantic chromaticism.

Once again, compositional problems which were ignored by composers of the fifties and sixties are being tackled: harmonic rhythm, arsis-thesis relationships, modality, additive rhythms, tonality, continuity. Furthermore, the group Hoketus is representative of two other trends in new music, the first being the 'de-hierarchising' of the musical material: that is, equal parts for all players and the influence of performance (music making) on composing. (When Hoketus plays a G sharp, it isn't only a G sharp, it is Hoketus too.)

The second, closely connected to 'de-hierarchising', is this: the music which Hoketus plays has not only sprung out of the western art music tradition but shows influences of other, non-western musical forms including pop and jazz. This musical attitude, probably a result of the democratisation movements of the sixties, is carried through to the decision-making process within the group. All the members decide collectively what they

[59] See also: Louis Andriessen / Elmer Schönberger, *The Apollonian Clockwork*, p. 15.

Jan Erik Noske (panpipes) and Bob Zimmerman (sax) from the group Hoketus.
Photo: Nederlandse Omroep Stichting, Hilversum

will play and where they will play and even how they will be composed for.
Composers who write for Hoketus, but who do not think sufficiently from
the group's perspective, are bound to fail. It is not knowledge of the set of
instruments alone which is necessary but also a knowledge of the musical
ideology of the musicians who play the set of instruments.

And with this, the ideal picture of composing as formulated in the nineteenth century, the most individual expression of the most individual emotion, changes. Composing for Hoketus is closer to the classical composers,
but at the same time also to composers who composed for orchestras such
as the Duke Ellington orchestra.

The intensive collaboration between performing musicians and composers is arguably the most radical aspect of the group Hoketus. As long as
the group goes to work without making concessions, then it will be able to
have a strong influence on the development of new musical thinking.[60]

[60] See note 49 on p. 123

About the open strings project

1977

From Louis Andriessen's rough books, 1977.

An important part of my instrumentation teaching at the Conservatoire in The Hague is the setting up of practical projects.

Last year, *Hoketus* was the result of a 'minimal music' project; this year the *Symfonie voor losse snaren* [*Symphony for open strings*] is the result of the 'open strings project'. The project is organised in a strict anarchistic way. One person has an idea; he involves another who pulls in a third, etc.

In 1969, I took my leave of the symphony orchestra once and for all with a piece half of which had to be improvised; the other half consisted of a gigantic string orchestra all playing continuous notes on open, albeit abnormally tuned, strings. This piece, *Hoe het is* [*How it is*] begins with a series of tonal chromatic chords (rather like Gesualdo) which shift sequentially. Thus you can really monitor whether the string players have re-tuned their strings accurately. (With one exception: about half way through, a magnificent three-part arrangement of the *Wilhelmus* [the Dutch national anthem] appears in G sharp minor on double bass, sounding like Pérotin. Later in the piece, the monitoring became more difficult, because the rest of the score was almost exclusively comprised of clusters. The *Wilhelmus* was included because the Concertgebouw Orchestra was to perform the piece and, at that time, was still calling itself the National Orchestra. I withdrew the piece before the performance as, three months before the concert, the Notenkrakersactie[†] broke out and my friends and I were thrown out of the Concertgebouw itself.)

The violin-maker Möller had explained to me how far you can go when you re-tune an instrument without damaging it.

Hoe het is was actually written 'against' the symphony orchestra. The strings have been the foundation and the heart of the symphony orchestra since its inception and, without doubt, will remain so until its death. Paralysing one hand of the entire string section and removing the possibility of producing a beautiful note and doing vibrato seemed to me to testify to a very negative attitude as regards the symphony orchestra. Later, that proved to be correct. When, I guess around 1975, a performance was being planned

[†] See page 37 / note on p. 121.

by the Frysk Orchestra, the orchestra, to a man, refused to play it. But for the wrong reasons: the scordaturas (the official word for mistuning) would be bad for the instruments.

However, one of the things which has remained with me from the only performance of *Hoe het is*, was the literally *unprecedented* beautiful sound of the Gesualdo-like opening bars. The idea of an 'open-strings string orchestra' was actually too good for such a nasty composition. Furthermore, when I met some pleasant student string players in The Hague, we decided to form an alternative string orchestra which would play only open strings. It was in this way that the project started and it resulted (having for a time rehearsed practice pieces – Bach, Milhaud, Purcell, some of my own fragments, South American beguines) in the *Symphony for open strings*

The group consists of twelve string players: five violins, two violas, three cellos and two double basses. The scordaturas are arranged by violist Koos Palmboom so that the orchestra has all the chromatic notes (according to equal temperament twelve-note tuning, between B and f") at its disposal:

This makes it possible to play a very wide range of repertoire, but there is only one of each note present. This means that each melody is played by as many people as there are notes in the melody. A melody such as:

requires four string players to perform it. Different examples of a playing technique such as this do exist. The closest to home is the English 'change ringing', pieces for a large number of big and small church bells in which each player operates one bell. In West Africa, there are orchestras of drums in which each player plays one or two drums.

I know of no examples in western musical culture except the comparable 'hoquet technique' in the vocal style of the Ars Nova and, to a certain extent, the 'punctual' music of Webern, for example. A playing style such as this requires a totally individual and specific way of bowing; the way in which you start the note and how, and when, it ends is totally different from normal violin playing. Furthermore, the rhythmic acuity of each part (the counting) is exceedingly important because each part is just a small part of the whole.

The *Symphony* which I have written for this orchestra only makes use of a limited number of the possibilities which the open string orchestra offers.

Compositionally and technically it uses symphonic techniques, recurring motifs, for example, but especially a development and something akin to a recapitulation. I have not used techniques such as these since the fifties. Perhaps that is my response to the current neo-Romantic trend – back to the symphony orchestra. In this sense my *Symphony* is ambiguous. The piece makes use of symphonic techniques, there are strong tonally-oriented fragments, even a quote from the twenties, but the orchestra can never sound like a real string orchestra because it is literally 'unhanded'. This apparent disadvantage proves to be an advantage. Because of the unprecedented sound you can write music which resembles existing music. What I am ultimately concerned with is not only inventing new music, but developing new ways of playing, and contributing other (new) ways for musicians to deal with their instruments and with music – in other words, an alternative musical practice. This applies to composers, too. It is much too limiting for a composer to concern himself with *notes* alone, the notes which you think have everything to do with your own attitudes as compared with the professional practice of your musicians. If you want to change music, and that is the composer's most important task, then you must change music-making too. As far as purely musical material (mine, as a composer) is concerned, whether you are talking about this symphony, or about *Melodie, Hoketus, Volkslied* or *De Staat* [*The Republic*], since 1970 my pieces form one story which is about unison, the intangible musical world in which harmony and melody gradually merge into one another.

PART 5

OWN WORK

Part 5

Own work

In the second half of this book, Andriessen talks about his own work, in interviews and lectures. The latter should not be taken at all literally. As he has already mentioned in the article on Ravel, he prefers to talk than to read from a prepared text. It is very unlikely that he will ever write any more than a short explanation about his work . (He does have plans for a book on *The Well-Tempered Klavier* by Bach and still hopes to explore Stravinsky's music further.) However, in order to give a more permanent form to his ideas on his own work, the lectures on his larger pieces are reproduced here.

We have chosen not to conceal the original spoken form for it is that improvisatory nature, or the appearance of it, which is so characteristic of Andriessen.

Stravinsky once defined the difference between himself and Arnold Schoenberg as follows: Stravinsky: "What the Chinese philosopher says cannot be dissociated from the fact that he says it in Chinese." Schoenberg: "A Chinese philosopher speaks Chinese, but what is he saying?"[61]

In a conveniently arranged summary of the 'contents' of the lectures, it would be precisely their essence which would be lost. The chain of references and anecdotes with which Andriessen describes his manner of working presents a characterisation of himself or, at any rate, of the way in which he talks about his work in public. Practice always occupies a central position. He finds that theory and analysis of the music comes out better in the isolation of the study.

He chooses what is of importance to him as a composer from the world around him. The consciousness that he is no philosopher, historian, man of letters or musicologist, gives him a freedom which the practitioners of these disciplines cannot always permit themselves. He can cross the dividing line between fact and fiction without ceremony. Consequently in his work he can accept speculations on Hadewijch's[†] idea of love as true.

He gives free rein to unresolved contradictions; he has been familiar with this since he got to know the Buddhist koans when he was seventeen.

---

[61] Louis Andriessen and Elmer Schönberger, *The Apollonian Clockwork.*
[†] Hadewijch was a thirteenth-century mystic and the subject of part 2 of Louis Andriessen's work *De Materie.*

In this respect, he feels sympathy for the early Romantics, who preferred to stretch a contradiction rather than give up their grand idea of reality by a forced synthesis. In reality, a reconciliation of these contrasts is just aiming too high.

By not presenting ready-made views but rather fragments with frayed ends and loose ends, Andriessen deliberately puts the ball back in the audience's court. Anyone who wants to know the details or to resolve the contradictions should try to work it out for himself .

The collection of works which Andriessen discusses begins with *De Staat* [*The Republic*]. "With the passing of the years, *De Staat* (1976) will probably increasingly be seen as the turning point in Louis Andriessen's œuvre," Elmer Schönberger wrote in 1986. He calls the piece "the delineation of a musical terrain which in the course of – so far – the ten subsequent years would be brought into cultivation." [62]

In the meantime, twenty-five years have passed since the premiere of *De Staat*. With the exception of *Mausoleum*, Andriessen here discusses all the larger works from this period. The lectures are arranged in chronological order of the compositions. [63]

He speaks about all those things which have been treated separately in the preceding chapters: his life, aesthetic ideas, other composers, ensembles he has worked with and lots more. The subject is composing and *everything* can play a part. In this field, too, he likes to overturn the customary hierarchies with a large gesture. As he said to his students: "Whether you work with complex figures or are inspired by the way your mother makes pasta, it can be important for your music."

Andriessen spoke about *De Materie* [*Matter*] to a general audience. In the case of the other texts, his audience consisted largely of young composers: students at the Royal Conservatoire in The Hague; participants in the International Young Composers' Meeting in Apeldoorn; and a composers' workshop in Radziejowice (Poland).

The lectures were mostly followed by questions and discussions. Interesting parts have been included in the texts. After the lecture on *The Last Day*, someone asked Andriessen if this piece wasn't a lot more personal than *De Staat*. At this, he looked back: "I believe that the fury in *De Staat*, BANG BANG BANG the whole time, is even more personal than *The Last Day* because at that time I was very angry about what was happening in

---

[62] Elmer Schönberger, 'Mono' in: *De vrouw met de hamer & andere componisten* [*The woman with the hammer and other composers*], (Amsterdam: De Bezige Bij, 1992), p. 155.
[63] Sometimes different lectures on the same subject have been brought together. The origination of the material is described in the short introductions.

the world, in my surroundings and in my soul. I had a lot to rage about. I wanted to do things, amongst others with De Volharding, and I must say that some things were successful. Musical life in the Netherlands has changed, so it has been a partial success. But I wanted to keep on shouting and De Volharding couldn't play my shouting any more. I needed more trumpets, faster rhythms and time changes. And then that – *De Staat* – came out of it. When you get older, you are increasingly distanced from what you are doing, partly because you have a better idea of what you are doing. That is not good; it is better in part *not* to know what you are doing. Of course you need some distance, otherwise you can't write. But it is good if you always try and do something which you can't completely control. Then true art comes into being. You've got to be content with that."

Interview on *De Staat*
by Ruth Dreier
Amsterdam, 1990

When the CD *of* De Staat *appeared in 1990, Ruth Dreier visited Louis Andriessen for an interview. As a music journalist, radio producer and programmer, Ruth Dreier has specialised in the Dutch-American connection. She is the host and producer of* 'LIVE! *at the Concertgebouw', a radio series heard across the United States. In the mid 1980s, while programme director of* WNYC-FM, *New York Public Radio, Dreier introduced the music of Louis Andriessen to listeners in New York City.*

This interview was made in the beautiful front room of Louis Andriessen's house on the Keizersgracht in Amsterdam. We met on an early spring evening when the long-setting northern sun was making a slow, spectacular disappearance from the sky. It hit the canal with blunt force, turning it now to silvery grey, now to a surrealistic blue in resonance with the sky above. Chartreuse leaves outside the tall house's ample windows sparkled in the changing light. Louis offered me an excellent red wine and began the interview himself:

LA: One of the important aspects of the piece is its polemic relation with the symphony orchestra. It shows a way of handling musicians, of choosing combinations of instruments which is anti-symphonic.

RD: You've answered my first question which was: "Fourteen years after the premiere of this political piece, is it still political?"
LA: The political quality of the piece is even more relevant now than in the early seventies because of the fact that it is written for an ideal ensemble, for musicians who are free to choose what they want to play, for musicians who want to play only the music they like. I don't want to have a discrepancy between the music and the production of the music as always happens when you perform twentieth-century music for symphony orchestras. I knew, while writing for this group of instruments, that I would have young, free-lance musicians who were dying to play the music.

It's even more revolutionary now than in the seventies because then you got support for that sort of thing. Nowadays, since there's less money around, particularly in America, people have to choose to work with their own bands. That's a very good solution. The problem is, when you write for your own band like Steve Reich did and a person like Michael Gordon does, you can't write in polemic with the symphonic tradition. When you want to write pieces that deal with polemizing the line of Bruckner up to,

say, *Le Sacre du Printemps* of Stravinsky, then you have to write big pieces
with a lot of instruments and long durations. That's *De Staat* [*The Republic*].

*It's of equal weight to a symphonic piece but it's not for symphony orchestra so
you prove a point that you don't have to use the symphony as an organism in
order to achieve profound ends or big sounds. That's another aspect of De Staat
– the sheer amplitude. Until this piece, the only time you heard loud music was in
the symphony hall or at a rock concert. There was nothing in between.*

That has to do with the piece having other sources than Bruckner and
Brahms. You will recognize scales and pitches from Indonesian music, for
example. But the loudness and the use of amplification, not only for loudness but for balance, is something that comes from rock'n roll.

*What symphony orchestra are you talking about? The general idea or a spe-
cific orchestra, like the Concertgebouw in Amsterdam?*

I don't talk about the Concertgebouw. They're a brilliant orchestra,
particularly for repertoire from the early nineteenth to the early twentieth
century. No, I'm talking about all orchestras; they're all the same and should
specialize in this period.

*Is there a contradiction in what you're saying? That 1) the orchestra should
stay with the repertoire that's best suited for it and 2) that you as a composer have
been left out, opted out, shut out of the orchestral world and you resent it?*

No that's not the problem. I've been performed. I have no rancour at
all. I wrote the piece because the musical language needed another approach to playing and another sort of musician. I'll give you an example.
The first non-Dutch performance was in Warsaw in 1977, and that was
mostly done with symphony orchestra musicians. I had to sing every note
for them because they articulated the piece like Bruckner and Mahler.
And it should be articulated like Count Basie and Stan Kenton!

I could write beautiful symphonic music; I have the technical ability.
But then I'm not doing what I am supposed to do, which is to develop a
musical language which has to do with other roots.

I like solo voices. Almost all those big pieces I did later, like *Mausoleum*
or *De Snelheid*, which was originally for orchestra, or *De Tijd*, are written for
solo voices. I use mass chords all the time, but I need solo voices.

*There's something strong in your music about the importance of the indi-
vidual voice and the shades of meaning when it plays with, or against, itself.
When you have people hocketing, or in unison, something comes through at a
deeper level about the individual voice of the player and, by extension, the individual voice of the composer. How do you make a big sound that isn't lost in the
weight of a massed section or a mass ideology?*

The record sleeve for *De Staat* [*The Republic*], 1977.
Design: Louis Andriessen, Floris Guntenaar. Photo: Floris Guntenaar

There is a strange philosophy of democracy here. All musicians should have the same information. All parts are difficult, all parts are equal in quality, in importance in the total voicing. The hocketing is a specific thing. First of all, it's from folk music, but I like the difficulty of it, the difficulty of producing together what you are unable to do yourself. I like the struggle of it.

You have to have such concentration to co-ordinate like that, which is fundamentally different from making a big unison sound. Here, if you lost your sense of self, you would be lost; you must maintain your integrity.

That's why I call it complex music, more than the so-called complex music. Because in my music, when you make a mistake, it's fatal, and in complex music it's not really fatal because you can't hear it.

One thing I'm sure of, my music structurally has more to do with Classical music than Romantic music.

Is there something frightening or even repugnant to you about the effect of wallowing in sheer sound, like the late nineteenth-century symphonists?
There's something in Romanticism which I don't like, which is that there's no space for the listener to fill in his own music; you are taken away with it.

I don't understand this text. It's very difficult, very ambiguous.
It's very clear. Plato wants to have extremely strong rules in this ideal state he was trying to define. And that's typical for totalitarian thinkers who are into power. The advantage of that kind of thinking is that it's very simple, its non-dialectical. Plato was a perfect example for me to use in explaining to what I call the 'vulgar' Marxists of the time that the problems were much more complex than they found. Because even they could understand that Plato is not right.
From the other side, Plato says in the final chorus that you should not change the laws of music because when you do that you change the laws of the state. I regret as a composer that he's not right. Imagine a situation in which music would have that power.
For composers that would be quite ideal of course! [laughter]
The angriness of the piece has to do with my regret that Plato was wrong. I have sympathy for a situation in which music becomes extremely important again, as in Plato, when people knew how important art was.

What language is the singing in?
Greek. I even worked with a guy who knows the difference between the Athens and the Spartan pronunciation so that it's as authentic as possible. That's what I always try to do: try to find the authenticity. That's the best argument in everything that you do – you should try to be as open-hearted as possible.

You just capsulized your whole effort, which is both anarchistic and conciliatory. When you're true to the spirit it can blow things apart and pull them together.
I'm glad you recognize that. But let me make it a bit more complex. I never try to find my own style. I'm not busy with "is this authentic?" I don't write to express myself. I use that which is surrounding me to write good music.

De Staat is very difficult to get a hold of. I can't file it. I like that about it; it refuses to be contained.
That's a compliment. It has a fluent tempo, quite contrary to my other pieces.

How is it laid out?

Basically, the construction is two times two. All the chords are based on four pitches, tetrachords. The orchestra is also divided into two, more or less identical, groups. Everything is by four – four oboes, four singers, etc. Four is the magic number for *De Staat* on all levels.

There are four texts also, like a mirror in a way. It's very important for me where the chorus sings. They come in right after the beginning, and right before the end is the final chorus so it's a symmetrical structure. But not completely because half-way through are the two basic texts and the end comes at the golden section.

That's what holds it together, inside of the variable tempi; it's almost like an object.

Yes, that's the way I thought of it. Before starting the piece, I thought it should be one big wall falling slowly over you. That was my vision: a sort of Peruvian wall – you know those Incan walls with all those stones? – in one big slow movement. GANG!

I'm stunned, when listening to De Staat, at what seems to be a direct connection to what Reich was doing, and also Glass, at the time.

There's not much Steve [Reich] in the piece. There's much more Terry Riley, some *In C*. *De Staat* was written three years before *Tehillim*, you should not forget that. When I gave Steve the record of *De Staat*, he was busy writing *Music for 18 Musicians*. I think that Reich is a very good composer. I met him at Misha Mengelberg's[†] place in 1970 or 71. That was his first concert here; he was completely unknown. But I knew about him already, from Frederic Rzewski.[††] Phil Glass was still in Steve's group then. I'd heard about his music from a German radio guy I met in a bar in New York City in 1970 or '71. He said I should hear *Music in Changing Parts*, which I liked very much.

Was that your first time in New York?

No, the first time I was in New York was in the late sixties. Some of us had founded a Charles Ives Society and were invited to the Charles Ives Centennial Congress. Amazing, eh? But my interest in America dates from much earlier than that.

It started immediately after the war when there was a guy on the radio who had a programme called USA *Cabaret*. His name was Pete Felleman. He was the first guy who made us listen to Stan Kenton, Shelly Manne, Monk and Parker, Miles Davis, all that sort of thing. That has been one of the most important influences in my musical life – except for the big tradi-

[†] A jazz pianist and composer.
[††] An American composer now living in Belgium.

tion we have laid back on our shoulders in Europe of course.

Another thing: my brother Jurriaan lived in the States during the early fifties and had a lot of success.[64] Then he came back to arrange a permanent visa and ended up staying here. But he brought back America. I met him when he returned, one of the first times a family member ever flew. That was in 1952. He flew back in a Lockheed Constellation – do you remember that aeroplane? That was not a brother, that was an archangel! [laughter] He brought back things like Bob Graettinger, who wrote a sort of Schoenberg for Stan Kenton's band; the string quartet of John Cage, Gershwin's *American in Paris*, Copland and others. That was very important for my education.

Early be-bop and cool jazz have influenced me very strongly, more than Mozart, Bach and Brahms. I was 14-15, and those are strong roots for a young composer. At first I couldn't really compose with it, because jazz was something to be improvised on the piano. So I played with my friends – all the Gerry Mulligan quartets, etc. – and the composing was more in the family tradition – French music, Stravinsky, Copland, that type of thing.

So there was a bit of a split between what you were doing at the piano and what you were writing on the page; was that resolved?

I cannot judge. You should judge that. Listen to *De Materie*, which I think is my main thing. The boogie woogie in that piece is a real good example of my piano playing!

There was a record, *8 To The Bar* it was called, of two gigantic black boogie woogie players, on two pianos. Twice as beautiful as one piano! [laughter]. Albert Ammons and Pete Johnson. Fantastic. When I was 14 years old that was the only record I really liked I think.[65]

Can you describe what the feeling was when you heard that music?

The first word was freedom, of course – the cry of freedom and anarchy, especially in the cool jazz. Parker and Gillespie were still fighting but *The Birth of the Cool*, with Miles Davis, was laid back for the first time. It was Gil Evans' work, the whole record.

What intrigues me in all of your music, which in some ways is more American than much American music, is how a child of a privileged home, your father a well-known composer, the whole family a distinguished one – how it was that you responded to freedom and anarchy?

I recognized the cry, but it's not what I dealt with. What I liked were the incredible changes Parker made on the chords of the standards! In fact,

---

[64] George Balanchine and Jerome Robbins choreographed Jurriaan Andriessen's *Berkshire Symphonies*.
[65] See also the chapter on *De Stijl*, part 3 of *De Materie*, p. 214.

that's what I'm trying to incorporate as the basis for the Kronos quartet I'm going to write.[66] I'm studying the changes of Parker.

Playing be-bop on string instruments is of course impossible, it's un-idiomatic, but it could be interesting because I know something about classical culture – as in string quartets – my roots being European and I have strong feelings for early be-bop. I have to say something about that.

I like the impossible, to put myself in a difficult situation. I see composing as an experiment. More than giving solutions to problems, I like to pose problems.

It seems like that has a lot to do with the players you are posing problems for.
They are the sort of people who can meet the problems. In fact, if Kronos had not asked me I would not have dared to think of writing a string quartet.

There's something in what you're talking about here – the groups you're mentioning are comprised of incredibly strong players, each member is an individual. I get the sense that when you talk about not writing for symphony orchestras, you're talking about a group sensibility in which the players have lost themselves; you're really talking about the death of something.
I consider *Le Sacre* to be the first piece showing the new world. It deals with both the classical tradition of the symphony orchestra and with folk music. That's the subject for the twentieth century, sure: diatonic folk music, rhythm, pulse, breathing and…

Sex.
[laughter] yes, and sex, of course. But when I hear performances of *Le Sacre* they sound like Brahms, like the grace notes for example. When we have this ideal ensemble, which we now invent tonight, that I would like to call the orchestra of the twenty-first century if you don't mind (and Reinbert de Leeuw should be the conductor), they will play the grace notes as you would hear two African women singing in the fields of Ghana, or Russian peasants. *Le Sacre* is about folk music and I want to hear that.

When you say folk music, I hear you talking about a raw human quality.
Yes. It's my main life attitude: to see that spirit and body are not each other's enemies, but that they develop each other. It's the only way to be a human being.

Who are you writing the music for? You've said elsewhere that you are aware of writing for someone and that your first listeners are the players.
In the sixties and seventies it was very important to meet your friends in the public, so you played on special occasions, for demonstrations and

[66] This was to be the string quartet *Facing Death*.

working class causes, etc. Now things have changed. I want to write music which I know will be understood by my public: middle class, left-wing, between 24-40 years old.

But I never think of that. I think of writing a kind of musical criticism which is interesting for people who are critical themselves – that's the best way to put it.

You have a kind of supra-criticism operating while you're working: examining as well as participating.

Composing means listening. You sit at a piano or the desk and you've written six bars and now it's time for the seventh bar, and who's going to do that? The way I do that is by imagining I'm sitting in a nice hall and this piece is being performed there – all your friends are on the stage, Reinbert's conducting – and the sixth bar happens and now what do I hear? I imagine this performance and then hear what I am going to write.

Like Roland Kirk used to say: "you've got to split your mind in two."
That's true.

That's interesting in terms of what you were saying about Classicism before. Is this a Dutch attitude? This distance?

Classicism? No, I don't feel it that way. It's French, it's latin... it's not German.

There's lots of space in Bach.
Bach is not German, he's a genius [laughter]. My father explained that Bach's genius has to do with using many different styles, like the Italian avant-garde of Vivaldi and all the others. He was a very hip composer. No, he was not hip, he used hip genres.

He was very aware.
Mozart was the same. He quoted the genres, then he put his own little essayistic criticism in it. He wrote his father, from Mannheim or somewhere, and said: "I'm sitting here and I'm going to write six violin sonatas *in a style they like here.*" These are the beautiful, important, violin sonatas, and he just wrote them in the style of 'those guys there'. That's nice, eh? I like that attitude very much.

Your music is never seriously serious. It's either humorously serious, or seriously humorous – always a space, always a sense of control.
In that sense, Stravinsky is my greatest example.

Also be-bop?
Yeah! Parker is cold cold cold. Good art is cold; it has reservations.

Here you sit in this beautiful canal house, where you've lived for almost twenty years, and it seems essential that there's water, a reflective surface, right outside your window. It seems like this situation, which is so comfortable and so gracious, allows you to write music with a lot of tension and energy in it.

If you want to use the metaphor of water, I agree. But your idea of the beauty of the canals in Amsterdam is a little bit naive. Why are these canals here? Because water is so dangerous in Holland. This is our way to control this terrible enemy. We have really big problems with this guy! We are used to a continuous fight with water – romantic idea, but it's true. The canals are our hate / love relationship with water.

It's lovely right now, with the street lights shining on it. But this is the demon right here; it's contained.

I'm not sure you can translate my approach that way. I prefer Vermeer to Rembrandt, for instance, who I think was one of the first Romantics. Vermeer, on the other hand, is typical for Dutch Calvinist art, that cold strictness. My passion has to do with my Burgundic Catholic upbringing. You have to be generous – overdaad schaadt niet.[†]

In the context of this country.

There's a word I use often, and never hear in America, which is bluntness. There is even bluntness in the structure of the canals, and you find it in my music. I don't like counterpoint, for instance. I like to be very direct and exact and that is very typical for Holland.

Maybe that's what you heard in Parker and Miles. They were doing for America what your Burgundian roots have done for you here.

That's possible, yeah. You hear the violence but you also hear the control.

I have the feeling that whatever you're working on, you have your eyes not on yourself, but on something that's in the middle distance – not too close but not too far away. The search for authenticity is to make that thing, to describe it, absolutely. That's something special about your music – you aren't stuck, you don't have creative cardiovascular disease.

[laughter] I will have this very soon. I need another cigarette!

You are focusing on something that's out there, not inside yourself. What I would say as a listener is that the real authenticity resides in the resonance and the reflection between you and this object.

I find this very intelligent and I completely agree. [laughter]

[†] A Dutch expression which means 'enough is as good as a feast', but with a sort of negation, so more like 'enough is not enough for a feast'.

On the conceiving of *De Tijd*

How the composer composes. Elmer Schönberger in conversation with Louis Andriessen[†]

Amsterdam, 1981

Elmer Schönberger (born in 1950) is a musicologist, author and composer. He has been writing for Vrij Nederland *since 1976 and, since 1982, has written the column 'Het Gebroken Oor'. He is co-author with Louis Andriessen of the study on Stravinsky* Het apollinisch uurwerk [The Apollonian Clockwork] *and has published music essays and portraits in five books. His most recent compositions are* Dr. Haydn's Universe, Verhuisbericht-Suite [Dr. Haydn's Universe, Message-of-Removal-Suite] *and the string quartet* Faites vos jeux [Place your bets] *which was followed by* Dovemansoren [Deaf Man's Ears] *with Theatregroup De Appel. In 1999, with Theatregroup Amsterdam, Schönberger made his début as a dramatist with* Kwartetten, *a work for four actors and string quartet.*

The premiere of De Tijd [Time] *took place in 1981 at the Holland Festival. De Tijd is set to a fragment of St. Augustine's* Confessions *and forms the third in a series of instrumental-vocal works. The first was* De Staat [The Republic] *(1976), to Plato, and for the second,* Mausoleum *(1979), Andriessen drew on the Russian revolutionary anarchist Bakunin. The first bars of* De Tijd *were composed in March 1980, shortly after the completion of* George Sand *(a text by Mia Meijer), the third of Andriessen's operas for the theatre group Baal. At the end of January 1981, when these conversations took place, the definitive score of* De Tijd *had, for the most part, yet to be written.*

ES: Do you compose regularly or in fits and starts?
LA: If I am working on a piece, basically I compose every day, for four to five hours on average. And always at the same time – let's say from ten to three. Experience tells me that if I do work longer, I will lose those hours a few days later anyway. I think it advisable to keep to a fixed daily schedule in order to work professionally. And if you ask me, it's just as important to be in good physical condition. When I am composing, even smoking and drinking coffee happen according to plan.

Do you start writing immediately when you begin at ten o' clock in the morning?
Before I start composing, I generally practise the piano for a bit. Scales, learning bars of Bach fugues by heart. Then I 'do sums' and search for chords, just as you would line up your herbs before starting to cook. I

[†] This interview first appeared in the journal *De Revisor* 1981 / 2, pp. 24-32 and, in English, in *Key-Notes* 13, 1981 / 2, pp. 5-11.

cannot imagine starting to compose, then discovering a few dazzling bars, and finally deciding to do a few sums.

You compose at the piano. Does that mean that it is the piano which actually does the composing?
When you are younger, you run the risk of your hands being in charge. You only think of chords that lie comfortably under the fingers. I think that there are still vestiges of that in my music, although an awful lot of the chords in *De Tijd* are completely unplayable on the piano. Stravinsky's music also bears traces of the piano, more so than Ravel's. The ninth in the bass, which Stravinsky likes so much, is a pleasant stretch too – though this is only of secondary importance. Actually, it has recently struck me that there is something very strange about my music. In *De Tijd*, for the first time in years, I am composing using very high notes; I have only been using the middle register for ages. Lodewijk de Boer[†] immediately understood why that had happened: the flap of my work table had been hiding the top end of the piano. I just couldn't get to it.

Composing for the same length of time every day probably doesn't mean composing the same amount every day.
No. The days you write three pages are the exceptions. Sometimes you have to be satisfied with three or four bars. Sometimes things can go *too* well. You have to remember that composing, when it goes well, is an emotional activity. Even Kees van Baaren,[††] the most disciplined and 'coolest' composer I have known, was in complete agreement with this. Emotion can be a dangerous guide. As soon as you feel that you are being carried away, you must stop and direct your attention towards something else – making coffee, skipping or running errands – so that you can return to your study with a clear head. The wonderful music I composed at night when I was twenty turned out to be banal the following morning. "Squirrel on a long journey" was on the piece of paper on which Carmiggelt[†††] had confided his most profound philosophical thoughts one night. There is another reason for stopping work when your emotions begin to take over: you feel that the notes themselves must calm down. If you sit tight and say to yourself, I must now listen very carefully, then what you are actually saying is, I must listen to what the notes themselves – the notes which are on the paper – want. Notes are alive and need time. In my experience, the slower the music, the more time you need to create it. Things which last a long time take a long time. In *De Staat*, it took less time to discover that the notes were the right ones than it did in *De Tijd*. After an 8/4 bar of, say, twelve

[†] Lodewijk de Boer is a Dutch playwright and stage director.
[††] Kees van Baaren (1906-1970) was a Dutch composer and teacher.
[†††] See note on p. 29.

seconds, consisting of a single chord, such as this one in *De Tijd*:

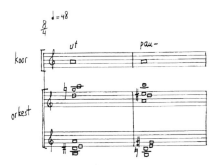

the choice of whether to let the A in the upper part go to G or B in the following bar is of far greater importance than when that a is one of a passage of thirty-six notes within the same time span. It's like when a girl takes off her clothes. The fewer they are, the more important they become. It is only the serial composers who have never really focused on time span. Rarely was rhythm so strictly calculated, and yet at the same time did it matter so little *precisely* how long a note lasted. Just as long as the rhythmic structure was irregular. This applies to all those marvellous piano pieces by Stockhausen too: all that noise and then one note – and it was always the right note too because Stockhausen is a good composer. But it never really mattered whether that note lasted three, five or six seconds. There wasn't any psychological time, just *real time*.

You have told me before, referring to your latest composition De Tijd, *that in the creation of a piece, non-musical factors are of greater importance than musical factors. Does that mean that the first ideas are non-musical ideas?*

No. Ultimately, that is not true. The first idea for *De Tijd* was that of a musical situation: a situation of sustained, glorified, musical stasis.

That sounds like the translation of a non-musical experience.

That is true. The reason for writing the piece was a unique experience which gave me the feeling that time had ceased to exist, the sensation of an eternal moment. It was more than a perfect, inner calm; it was a euphoric moment, so powerful that I later decided to write a work about it.

As a starting point for a composition, I do find that fairly abstract. Can it happen that large-scale, 'free' pieces (not opera, film music and other 'functional' compositions) develop exclusively from a purely musical idea, a 'find'?

I think you have to look at each case separately, although it is true that purely musical ideas which give you the impetus to move forward appear mostly in functional music. But the idea behind *De Staat*, for example, was not so abstract. *De Staat* had to become a sort of inflated *Volharding*. Things which I couldn't do with De Volharding orchestra because of technical limitations, I had to achieve another way. *De Staat* was, above all, a musical vision. I likened it to a very high wall which slowly falls on top of you. That was the non-musical description of a musical experience. It was different with *De Tijd*. The musical idea into which I translated the experience I just described was much less concrete. I was busy with it for nearly two years before I put the first note on paper.

Busy doing what?
Reading a lot of books, searching for texts. I knew for certain that it had to be a vocal work. After *De Staat*, set to texts by Plato, and *Mausoleum* set to Bakunin, to search for yet another text might be regarded as something like automatism. But it does not detract from the fact that I think it is perfectly legitimate to seek inspiration as regards form, duration, movement, or anything for that matter, from a text. You look for a text which says what you want to say and, at the same time, is a means of realising musically what you want.

De Staat, Mausoleum *and* De Tijd *are long works for large forces. Could the use of texts be due to your fear of large-scale forms?*
I don't think so. If you're going to Haarlem and you take the car, it doesn't mean you are afraid of walking. Using of texts is an obvious thing to do. Large-scale musical forms, with the exception of Bruckner, perhaps, are always about more than just music,

Had you ever written a piece before which needed so much preparation time as De Tijd?
No. When I was writing *De Staat* and *Mausoleum* I didn't begin writing notes from one day to the next either, but the preparatory work was as nothing as compared to that of *De Tijd*. This had to do with the subject and with the fact that I had never before found it so difficult to find a musical solution for what was in my head – and clearly, in this case, what was in my head was not a 'tangible' enough musical experience. I kept telling myself: just listen very carefully because you know perfectly well what you want to hear. Evidently I didn't. I can scarcely reconstruct what I did in those two years. It began with Dijksterhuis' *The Mechanization of the World Image* and Dante's *Divine Comedy* and it ended with Dante's *Divine Comedy* and *The Confessions of St. Augustine*. In between lie piles of books with seven centuries of reflections on time and a trip to Florence, where, apart from peace and quiet, I was looking for a philosopher – a contemporary of Dante's.

A composer from the post-Einstein era looking back to the late Middle Ages.
Not only, no. I also threw myself into *Reader's Digest*-type books on the

theory of relativity, into books on clocks, books on the calculation of the calendar, histories of mathematics and astrology. I even tried to get to grips with Hans Reichenbach's *Space and Time* – but after about ten pages, I could make neither head nor tail of it, due to a lack of scientific education. Texts from the period of, let's say, Newton to Einstein, written when we knew what time was, were also out of the question. I noticed that I was dealing with a philosophical unknown – which, since Gauss and Einstein, is the case once more – and that meant that I had to delve much further back in history. I then ended up in the labyrinth of the fourteenth century where I could only find my way with the greatest difficulty. Initially, I was looking for two types of text: metaphysical and scientific. Firstly, texts which could put my experience into words and secondly, texts on the measurement of time. At the time I thought: Dante is the poet; now for his scientific counterpart. It was my intention to combine these two types of text. It could have been a simple closed form like this:

in which the vertical lines stand for short, scientific statements on the measurement of time in the fourteenth century and the horizontal line stands for a continuous poetic text in the form of a sort of cantus firmus.[67] The contrast between these texts is much the same as that between the two books which began it all: Dijksterhuis and Dante. The same contrast is reflected in the possibility of using either an open form or a closed form. That was the biggest compositional problem of the piece, beside which all the other problems (harmony, instrumentation, texture) were of less importance. Cutting through that knot was the hardest decision of all.

How did you envisage this open form?
As three simultaneously audible musical structures, which repeat themselves after a long time, but which are of unequal length, so that, if you begin at point A, you will only hear exactly the same music again after twenty-seven hours or three days. Texts especially suited to this I found in Oresme's *De proportionibus proportionum*. But I was side-tracked by Oresme in the labyrinth. I have an entire notebook full of extracts from his work. In *De proportionibus proportionum*, Oresme formulates nine conclusions which relating to the coincidence of movements, and when these coincidences happen. The ninth conclusion is as follows: "It is possible that there

---

[67] cantus firmus: a pre-existing melody in an inner part (usually taken from plainsong) against which other tunes are set in counterpoint.

are three movements which coincide only once in eternity, and it is impossible for them to coincide more than once or to have coincided at other times or to coincide at other times in the future."

Could you repeat that?
It won't help. You would have to understand the eighth conclusion and the seventh and so on. It shut me up for ages but ultimately contributed nothing to my piece.

But even if nothing comes of it, no 'settable' texts at any rate, you are at least learning more about time.
If only that were true. The problem itself just looms larger. That's part and parcel of this particular subject. You accept it, because you realise that you are reading in an ambiguous way. The question is not what should one think about time but what has been thought about time. Ultimately, the question is: what ideas that have been written down are inspiring in terms of the creation of this piece? That must be the criterion. Many composers wouldn't dare to admit that, but I do. One reads with the eyes of a composer. If one really wanted to get to know something about time, then one would have become a physicist or a philosopher, I think.

In your notebook I see entries about many more philosophers.
Yes. On Ockham, Oresme's teacher, Cusanus, *De docta ignorantia*. I was side-tracked by all of these. And this one, *Das Zeitproblem*, an impenetrable analysis by A. Maier. Can you believe it? Only part 2 of volume 4 of the (as yet incomplete) *Studien zur Naturphilosophie der Spätscholastik* to which this presumably ancient, toothless, female German scholar who lives in Rome is devoting her life. This was another side-track although, as I was looking for a translator for the Latin texts in this book, it did at least bring me into contact with the theologian Burcht Pranger who, in his turn, brought me into contact with quotations from the work of, amongst others, Alain de l'Isle. Gradually it dawned on me that the relationship between science and non-science was much more complicated in the fourteenth century than it is these days. Alain de l'Isle came close to the truth (as I see it) when he announced: "punctum in puncto non est nisi unum punctum." ("A point in a point is only one point.") The subsequent sentence describes more or less the experience I had (a similar sentence can be found in Dante): the description of eternity in the description of a point. "A point, for example, the centre of the world, and a point in time, that is to say, the present time, display some resemblance to eternity after all, which is of no little use, especially when thinking about eternity." You can deal with someone like that.

Once you perceived that the divide between science and non-science in the fourteenth century was not so clear, this must have had consequences for your choice of texts.

Yes. Before I came to that realisation, I tried to bridge the gap by searching for a system in which texts from both worlds could be present and in which the choice between the open and the closed form did not have to be made. I was considering a form in which those circles – the self-repeating structures of unequal length to which I have referred before – would be cemented by music with a fixed duration.

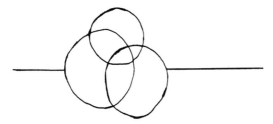

On reflection, I found the idea of an open form not challenging enough. The consequences of having independently moving musical structures would be that those structures could scarcely be made controllable. In the end, I opted for closed form and one sort of text. But which sort? That was the question. At first, I thought: you really mustn't use metaphysical texts – no poetic descriptions of that emotional emptiness. No, the music must sound like that emptiness and in contrast to that, the text must deal with the measuring of time. When this didn't work out – by that time I had the feeling that I simply had to start writing, otherwise I could carry on like this for ever – I decided to turn the concept through 180° and concluded that the text was evidently concerned with describing a point in eternity (and was therefore metaphysical), and that it was the music's task to measure time. At that point I returned to *The Confessions of St. Augustine* which, like Dante, had been a constant in the background all this time. Increasingly, I had the feeling that Augustine had said what I wanted to say. Augustine asked himself this question about time: "Quid est enim tempus... What, indeed, is time? When no-one asks me, I know what it is. Whenever I want to explain it to someone who has asked me, I don't know." Eventually, I chose one paragraph and was supported in my choice by the knowledge that Augustine was not just some old Roman bishop but originally an odd, Eastern tear-away, regarded by Russell as an important philosopher. Quite by chance, I composed the last few bars of *De Tijd* last year in December in Tunisia, less than sixty kilometres from Augustine's birthplace.

> ... if only their minds could be seized and held steady, they would be still for a while and, for that short moment, they would glimpse the splendour of eternity which is for ever still. They would contrast it with time, which is never still, and see that it is not comparable. They would see that time derives

its length only from a great number of movements constantly following one another into the past, because they cannot all continue at once. But in eternity nothing moves into the past: all is present. Time, on the other hand, is never all present at once. The past is always driven on by the future, the future always follows on the heels of the past, and both the past and the future have their beginning and their end in the eternal present. If only men's minds could be seized and held still! They would see how eternity, in which there is neither past nor future, determines both past and future time. Could mine be the hand strong enough to seize the minds of men? Could any words of mine have power to achieve so great a task?" (St. Augustine, *Confessions*, translation: R. S. Pine-Coffin.)

When, having made the decision to use that one paragraph, I looked up exactly *what* I was using, the paragraph turned out to be from the eleventh chapter of the eleventh book. I then went back to the *Divine Comedy*, asking myself whether it was really conceivable that a book that had been my companion for two years should disappear, unused, back into the bookcase at the last moment? Initially, Dante had stood exclusively for the poetic, metaphysical approach to time. 'Paradiso' for the most part deals with the purifying experience which I myself had felt and had understood as the cessation of time – the euphoria of love, if you like. At that time, I hadn't realised that Dante, as well as being a poet, was a man of science, a historian and a politician, and that the *Comedy* was, in effect, an encyclopaedia containing everything there was to know at that time. And even things that couldn't be known – Dante even mentions the Southern Cross which was first seen two centuries later by Vasco da Gama. So I looked through my notes and found the sentence which says it all exactly. I put this sentence above my piece as an epigraph.

"… mirando il punto a cui tutti li tempi son presenti" ("…gazing on the point beyond, To which all times are present…" translation: Laurence Binyon.)

And what do you think transpired? It was the seventeenth line from the seventeenth *canto* of *Paradiso*. I thought: yes, that works.

You say that as if it were significant.
At a moment like that it *was* significant. I then did a lot of little sums with those figures. Smallest common multiples, greatest common denominators.

So at the moment you had finally found the text, you had…
I still had nothing: a text, an image of a *Threni*-like[68] piece, reserved, without expression, precisely notated and controlled by strict numerical relationships from beginning to end. I also knew that the piece had to have

---

[68] Igor Stravinsky, *Threni: id est Lamentationes Jeremiae Prophetae* (1958).

something to do with A (possibly D, E – those sorts of keys). These sorts of keys stand for brightness, the open strings of the violin. *De Tijd* did indeed turn out to be an A piece and I am convinced that that is connected to the fact that *De Staat* ends on G sharp and *Mausoleum* on F / G. An observation like that is no use to anyone except sycophantic ladies, but it is of great relevance to me.

But did you also have a central musical idea, in the sense of a specific intervalic construction, a rhythm or a harmonic starting point?
I had two chromatic dominant seventh chords, initially only one. But that was certainly a chord with a long history to it. Years ago, I had once formed a plan that, were I ever to compose something for symphony orchestra, I would write a piece consisting of one single dominant seventh chord which, in compositional terms, would say a whole lot of things about that one chord. Although I eventually abandoned this idea in its radical form, traces of it (somewhat toned down) can be found in *Symfonieën der Nederlanden* [*Symphonies of the Netherlands*]. I also used it in *Orpheus* at a very different, low pitch in the organ part for about seven minutes to support a well-nigh incomprehensible monologue of Apollo's. Come to think of it – that monologue was also about time.

De Tijd *is non-tonal, yet you are using a tonal chord.*
As far as form is concerned, I regard the search for solutions to the antithesis tonal / non-tonal as being the most important subject in contemporary music. The tradition of strict atonality or anti-tonality offers, as has been proved, few guarantees for the development of composition.

And did the entire work develop from that one chord?
Yes. Initially, the chord was in this form:

a dominant seventh chord with a major and a minor third and no fifth. It was only later that I realised that, given what I wanted to do with the piece, it would be better to choose another form: a dominant seventh chord, still without a fifth, but with an added tonic.

What made the second form of the chord more suitable?
The task I set myself was this: create a situation which is characterised by a combination of tension and non-tension which is difficult to describe.

In principle, it is possible in music to do two things simultaneously. If you are thinking about harmony, it is obvious that you would let your thoughts drift towards the dominant seventh chord, because the dominant seventh chord is a chord which demands resolution. If you build in your resolution by using an added fourth (the tonic, therefore), then you have at your disposal (in principle at any rate) a 'sound' that both has to be resolved and that, at the same time, has already been resolved. It depends on the context whether the thesis-like character of the chord (the resolved chord) or its arsis-like character (the chord demanding resolution) predominates. Technically speaking, you could call *De Tijd* a succession of dominants: an endless suspension of which the resolution is always present.

At a later stage, you started working with a combination of two dominant seventh chords.

Yes, two dominant seventh chords, without the fifth but a fifth apart.

This appears in one of the earliest drafts: a fragment for eight-part choir, a rhythmic canon in augmentation based on seventh chords a fifth apart. That's how it began. Just by writing. During the year I didn't compose but just sat at home on the sofa the whole time thinking about the meaning of composition, Harry Mulisch[†] gave me a presentation copy of *De Verteller* [*The Storyteller*] in which he had written the dedication: "Just do something – that's the best thing".

That was good advice. You didn't do anything more with that fragment for eight-part choir. Is there such a thing as the problem of the first bar?

That really does depend on the piece. Generally, it's a question of getting a bright idea. Sitting at the piano, listening and something will come to you. In the worst-case scenario, nothing does. *De Tijd* was a case in point. But even so, at a propitious moment you do begin . You write something down, without there being talk of a bright idea. You just have to get on that bike and pedal. Without exaggerating, raising a leg takes an enormous amount of effort but when, on a certain morning, you at last write something down (and then it will be mostly wrong anyway), you are at last cycling – in any event, more than when you were standing next to your bike. Dick Raaijmakers wrote a piece about it. *De Fiets* [*The Bicycle*]. Ex-

[†] see note on p. 57.

cept that *De Fiets* is about dismounting. Mounting is more difficult. Had I been Dick, I would have taken that as my subject. Page one of *De Tijd* consists mainly of rubbed-out notes. I got on my bike three times and it was only at the third attempt that I could cycle on. As I've said, practically nothing was settled except the vision. I had a vague notion that I would choose the linear, closed form but I didn't know then if that form would require forty-five or sixty minutes. When I had completed the first page, I still had the idea that the piece would revolve around six notes and that these notes should sound throughout the piece in a high organ register – like an endlessly-sustained chord on the sho.[69] Actually, now it's completed, there isn't an organ in it at all . From this, you can see that the form only developed during the compositional process. All those calculations, all those plans were dictated entirely by things I had done previously.

We are now on the first page of De Tijd. *This is preceded by a period of two years in which you have read more or less everything there is to read about the philosophy of time. Are you not running the risk of writing a piece in which you 'prove' that two times two is four?*
    That is not inconceivable. But you don't, of course, do all that preparatory work just to gain an insight into the subject of your piece. You are, at the same time, investing in your own future, in terms of thought as well as of composing. With an all-encompassing subject like time, you know in advance that the ultimate piece cannot be more than a minuscule reflection of the things which have occupied you.

Would you have written a piece like this if you hadn't immersed yourself in philosophy?
    Burrowing as deep as possible into the labyrinth has the advantage of greatly increasing your range of options and this, in turn, has the advantage that the limitations which you finally impose on yourself are well-founded and not the result of idleness and laziness. With a subject like this, it couldn't have gone any quicker, nor should it have.

Does that have anything to do with a special attitude to the work ethic?
    Not as far as *De Tijd* is concerned but, in general, yes. You have to work hard, otherwise it isn't good. The pieces you have worked hardest on are the pieces closest to your heart, which does not necessarily mean that they are your best pieces. *Melodie* is a case in point: a minimal number of notes which cost a maximum amount of composing time. The opposite is also

---

[69] Sho: little Japanese mouth organ consisting of an air reservoir with seventeen little bamboo pipes. In the gagaku, the sho plays sustained, shrill chords. These chords form the static 'breathless' background to the actual musical action.

true. Multatuli[70] regarded *Max Havelaar*, which he wrote in a very short space of time, as a pamphlet. But it is his masterpiece.

Does the first musical idea consist only of 'abstract' intervals, chords or notes, or does it already have its own instrumental colour?
The latter, usually. But the colours were wrong in *De Tijd*. In the fourth bar, I had flutes and above them strings and organ for a long time. I only took the decision to have the first eight bars played exclusively by strings much later on.

How long was it before you had a more or less defined picture of the whole piece?
Usually, the first ten minutes of a large scale work are the most difficult. This was certainly true of *De Tijd* , although the puzzling fact remains that those first ten minutes are actually extraordinarily boring and obvious. Apparently, those chords had to satisfy all sorts of strict, and as yet unformulated, conditions. After twelve minutes I knew that I would achieve much more by using a process of gradual accelerations which I had, by then, already initiated.

Did that knowledge have any consequences for what you had already written down?
It could have done, but this was not the case. Although at this moment, now that the short score is done, I'm still not quite certain if I should begin with a tutti or not. In general, I tend to adapt what comes later to what is already there. That is not just a form of laziness. If you don't know how to take things forward, then the only thing you can rely on is your hearing. If I get stuck I imagine – quite literally – that I am sitting in the hall where the piece is being performed. I imagine the plush seats, the temperature in the hall, the humidity; I listen to the piece and then listen very carefully to what should come next.

You then play through the entire piece.
Sometimes. Maybe once or twice a week. You could compare it to what is known as a run-through in the theatrical world. You do it at a tactical moment, not only when you're stuck, but also if it's going well. And that's a good reason for doing it at the beginning, and not at the end, of a composing day. A run-through gives you the opportunity to stand back and to put yourself in the listener's place.

The rules of composition are rarely unambiguous. Doesn't the problem of

---

[70] Multatuli (the pseudonym of Eduard Douwes Dekker, 1820-1887) was a Dutch writer and anti-colonialist.

composing lie less in the finding of solutions than in choosing between differing solutions? In other words, isn't the big problem that of making the correct choice?

You train yourself to become quicker and quicker at knowing whether something is good or not. But even so, there are always situations where you have to choose between more than one solution. Often, the best solution is the one which lies closest to the original idea of the piece. You choose the conventions which you have created yourself: when in Rome, do as the Romans do. The rules which a piece lays down for itself merely consist of a limited number of links, chord types, rhythms etc. In *De Tijd*, the problem of the correct choice often proved to be the problem of the correct modulation or, better perhaps , the correct transposition. Take this point, for example:

I knew that the choir would come in here with that chord, but should I make a sudden modulation or not? Finally, after much hesitation (do I continue in C or in F?) I went for the obvious solution: back to the beginning – A.

Can the wrong choice sometimes produce a good result?

We're talking more about mistakes or slips of the pen here. It often happens that such mistakes, just as in improvised music, can be turned to your advantage. That is more like tinkering around. But a few times in *De Tijd* the music simply didn't match the text – I was bars short. I turned that mistake into a rule by always having the last words sung in very small note values. With hindsight, that turned out to work very well.

Going back to March 1980 for a moment, the month the first page of the manuscript is dated. You haven't said anything about the consequences that your choice of text had on the definitive shape of the piece.

Of course, choosing a text like that had all sorts of implications. Precisely because the text was *not* about counting and measuring, I decided to 'count' the piece very strictly. Every duration can be justified. I even bought a calculator especially for this purpose. The form of the piece is determined by two numbers: 2 and 3, numbers which spring from my contact with medieval writings. These are the same numbers which dominate the building of medieval cathedrals and which you find in medieval music where the bars are divided into duple time and triple time – tempus imperfectum and tempus perfectum. Tempus perfectum was indicated by a circle. The circle, a thing with neither beginning nor end, I associate with metaphysical thinking and with the open form. I associate tempus imperfectum with lines, little fences, regular divisions. You find the number 3 in *De Tijd* in a consistently sustained iambic rhythm. That iambic rhythm is constantly subject to acceleration, in time sequences such as 6-12, 5-10, 4-8, 3-6, contrasting with the binary rhythms which are regular. To do justice to the iambic rhythm, you have to have mastered the triple time note values, 3/3 time, for example. In *Mausoleum*, I wrote out those sorts of bar types whereas in *De Tijd*, I only used binary notation. It makes no difference to the sound, but it is quite remarkable that for centuries now, music has only recognised binary notation. Binary notation says nothing about the number of beats per bar (waltzes are also written in binary notation) but only about the number of parts into which the beat is divided. These divisions are crotchets, quavers, minims; the third part of the apple doesn't exist. Binary notation is an invention of Ars Nova, of rational thought processes. I imagine that binary divisions of time are also to do with a rational view of time as something linear.

In De Tijd, *has anything remained of your original idea of making time audible by means of circles turning independently of one other?*
The piece is based on the combination of two differing tempi, but the result is controlled down to the smallest detail. The passing of time has to be audible and, to achieve this, you have to be sparing with your musical statements. But in order to focus the attention – since without attention time does not exist at all – I have composed almost imperceptible accelerations into the forward thrust of the piece, which create precisely the impression that everything is staying the same. But not exactly the same; more like the way in which the towers of a cathedral are the same and yet not the same. *De Tijd* is based on a sort of 'parallelismus membrorum',[71] combined with the principle of accumulation; something is always being added but nothing is ever taken away, except in the instrumentation.

Composing De Tijd *was just as much a question of emphasis as a matter of measuring and counting.*

---

[71] 'parallellismus membrorum': syntactic or semantic conformity between two successive pieces of text: *Cleanse me with hyssop, and I shall be clean; / Wash me, and I shall be whiter than snow.* (Psalm 51).

Yes. I cannot always tell in advance which feeling will be the stronger: that of the 'same' or that of 'not-the-same'. Perhaps the impression of 'sameness' only appears after repeated listening. The penultimate chorus may sound completely different from the opening chorus on a first hearing, but the chords are in essence the same, just arranged differently. I still don't know precisely how the piece will work. A few weeks ago in Copenhagen, I imagined that I had suddenly acquired an extraordinarily good insight into music. At the time, I wrote to a good friend: "Perhaps I have really succeeded in conveying what Augustine said about time: that it cannot be measured, because there is only a past and a future (and this while I was trying to write a piece about the moment in which time stands still: *il punto a cui tutti li tempi son presenti*. But this is precisely what *all* music is – the sustained *present*: "you forget time"). When I played the piece to Elmer shortly before I went to Copenhagen, one of the things he said was: "As you are listen, you find you are in the process of trying to remember something – what have I just missed? what happened?" And the second thing you can do when you hear the piece (and you are evidently 'bored') is to sit and wait for what has yet to come. If that is the case, then I have succeeded but in a way which is completely contrary to how I imagined; thus the piece is absolutely the converse of all other music.

So that waiting is a sort of waiting for Godot. You are waiting for something which doesn't come; as a listener, you are not driven on. You are listening to music which is there again and again.

Perhaps that is 'classical'. Romantic music is going somewhere, while Classical music just is there and, at most, gives the impression of being about music which is going somewhere. The three crescendos at the end of the first part of *The Rite of Spring*: and then… and *then*… and **THEN**… And then you simply get something else.

In Copenhagen you gave a lecture in which you described the orientation of your piece as springing from a classical perspective.

That was nothing new. I believe that I have been using that term for my music as a result of two incidents. In the first place I heard on the grapevine that Karst Woudstra[†] had condemned me because "that Andriessen, he's a bloody classicist". I took that as a compliment. The second incident occurred after the premiere of *De Staat*. Hein van Royen[††] came up to me to say that he thought the piece was very beautiful, that he was glad that he had heard traces of Stravinsky in it (I always regard that as a compliment) and that although it *seemed* like a Dionysian piece, in fact it was cold music. I said to him: Hein, that is an interesting view. I do believe I

[†] Karst Woudstra (b. 1947) is a Dutch playwright and theatre director.
[††] Hein van Royen was the then artistic director of the Concertgebouw Orchestra.

agree with you.

I can imagine that there are people who say: what is so Classical about De Staat? It is so compelling, so moving, it is impossible to withdraw from it.

It's worse than that. After the premiere of *Mausoleum*, a couple of student social workers steeped in education theory gave me to understand that my music was fascistic. In my view, the word 'compelling' is not appropriate unless, like me, you use the word in connection with things that appear to compel. Things which are really compelling are nearly always banal.

Mahler is really compelling.

I don't find Mahler at all compelling. Why? Because I am being compelled by it so much. It's tugging at my arm but in the wrong way. I switch off after two bars. I don't give a damn – it passes over me like a thunderstorm. What I like about art is art that is not real. Art which is trying to intensify reality passes me by. That's why I like Fellini better than Buñuel. The Italians are masters in simulating compulsion. What could be more pleasant than sitting in a mountain village square in northern Italy, sipping a glass of grappa and suddenly hearing from the bell tower of the local church the sound of a needle being placed on a gramophone record by a trembling hand, amplified a thousand times – tschkr, krg, krg and then a resounding ding-dong ding-dong.

Let's just go back to De Tijd for a minute. I understand that every 'time span' in the piece is perfectly justified. Do you think that makes a difference when you listen to it?

I think that the listener would certainly surmise that the form of the piece has been strictly calculated but I also think that, essentially, it won't matter to him. Very few people would be tempted to 'count' the piece. I regard that as a positive quality. Nevertheless, when talking about the piece, you tend to place strong emphasis on the calculation aspect. This is because I trust my hearing more than I trust my rational thinking. And furthermore, counting is 'explainable'. It is infinitely more difficult to explain why one chord progression is more beautiful than another. Anti-Romantics, and I regard myself as one, shrink from talking about it because you quickly fall into an odd sort of nonsense language. What more can I do than to play you those chords and then tell you why I get tears in my eyes from them?

Give an example.

This is a pretty exceptional progression because, in the rest of the vocal parts, there are virtually only repeated notes with, now and again, a small shift of a major or minor second upwards or downwards. Here, something more is happening – a descending chromatic line F sharp-F-E. That is an unusually beautiful combination which emerged more or less by chance one morning and it recurs repeatedly throughout the piece. Now the big question is: how do you explain the beauty of this combination? What you *can* say is that, provided it is the right harmonic progression, a descending chromatic line like that embodies an immense musical tradition to which you are immediately referring. From sublimely beautiful Monteverdi madrigals, via Mozart operas, to Verdi's Requiem and Carmen's death. All that is in there.

Is it conceivable that you set up large-scale, non-functional compositions that are less strictly structured?

Yes. *De Staat* was much more free than *De Tijd*. In *De Staat*, I had not settled on much, except that I wanted it to have something to do with four-part chords. To make it easier on myself, I then made a plan of the form, where the choruses were to be, proportions, timings etc. That apart, I wrote the work completely freely, playing and improvising. In my opinion, you can hear that in it, too. It wouldn't have worked with *De Tijd*. If I had begun *De Tijd* absolutely freely, I would presumably have ended up in a musical morass. In a way, it is easier if you set yourself restrictions. If it rains, you put your Wellies on; that is practical.

It isn't lack of confidence, on your part, in your intuition?

No, I have so much confidence in my intuition that there is always room for something else. It was precisely because I had so much confidence in my intuition that I dared to write an opera for Baal in six weeks, and it wasn't at all bad. But an opera like that doesn't give you the feeling: success at last! At least, less so than a piece like *De Tijd*. When I was about two-thirds of the way through, it suddenly struck me during a run-through at the piano: if this turns out well, I will have achieved something I have wanted ever since 1972. I recall one evening when I was visiting someone. I was full of plans for large scale works (I had yet to write *De Staat*) and I shouted out, somewhat agitatedly: I want to write a piece, all terrifying blue pillars. Very long. Loud noises. Silences. And during that run-through, between the chords, I still remember exclaiming: to be able to do that, you have to be forty.[72] I think that only now am I free from those blue pillars. Although I am not entirely sure of that. Perhaps it has to be worse. Perhaps it is an even greater vision.

Yet more monk's work, as we say in Dutch.
　　It *was* monk's work. *De Tijd* was, for me, an exercise in asceticism. Writing it has been a sort of retreat. I wanted to lock myself away in a piece because I had been demanding things from myself for a while which I couldn't sustain. One of these things was writing pieces that the world (at least, this is how I felt) – whichever world you like – expected of me. I had the feeling that the success of *De Staat* had robbed me of the freedom I used to have when I was twenty, the freedom of only doing what you want to do. I suddenly had the feeling that I had to accomplish everything, all at once.

That doesn't detract from the fact that De Tijd *is the third in a series of large-scale compositions which began with* De Staat.
　　Perhaps it is also the huge 'black hole' of the series. The emptiness of a very large piece.

---

[72] In 1979 Louis Andriessen turned forty.

De Snelheid

Amsterdam, 5 October 1998

Lecture in the music centre De IJsbreker in Amsterdam for composition students at the Royal Conservatoire of The Hague, 5 October 1998.

Last week *De Snelheid* [*Velocity*] was performed. That in itself is already unusual, because it is extremely difficult to play. And it was a good performance too.

As the title implies, the piece is about the perception of speed in music. Conductor Oliver Knussen did what no one had done before: he put groups of bars together into one large bar. Beethoven had already achieved this in his string quartets, especially in the scherzos; you can see this in his indication 'ritmo di tre battute'. It is very simple: you write 123123123 and you hear one – two – three.

This is actually the subject of *De Snelheid*, which brings us immediately to very profound and fundamental thoughts on how to write music – why do you write a particular bar in a particular way?

The entire piece is written in very short bars. On each page there are ten bars, even when the tempo increases, and I want to keep it that way when it is printed [the piece is currently only available in manuscript copy]. All those barlines send musicians round the bend but, for me, this is not a reason to write the same notes in longer bars.

The subject of the piece is not only how we perceive speed, although that is a very important question. I also wanted to write in a certain genre with its allusions to a historical background: the scherzo, of which more later.

'MATERIE'

De Snelheid has the same origins as *De Materie* [*Matter*]. After a concert in Copenhagen which was part of the Young Nordic Music Festival in the Niels Gade Conservatoire, we were walking down a magnificently carved nineteenth-century wooden staircase. We had heard a piece by Hans Gefors for double bassoon and double bass. We are always taught that these instruments are from different families, the wind and the strings, but I suddenly realised that they are from the same family; they are both made of wood. Yesterday, I found, to my surprise, a piano manuscript of *De Snelheid* with the word 'Materie' on the front page. I had completely forgotten about that.

I had, then, originally wanted to write something which had to do with matter. I think that is one of the historical reasons behind the fact that the pulse, which is the most important voice in the whole piece, is played on wood-blocks.

LOUD AND FAST

The other event which is important in relation to *De Snelheid* took place in Italy. I can't remember now if it also influenced the chords in *De Materie*, which I wrote at the end of the eighties.

Sometime in the seventies, I was driving, with Reinbert de Leeuw and Frans Brueggen (the recorder player and currently conductor), back to Frans' house; he was the only friend of mine who was rich enough to buy a house in Italy. We had enjoyed a fantastic meal and although we were not what you might call drunk, we were in high spirits. Lodewijk de Boer, the playwright, was also there. On that winding road through the mountains – and there wasn't a straight bit of road that was longer than ten metres – we switched off all the lights. The question was: how long could we keep them off? It was our version of bungy-jumping, but more dangerous. On one of these trips we had loud music on – Prokofiev or Tchaikovsky – and someone suddenly shouted amidst all the commotion: how fast do we have to drive to go as fast as the music? Now that is a profound philosophical question. This experience has remained with me and proved important when I began composing the piece which was to be about the perception of speed.

SCHERZO

I am certainly not the first to think about speed in music. All the scherzi in the symphonies of the nineteenth century are about speed. In the period from Mozart to Bruckner – and this also applies to the better composers that came after them – the third movement of the symphony became continually faster. The phenomenon I mentioned earlier – of bars being grouped together – appears fairly early on. Nowadays, a good Mozart conductor will take the third movement in one, if he wants to be hip and modern.

In the meantime, in the second half of the nineteenth century, a virtuoso one-movement orchestral work was developing outside the symphonic tradition, usually referred to as a symphonic poem. This is actually an extended third movement, a great scherzo like those written by Bruckner in his symphonies. The scherzo as a symphonic poem is chiefly a Russian and French affair; at that time there was a lot of close cultural contact between those two countries. Glinka, Rimsky-Korsakov (*Capriccio espagnol*), Tchaikovsky and Stravinsky (*Scherzo fantastique*) all wrote their virtuoso scherzi for the most part in a very quick 3/4 or 3/8 time. A French example is the *Danse macabre* by Saint-Saëns. Later, I used it for the last part of *Trilogy of the Last Day*, which is actually also an essay on the virtuoso scherzo.

Another example which I had in front of me was *L'apprenti sorcier* [*The Sorcerer's Apprentice*] by Paul Dukas, written in 1897, a very good virtuoso scherzo. It may be familiar to you because Disney used it for a film which follows Goethe's story fairly precisely. The sorcerer's apprentice uses a magic spell to fob off his work onto some brooms, but he doesn't know how he can make them stop.

I remember once, when I was about four or so, my father invited me to stay in bed with him. It was probably a Sunday morning because my father always worked hard and was often away. Apart from telling me stories, he counted my toes. I never had ten; he always made it nine or eleven. It was quite unforgettable listening to him telling me the story of *The Sorcerer's Apprentice*. I found it rather frightening – a horror story.

Impressions and crazy memories such as these and the knowledge that you don't have ten toes are very important for your development as a composer, I think.

The last brilliant scherzo, the piece to end all virtuoso scherzi, is *Jeux* by Debussy. Do me a favour and listen to it. People don't know it these days. In the sixties, when you were only allowed to write twelve-note music and to have lessons with Boulez, that was the only piece of Debussy which was considered to be well-worth analysing. *Jeux* was fine even in a twelve-note world. If you want to know more about that period, the taboos which prevailed at that time are all very interesting.

I regard Dukas as a very sharp and intelligent composer. He was a friend of, and source of inspiration for, many people around him in Paris and he also wrote about music. What interested me about *The Sorcerer's Apprentice* was what my father taught me much later: that Dukas always writes a very short 3/8 bar, except in the slow introduction and towards the end. The piece shows you that this 3/8 bar is only partly responsible for the fact that the piece sounds fast. The simplest example is the most important theme:

What he writes (see above) is three times as slow as what we hear:

Why do our ears make something else of it? How can we describe the perception of this tempo? It has to do with harmonic rhythm. Oddly enough, this topic was not even under discussion in music for a period of about twenty years. You didn't concern yourself with harmonic rhythm, nor did you write any harmonies which were related to each other. This is now no longer the case, and I am hopeful that this new view of harmony has implications for the future of music. Because, without voice leading, there isn't much sense in composing. In the eighties, this subject was much more revolutionary than it is now, because people who concerned themselves with regular pulse rhythms or chordal relationships were completely out of fashion. I did occupy myself with this subject in the early seventies and, even then, I thought that it was high time that the problem of harmonic rhythm was put on the agenda.

SYMPHONY ORCHESTRA

With all this in mind, and because I had a commission for a symphony orchestra to deal with, I decided to write a virtuoso scherzo. This makes *De Snelheid* what it is. Fifteen years earlier, I had decided that I would no longer write for the symphony orchestra and I was very definite on the subject. Moreover, through my experiences during those first rehearsals of *De Snelheid*, I became even more confirmed in my views.

The musicians began to complain. They found the music too loud. In America they can refuse to play if the volume exceeds a certain number of decibels. Americans are very precise. So the following day, a union guy stood there with a decibel metre. (You think I'm kidding, but I'm not). It wasn't more than 95 decibels, far under the limit, so they couldn't refuse to play. The next day, they had solved the problem with a large basket full of earplugs which they put in for every rehearsal and performance.

The performance by the San Francisco Symphony Orchestra with Edo de Waart is one of the very few performances of *De Snelheid* by a symphony orchestra. The BBC Symphony Orchestra has done it too. In London, I remember the way in which each orchestral musician passed me as I went to get a coffee during the break in a full rehearsal. Not only did they not greet me, they even turned their heads the other way.

So, I've had my share of symphony orchestra experiences, which doesn't entirely surprise me. These days – and I think this is a lot better – a piece like *De Snelheid* is not played by symphony orchestras but by larger ensembles for new music, such as the Asko / Schoenberg or Ensemble Modern, who gave a good performance in March 1995 under Sian Edwards.

So the commission from the San Francisco Symphony Orchestra was very exceptional for me. This was the main reason to involve Dukas.

At that time, John Adams was composer-in-residence in San Francisco. This is the only hope of a young American composer to fulfil some sort of social function, but it is a boring job. Of course you earn some money, you can do some composing and you can go to parties. But it doesn't mean anything because the orchestras simply play what the guys in charge want them to. We're talking about the seventies now and John was completely unknown. He was a fan of my music and wanted me to write for the orchestra, because that's what *he* wanted. And he got his way. There was a private donor (as there always is in America), who gave the orchestra the money to commission me. I couldn't say no. Just imagine: a young composer being able to travel to America.

The fact that the commission was for symphony orchestra was reason enough for me to revert to an older project, namely writing a virtuoso scherzo. But because I didn't like symphony orchestras, I had, first of all, to change the orchestra – throw out half of the instruments and replace them with saxophones, Hammond organs and bass guitars so that it sounded different from an orchestra. But not only that, I also wanted to 'unpick' the essence of all virtuoso scherzi. That brilliant, positive approach to speed (like *Romeo and Juliet* in a car that's travelling downhill), that feeling of victory, seemed to me to be characteristic of virtuoso scherzi. Even *The Sorcerer's Apprentice* has an element of victory, of ecstasy. I wanted to do the same thing but the other way round, like a wheel that's turning in the wrong direction; a piece in which the speeding-up process finishes in a dead end and slowness wins out.

I did not have a good explanation for why I wanted that. It probably has something to do with an interesting musical phenomenon: that as the harmonic rhythm speeds up, there comes a point where you become indifferent to it. Reger illustrates this well; his incessant activity becomes so frenetic that you end up 'on the outside'. This probably accounts for why Reger is not as good as Strauss. Strauss is able to hold your attention, even when the rhythm is very fast. I think that Strauss was more intelligent than Reger because he realised that very fast movement, or a quick pulse, needs a slower harmonic rhythm. Reger messes everything up completely. I am telling you this because it is all relevant to *De Snelheid*.

OONG-KAH

To begin with, I divided the orchestra into three groups. This was because, earlier, I had discovered a playing technique which I found very helpful in writing music; it sounds interesting but is both unusual and very difficult to bring off – the hoquet-technique. I had done a piece on this subject with a group of students.[73] (The group, Hoketus, was extremely successful and gave concerts throughout Europe.) I used the hoquet-technique for *De Snelheid*. Two of the three orchestral groups are identical. They are small wind orchestras: saxophones, trumpets, trombones, tuba and piano. They play staccato chords together, continuously – BANG, BANG, BANG. Sometimes the chords are played very fast or they become the melody, and sometimes they form very slow, staccato melodies. The third orchestra represents the instrumental interpretation of the slow music.

But perhaps I should begin with the percussion. Since the perception of speed was my subject, the percussion is the most important voice; the three orchestras try to follow the percussionists.

There are three percussion parts. The two wood-block players belong to the two quick orchestras. Sometimes they play in hoquets, sometimes they don't – it depends on where they are in the acceleration. Even on the first page, the third percussionist is there in the middle; this is the low voice. He plays a simple rhythm throughout on two bass drums and two tom-toms, at ♩ = 60: OONG-KAH. There are all kinds of exceptions and variations, but the idea is simple: he is playing a slow march. I have used all sorts of metaphors for it – bellows, a large body breathing very slowly and regularly, a sleeping giant. I also call him Buddha because he doesn't change. He doesn't move. The only thing that happens is that the rests in this slow march become ever shorter.

At the end of the piece, the three orchestras come together to accompany the Buddha in a tutti:

You could call this the dénouement of the musical 'story'.

I think that the two wind orchestras are a sort of express version of De Volharding, the wind orchestra which I set up in the seventies. As I have

[73] During one of Louis Andriessen's projects at the Royal Conservatoire in The Hague in 1976, the group Hoketus and the piece of the same name came into being. See Part 4, p. 137.

already said, I had rejected the symphony orchestra and for these reasons I wrote a scherzo which goes completely wrong. It goes wrong chiefly in the strings, the soul of the symphony orchestra. The two identical wind orchestras on either side at least try to follow the accelerando on the woodblocks. Sometimes it works, sometimes it doesn't. But the bass drum (the third voice) is followed by the strings and some other instruments such as the harp and the Hammond organ. They keep to the slow rhythm, continually depressing the tempo or trying to influence the quickening of the wood-blocks and wind instruments. The wind orchestras are the 'sons of De Volharding', which I have put into the symphony orchestra to give the musicians a hard time and to make their lives difficult.

TREPIDUS

It is important to tell composers that I had to make a difficult decision when I was writing the piece. I was running late and I really hate that. I was only writing fast notes. The piece had to be finished some time in March, and around Christmas 1983 I was only about half way. I didn't like it. The piece was too virtuosic, too nice, and it had to be 'terrifying'. Around Christmas I suddenly decided to remove all the fast notes from the strings, from the fourth minute onwards. The strings should only play with the Buddha. The decision to remove three months' work was painful. These were such good harmonies and melodies and so I furtively put them away. But you have to be strong: kill your darlings. This is sometimes difficult but good material is not necessarily good for the piece – the piece must tell you what is good and what isn't.

About five years later a good friend of mine, the pianist Gerard Bouwhuis, asked me for a piano piece. So I wrote *Trepidus*, ninety per cent of which consisted of material from *De Snelheid*, using all those brilliant six-part chords.

COWBOY FILM MUSIC

The last thing I want to touch on is harmony and melody. In one way or another, things sometimes fall right into your lap – you get a commission from an American orchestra. The Grand Canyon sound of San Francisco imposes itself on me, and I decide that there must be cowboy music too (which I ultimately included in *Rosa*). The fact that I opted for a contrast between speed and slowness in *De Snelheid* has to do with the American approach to freedom – in short, like driving from one coast to the other on a motorbike, your hair flying in the wind. Freedom it may be, but although this country can keep itself in grain, everything else has to be imported. This concept of freedom therefore pre-supposes that there is the freedom to exploit the rest of the world.

In American music, especially in symphonic music, you often hear nice, simple, fast rhythms in the strings, and suddenly a splendid slow melody pops up; beautiful panoramas unfold. I started *De Snelheid* like this too – establish a fast rhythm and then this melody:

This is a sort of homage to American cowboy film music. At the time I didn't really dare to write *real* cowboy film music as I did later in *Rosa*. From the melody which I first wrote, a scale appeared (for those of you who would like to know the details: C sharp melodic minor with an added diminished fifth).

In this scale there are two minor chords – C minor and C sharp minor:

That was everything in the piece. All the fast music which supports the wood-blocks is based on this material; all the harmonies, with a few exceptions, are six-part chords from this C sharp minor and C minor scale. The opening melody is a homage to California – blue skies, wonderful panoramas – and it is continually repeated, sometimes very slowly, sometimes very fast, and sometimes fragmented, like Bach in his chorale variations. The melody itself sounds like Ferde Grofé.[74]

On the first page the bass drum rhythm appears, ♩ = 60 and this doesn't change. At the end, when the tempo is quadrupled, I take up the tempo from the beginning again, the value is one quarter of the beginning.

---

[74] Ferde Grofé is known to American students as the composer of the *Grand Canyon Suite*.

SYSTEM OF ACCELERATION

The acceleration

page	bar	beat	pulse	
1	$^5/_{16}$	= 45	= 225	
14	$^6/_{16}$	= 45	= 270	quicker pulse
20	$^5/_{16}$	= 54	= 270	shorter bar
26	$^6/_{16}$	= 67.5	= 405	quicker pulse, longer bar
41	$^5/_{16}$	= 81	= 405	shorter bar
54	$^2/_4$	= 135	= 540	quicker pulse, longer bar
63	$^3/_8$	= 90	= 540	shorter bar
87	$^2/_4$	= 90	= 720	quicker pulse, longer bar
95	$^3/_8$	= 120	= 720	shorter bar
109	$^3/_8$	= 90	(540)	pulse = tremolo, bar slows down
112	$^5/_4$	= 45	(900) =	= 225

The acceleration accelerates (10 bars on each page).

This table, which I wrote fifteen years after I composed *De Snelheid*, is a precise analysis of the system of acceleration and is only interesting for people who like numbers.

It is a gradual acceleration in terms of tempo and perception of tempo. Sometimes the tempo stays the same and the bar type changes but mostly it is regular. There are some exceptions – short codas and short extensions. I have always written ten bars to a page.

At a given moment, I decided that the acceleration merely had to be apparent; it is in the structure, not in the music you hear. At the bottom of the table (above) you can see that a very long 5/4 bar is precisely four times as slow as the beginning but it sounds just as fast. The only person who really gets faster is the conductor, because he keeps having to turn the pages faster. Sian Edwards with Ensemble Modern was like one of those frightening school-ma'ams who beats the children like the devil. It looked marvellous. But Oliver Knussen's division of the piece into groups of bars I also found very refined and special. He was able to suggest the slow tempo which is always there under the surface and that is probably why his performance was so good. He even put in an accelerando, as if it was Liszt or Tchaikovsky. That sounds very good.

COMPLEX AND CLEAR

Later, I changed *De Snelheid*, the most important change being that I made holes in it. There are three elements in the piece and on the whole they happen automatically: melody, the acceleration and the regular bellows (which are always slightly *irregular*). I followed my intuition and took bits out here and there.

The reason for this was that I thought it was too muddy. People often hide behind the word 'complexity' but I think this easily becomes 'muddiness'. If something of everything happens at the same time, then things can become uninteresting. It has nothing to do with the complexity of the material but with the lack of clarity of what you want to say. I remember a discussion with my friend Jacq Vogelaar, one of the most intelligent philosophers / writers of the seventies. During our conversations I often criticised Adorno.[†] Adorno is important to us, because he wrote about what he called the philosophy of new music. Roughly, he maintains, in a very profound way, that Schoenberg is better than Stravinsky. For all sorts of reasons, but especially musical ones, I thought precisely the opposite. The subject of complexity is not only present in his ideas on Schoenberg and Stravinsky, but also in his way of writing. Sometimes I thought Adorno's ideas were particularly relevant. I will not say that I agreed with him, but he did put the right subjects on the agenda. He just could have written about them more efficiently. Vogelaar defended Adorno with the historic words: "If a subject is complex, then it must be written about in a complex way."

Later, to my surprise, I discovered a long essay by Robert Craft on Adorno's book. It must have been around 1970, because the English translation of *Philosophie der neuen Musik* [*The Philosophy of New Music*] had just come out. And in Craft's article I found my arguments against Vogelaar.

Even very complex situations must be able to be explained clearly. Obviously not to stupid people. I can imagine that a physicist trying to explain quantum mechanics to me would not succeed, even if he is very clear. So, to a certain extent, Vogelaar was right. It also depends on how you define things. Many things which we think are very simple are very complex.

I remember a theory class involving the Hoketus group at the Conservatoire, in which Diderik Wagenaar and Klas Torstensson were discussing complexity (Klas was our Xenakis). Diderik said that the *Bolero* was a very complex piece. Klas hadn't heard it since he was sixteen. It is a difficult subject: how complex is Ravel's *Bolero*? Complexity is something that can't be analysed. Some laws we don't yet know – musical laws, aesthetic laws. This does not only apply to the *Bolero*, but also to a Mozart symphony. That's the difference between art and science. In art there *must* be laws of which we are not yet aware. Why do people think about *Hamlet*? Either because it appears to be interesting, or because we don't understand it, or because we can ascribe different interpretations to it. It is, to an extent, irrational.

I like to take as much responsibility as possible for what I write. But if

---

[†] Theodor Wiesengrund Adorno (1903-1969) was a philosopher who founded the Frankfurt School of Philosophy. He was also a composer, and as a student, studied with Alban Berg.

you make a piece as conceptual as possible, then a moment comes when you do something without any reason. I would never admit to doing something *just like that*. I would have to rethink the note – B flat, of course, but why? We cannot rationalise the law behind it. This is a great advantage of art; there are laws we don't yet know, and probably never will know. It's like falling in love. Partly, you understand why this is the most interesting person you know (and you seem to know him or her very well). But at the same time, you realise that you will never comprehend anything about this person and that is why you fall in love.

Recently I was in Riga, the capital city of a country that has not existed for fifty years – Latvia. There was a film festival devoted to Eisenstein, who was born in Riga. Someone had heard of the 'Eisenstein Song' in M *is for Man, Music, Mozart*. I went to Riga for the opening and the complete Volharding showed up because of that song, which had little to do with Eisenstein – but this didn't bother them. De Volharding stood on this large stage and as they were slowly moving to their positions with the singer Astrid Seriese, suddenly a guy with a big knife cut the film screen right down the middle. There was a bright red light behind it – very exciting.

I regard M *is for Man, Music, Mozart* as my 'vulgar' side (sometimes we have to occupy ourselves with such things). Later I heard that the public – eight hundred connoisseurs of avant-garde film – found the music very complicated. What do we call complex? I regard the music as very simple, but obviously not for film-goers. Complexity is bound up with visual perception.

Some things which sound very simple are very complex – Janáček, for example, is very complicated. On the other hand, I think that a lot of so-called complex music is very muddy.

ESCALATION

Now that I have heard *De Snelheid* again, I remember that Ravel's *Bolero* was a model for the piece. The idea that the percussion is continually present comes from Ravel. It is interesting that he simply puts in a snare drum from the beginning to the end. This one part is performed by five, six, indeed as many percussionists as possible who take it in turns, otherwise these symphony orchestra players would get too tired.

I knew that I wanted to write a sort of *Bolero*. In the seventies I found it an important, revolutionary work because it is a conceptual piece and conceptual art was hip at that time. The concept is escalation, a word that we often used to describe all sorts of music at that time. Peter Schat wrote *On Escalation*. It means: 'exacerbate the conflict', just like the Vietnam War. As Ravel pointed out, the concept of the *Bolero* is more important than the piece itself: "If you have the concept, every student can compose the piece." It is polemic and a joke, of course, but in a way it is also true.

In *De Snelheid*, the escalation is in the tempo, not in the instrumentation. *Bolero* is a positive piece; *De Snelheid* has an element of killing, just like *The Rite of Spring*. Stravinsky could only write that music because the girl dies. You can compare the end of *De Snelheid* to that.

In this piece I wanted to explain that tempo is not defined by the speed of the pulse, as many composers think, but by harmonic rhythm. The best way to demonstrate this is by combining a very fast pulse with a very slow harmonic rhythm: II-IV-II-(V). The harmony at the end of this piece is a very slow harmonic rhythm (see the example on p. 180).

The idea is that the heavyweight is the only one which remains and which cannot fall silent. The wood-blocks become so fast that in effect they play a tremolo which cannot any more be defined as a tempo. Just like hummingbirds; they move very quickly yet stay on the same spot. In cartoons, you are always seeing little figures that jump and only land after a while.

When you run as fast as possible, you don't move any more – like the wood-blocks. You are going as fast as you can, so you have to stop. Shortly after that point, thanks to thorough calculations, the three orchestras come in together following the rhythm of the bellows.

Right at the end the wood-blocks make a re-appearance. This is probably connected to horror films. Even when the hero has killed the nasty monster, it always comes back.

De Materie: introduction

Amsterdam, 1988 / Nijmegen, 1997

De Materie, *Introduction and Part 1. Combination of a lecture previously published* in Vrij Nederland, *10 December 1988 and a lecture at the Catholic University Nijmegen given on 2 April 1997.*

FOOTBALL

When we used to play football, two teams always had to be chosen first. You know the system: two little lads could choose someone from the group in turn. Because of the fact that I was always chosen respectably quickly, I naturally concluded that I was a sought-after little footballer. Subsequently I realised that it wasn't because I was so good, but that I had a clever psychological strategy for convincing those little boys that I *was* a good footballer.

I must say, regrettably, it doesn't work with composing. Sometimes it does seem as though someone who can talk well about his work also composes very good pieces, but that is often not the case at all.

Musical intelligence is only indirectly connected to general intelligence. It is even conceivable that one can be stupid and yet very musical. This is a conundrum which not many people willingly contemplate. The reverse, of course, is also true – there are very intelligent people who are not in the least musical. This was demonstrated very clearly to my father for the first time when he was a prisoner in St. Michielsgestel, an invention of the Germans. Every time the Resistance achieved some small success, a number of well-known Netherlanders were imprisoned and when another horrible thing happened (at least according to the Germans), they were shot dead, murdered.

So my father was sitting there, surrounded by all sorts of important Netherlanders, people such as Willem Ruijs, Lou Bandy[75] and of course many professors and scientists. It was then that he realised then that the intelligentsia often had a certain aversion towards art. The reason for this, according to my father, was that, despite the fact that art doesn't really let itself be understood, in one way or another it still can really carry people

---

[75] Willem Ruijs was a famous ship owner, Lou Bandy a popular singer.

away. For a scientist this is a slightly irritating phenomenon and I actually agree with the scientist – it certainly *is* irritating.

FORMALISM

The large measure of formalism which forms the basis of *De Materie* does not in itself offer any guarantee that the work will be beautiful. I don't want to say "on the contrary" because that isn't true either. I believe that, in art, there is a need for some sort of organisation; organisation is, in fact, the friend of chaos and chaos is an essential characteristic of art. A work like *De Materie* in particular is put together quite strictly and yet it often sounds as though it has been hurled onto the canvas in a joyous, Karel Appel-ish sort of way. Appel did, of course, take a quick look to see where the mess would land before he allegedly threw the paint onto the canvas. There was no question of his 'just making a mess'.†

De Materie was produced in 1989 by De Nederlandse Opera. It isn't an opera but rather a large theatrical four-part work, and it is essential to me that all these four parts are independent. They are also very different from each other. For the enquiring amongst us, it is probably more important to establish what is common to all of them and what the relationship is between the differences and the similarities. This is actually the most difficult and most profound subject and you can only move on to it after you have first discussed all the similarities between the four parts, and also the characteristics of the fours parts and the extent to which those characteristics develop. When you have got all that lined up – in so far as it is possible – then you can talk about the *relationship* between the differences and the similarities. I have more or less got round to it, but composers have to compose their next piece and I don't have the time to do too much meticulous academic work on pieces that are already eight years old.

The four pieces were not composed in the order they are performed: part 3 was composed before parts 1, 2 and 4. When part 3, *De Stijl [The Style]*, was completed and had already been performed, I started work on the other parts. There were practical reasons for this sequence.[76] This is often the case and that is good – structures (or inspiration) are often directly related to musical practice.

From that first vision, that first idea, it was clear that the work had to be called *De Materie* and had to have four parts. It was not until a lot later that I discovered that, in Christian symbolism, the figure 4 stands for all earthly things, literally, in fact, 'de materie' [matter].

Formalism, if I can use that word, produces a peculiar phenomenon. I lay down many things in fairly rigid structures which are associated with

---

† The Dutch Cobra artist Karel Appel is famous for the quote: "I'm just messing around a bit."
[76] See the cna[ter on *De Stijl*, p. 214.

counting and calculation. Subsequently, things turn out to fit and to be right without my having done a great deal to achieve it. But some connections also remain hidden from me. When I was preparing this evening, I again discovered something which I hadn't realised, namely that the melody on the letters B A C H, which I often use, also consists of four notes. Everyone knows that, of course, but here it is wonderful because of that central – I would even go so far as to say magical – role of the figure 4 in the whole *Materie*. It is evident that knowledge exists and is available but you don't consciously have it at your command.

In *Architektur und Harmonie* by Paul van Naredi-Rainer[77] there is a lot of information about the early use of symbolic numbers in architecture, from the Greeks to the early Renaissance. From this book I learned that 4 stands for all earthly things and for sound structure. In architecture, this connection appeared at a very early stage. The temples in Jerusalem, the Holy City, were square; the temple in the Castle of the Holy Grail was square. Very early on, architects were aware of the fact that 4 (square or oblong – these were interchangeable) is an essential figure for justice, and also strictness and the correctness of human behaviour.

I had previously learned that 3 is one of the Christian symbols for God. This is the second important number within the larger and smaller structure of *De Materie*. It may sound a little bookish but before long, strict, limited forms are needed whenever you have a vision of a large four-part work which has to summarise different ideas on the culture of the Netherlands – it's comparable to a chess board with four castles at the corners.

MIND AND MATTER

It all began with a vivid experience in Copenhagen – after ten years studying Marx (we'll just skip over that this evening). I was walking down a flight of stairs after a concert of works by a few young composers from Copenhagen, in which I had heard and seen a piece with a double bassoon and a double bass next to each other, two very low, grumbling instruments. I realised that although the two instruments certainly were from different families they were also from the same one because they were both made of wood. You did different things with it, but the material, the matter – and this was when the word first hit me – was the same. At that moment, I regarded this as an extraordinarily profound perception. It is a good way of understanding how things are sometimes connected in a totally surprising way, often in a very obvious manner. The material something is made of, for example.

The word 'matter' has been coined to some extent by Marxist philoso-

---

[77] Paul van Naredi-Rainer, *Architecture and Harmony* (Cologne: Dumont, 1982).

phers and you encounter it again in the term 'historical materialism'. It has to do with one of Marx' statements, often quoted by me: "It is not the mind which controls matter, but matter which controls the mind, the working of consciousness." I still think this is true and you can regard this statement as the motto of the piece.

Marx himself was a respectable bourgeois. At the time, artists and philosophers congregated in the salons, with the women wearing long white tent-dresses and howling sycophantically at a Chopin nocturne, which Chopin probably did not appreciate at all. With this picture of late-Romantic philosophy in your head, a statement such as Marx's proves to be extraordinarily interesting, rather rigorous and modern. It has always had my sympathy– it goes right against the prevailing emotional trend. But he is not totally right; it is much more complicated than that. Having grown up in an environment of thieves, you should, according to a famous statement by the anarchist Bakunin, actually only be able to become a thief. I do think that is a respectable way of thinking about it, but then there are embarrassing examples of newspaper boys who become millionaires. In other words, the mind really does have a significant influence on your material being, on your attitude towards the world and on your position in the world.

For example your mind controls your own body. I can give an example of this, a deeply non-Marxist story which I experienced myself. Because of mischance or a bad upbringing, as a boy I never went to the dentist. You didn't go in those days, even though my mother did talk about it, but evidently I never had toothache. When I was twenty-three, I was doing my final exams – Theory, Piano and Composition – at the Conservatoire in The Hague. Afterwards I went to visit my girlfriend. As I was waiting for a tram on my way home, I suddenly felt the most immense pain in my cheek. I had never felt that pain before, but I immediately thought: "Of course, that's what they call toothache. How dreadful. Dentist tomorrow." Sure enough, it turned out that I had two rotten teeth. This is what we can learn from this: those rotten teeth had been sitting there for a year, maybe two or more, becoming increasingly rotten. But clearly, I had to take the exam before I could feel pain. Everyone knows striking examples of that sort of case from his own experience or that of his neighbour's nephew. Evidently, the mind does control matter to a certain extent after all. You can argue about whether pain comes under matter. I think it does. In any case, it's pretty troublesome if you've got it.

SYMPHONY IN FOUR PARTS

De Materie had to consist of four dramatic situations, each displaying a specific historical aspect of the culture of the Netherlands. Because of the figure 4 and the fact that the four different parts each have their own historical context, the piece is much more like a symphony than an opera. Since late-Romanticism in Italy in particular, operas have been through-composed. In Handel's and Mozart's time, they all still consisted of little pieces of music one after the other but thereafter, as operas became realistic dramas (frequently with women who became very sick and feared they would die), the music had to be through-composed, 'aus einem Guß' ['a unified whole']. Until now, that has been the structure of an opera and, because *De Materie* has nothing to do with that structure, I believe it is much safer to see it as a very large instrumental, symphonic work. The only thing is, there is a lot of singing in it and that is not so often the case in a symphony. Those Mahler symphonies in which there is singing are a rare example. That man should simply have written operas. But due to a confluence of circumstances that didn't work out (he probably didn't have a good librettist). He also hated the opera 'business' because he always had to conduct things himself. It's no picnic with all those divas – certainly not in Vienna in 1890.

TEMPO

The fact that *De Materie* is actually a very big symphony means that the four parts have different tempi. As you know, a symphony has four movements: one quick, one slow, then a little dance and then a very fast finale. I have more or less adopted this arrangement, although at the time I wasn't really aware that I was in the process of composing a symphony. It is certainly a very long symphony because each part lasts twenty-five minutes.

This duration is the result of a formalistic choice of relationships:

$$4 \times 25 = 100$$
$$100 = 10 \times 10$$
$$10 = 1 + 2 + 3 + 4.$$

The sequence 1, 2, 3, 4 is of great importance in the piece, but first I should say something about the tempi. Before I started work on the first part, I tied myself down as regards the relationships between those four tempi. The essence of the whole piece is actually that they should be in the ratio 4:3:2:1. In this case, three tempi are about the same: 2 is actually twice as slow as 4 and 1 is twice as slow as 2. In fact, composing is very easy. If you know these sorts of things, you know quite a lot.

The ratio between the tempi ultimately became 8:6:5:4. The tempo of part 3 was fixed because I had already composed it. There a ♩ = 90, so ninety of them can sound in a minute. These days, in good Dutch, this is called '90 beats per minute'. You can hear this on a metronome, an invention of Maelzel. With it you can thus measure precisely how quickly things go and how long they will last.

   With this in mind, I fixed the tempi of the remaining three parts. The
ratio 8:6:5:4 is approximately the ratio 4:3:2:1 times two but it is much
more effective because the tempi differ more widely from each other.

   When the tempo gets slower, the pulse gets quicker. That is a version of
an ancient law of nature which forms the basis of the whole work: something that is always getting faster becomes increasingly heavy and apparently smaller too. This odd contradiction in nature, the connection between tempo and mass, was a reason for me to use it as the structure of the
whole piece. The figures are as follows:

	TEMPO	NOTE VALUE		SMALLEST SUBDIVISION OF THE BEAT
Part 1	♩ = 144	quavers	288:	2 in the beat
Hadewijch	♩ = 108	triplets	324:	3 in the beat
De Stijl	♩ = 90	semiquavers	360:	4 in the beat
Part 4	♩ = 72	sextuplets	432:	6 in the beat

In part 1, a ♩ = 144 and the beat is divided into quavers. Very occasionally
you hear semiquavers, but in general, the quaver is the shortest note value.
The note value is therefore 288; there are 288 of them in a minute. You do
frequently hear longer note values, for example a note consisting of three
semiquavers, thus one-and-a-half quavers.

HARMONY: 1-2-3-4

   The ratio 1-2-3-4 is present in the harmony from the first to the last bar.
The most important chord, a compositional *tour de force*, consists of three
intervals, four notes: a prime, a second, a third and a fourth. This is the
chord:

The prime is an interesting dialectical problem. Is it an interval or isn't it?
What is the difference between two people playing the same note and one
playing that note?

   The great advantage of this chord is that it is a combination of a tonal
situation, namely the dominant together with its resolution, and at the
same time also the combination of an augmented and a perfect fourth, an

exceedingly chromatic norm. And with this comes the freedom to create a situation which can distance itself from purely tonal functions.

Another basic element (but this is more for the professionals) is that the whole of *Materie* emerges as it were from the fundamental triad, from the keynotes of the four parts. The entry of the chorus in the first part is an E flat minor chord: E flat-G flat-B flat, simply the root position. Part 2, the slow movement, is based around F minor, the third part was already written in G major and the large final part ends in A major. This also happened in German Romanticism: when the sun rises, it is very often in A major. It works like that too. If you know the piece well, then you feel that G is continually present in *De Stijl* and when we get to the Ascension, which part 4 is about, it is A major which shines in your heart. So there are appropriate references to great Romantic pieces.

To my utter astonishment I realised (but not until much later) that these four fundamental triads have all twelve notes. It is a good example of the contrasts between mind and matter, and that is what the piece is about. I had never noticed before that you can do this with four triads, two major and two minor triads. That was a pretty majestic discovery. Things often happen which lead you to think: "It's right that way." I call that grace.

During a rehearsal of *De Materie*, with conductor Reinbert de Leeuw.
Photo: Frans Schellekens

De Materie: part I

Amsterdam, 1988 / Nijmegen, 1997

When *De Stijl* [*The Style*] was ready, I began work on the piece about Hadewijch. I had that hazy vision about *De Materie*. When I formed my ideas as to how the first part should be – my *Leben des Galilei* [*Life of Galileo*] coupled with Amsterdam around 1600 – I took my synopsis to the then director of the Nederlandse Opera, Jan van Vlijmen. He read it and said: "That's a good idea, we'll do that." That was a bit of shock, because the piece really didn't have anything to do with opera. Jan van Vlijmen also said: "There is only one man who can design this non-opera, these non-dramatic works, and that is the American genius, Robert Wilson." That also surprised me, because I thought that Wilson only did his own things. However, it turned out well.

In the meantime Jan van Vlijmen was dismissed – for the wrong reasons, in my opinion. I thought back to our conversation, in which he had also said that he didn't think it was a good idea to give previews before the premiere of the whole piece. So I simply had to start at the beginning. That took me six months because I wanted to create a first part that would be as interesting as Brecht's *Galileo*. *Galileo* is an exemplary combination of spirituality and matter and that's what I was after. I wanted to show, in four different ways, how the mind, the person, deals with tangible surroundings.

As far as that is concerned, Galileo – certainly how Brecht writes about him – is an ideal example: how he retracts his theories because he wants to assure himself of a good meal and a peaceful and comfortable life. That is the moral of Brecht's play, if I can summarise in such a generalised way. But I knew very early on that the action must take place exclusively within the culture of the Netherlands. I have a peculiar aversion to scrounging. I prefer to leave songs on texts by Jacques Prévert to other composers. You have the most feeling for your own roots. Moreover, your own culture concerns you; you have taken it in with your mother's milk.

So I went on the hunt for a Dutch Galileo. It cost me a lot of time, in telephone calls and reading books. In the end I chose someone of whom most of you, I hope, have never heard – Gorlaeus (David van Goorle) who died, aged twenty, in 1609.

It goes without saying that you have to read many history books, including those about the dissidents of the Golden Age. A little book by Klaas van Berkel: *In het voetspoor van Stevin* [*In the footsteps of Stevin*] was very important. I thought Stevin, despite his being a bit of a bureaucrat, was an interesting man. I briefly considered making him the main character in the first part, but then I got hold of a thesis by the same Klaas van Berkel. It concerned Isaac Beeckman, an extraordinarily interesting man. We are still fighting about whether he was the inventor of molecular theory or not. At the time, I thought: "Now things are improving."

I tracked down Klaas van Berkel in his Institute for the History of Science in Utrecht. I had a long talk with him there. After I had explained to him that I had devoured his book on Beeckman from beginning to end I told him that I would like to use this Beeckman, but that I found him a bit boring. He certainly was comparable with Galileo, because he developed good ideas in all fields, but he was also an ordinary schoolmaster in Utrecht, headmaster of one of those Latin schools. The one amusing detail that I remember from the thesis is that, late one evening, he climbed up a tower by a spiral staircase with his students, who were all supposed to be in bed, and they lay on the roof to look at the stars. I could really see that on a stage, a large tower like that and all those little children climbing up it, but it wasn't really enough of an idea after all.

Van Berkel muttered under his breath: "Yes, perhaps Gorlaeus." But he remained very hazy about it and directed me to the as yet unknown Michael Zeeman.

Before I created *De Tijd*, I had read Dijksterhuis' book *The Mechanization of the World Picture: Pythagoras to Newton* and Gorlaeus turned out to be in it. The way in which Dijksterhuis devoted himself to a historiography of learned physics that would be as precise as possible kept me very busy. I asked myself how I could conjure up these things as scientifically as possible in the music and for this reason, I went on the hunt for this Gorlaeus.

He proved to be an extraordinarily exciting boy who died very young and of whom virtually nothing is known. All I found was a journal article about him from 1923, a fairly extensive description of the content of two books, the second of which, *Idea Physicae*, was called a sort of *tractatus logicus* by the writer of the article. In this book, Gorlaeus frequently challenged many of the Aristotelian theories of the day. And so he reduced Aristotle's four elements to two. This tampering with Aristotelian laws of nature was anti-Catholic and for this reason it interested me; I also wanted to reflect the revolutionary ferment in the Netherlands at that time. The Catholics had accepted anti-Aristotelianism since Aquinas but not the atomic physics of people such as Democritus.

The first generation of nuclear physicists – Beeckman, Gorlaeus and others (predominantly in Holland) – used Democritus' atomic theory in their examination of matter. This, of course, had to do with the fact that they were Protestants, literally protestants. The intellectuals were Calvinist and anti-Catholic. At the time that nuclear physics – now proved to be the correct theory of matter – was being developed in the Netherlands, we also slung out the Spanish and that, as you know, was pretty difficult.

Gorlaeus' *Idea Physicae* could not be found – not in the university library, nowhere.

There was a copy of his first book in Leiden, but I had the feeling that I needed the *Idea Physicae*.

As I was searching for a completely different book in the university library, I suddenly thought: "Why not just have a look in the twenty-three bulky volumes of the catalogue of the British Museum?" And sure enough – sometimes you're lucky – I found simply 'Gorlaei Davidei, *Idea Physicae*.' After a lot of effort, I finally received a photocopy of a few chapters that I suspected might deal with particle theory.

REVOLUTION AND SHIPBUILDING

In the meantime, I had started composing the first part. I had yet another subject in mind for that first part. It would be about revolution – Paris 1789, Amsterdam 1968, but also in a more general sense. My musical metaphor for the eruption of intellectual, and also physical, violence was shipbuilding. From the first moment I knew that it was good.

Then you race to the maritime museum and you read yourself silly about how it all happened. Luckily – things were really going my way again – there was a large book there by a certain Witsen, probably an ancestor of the later Witsen, the painter. And in that book was all I needed to know about building ships between 1600 and 1672. Actually, I didn't think I needed much more than a list of all the necessary tools and nails and bolts and screws and nuts in a 'fluit' such as this (because that's what a wonderful three-master with high stern and high prow was called). But after I had been through Witsen's book once, I thought: "Now I know how a ship must be built, let's do it in the piece too."

In this way, the first part slowly began to take shape.

Eventually, the choosing of the texts became less and less difficult. I'll talk about the music later. After the orchestral introduction, which is very momentous, the chorus comes in at a very specific point, of which more later too. We hear two fragments from an important Dutch historical text, the Acte van Verlatinghe [The Act of Abjuration]. This is the first official document in which we withdrew our allegiance to the Spanish king in 1581, before the Twelve Years' Truce. That was of very great significance, because on that day – and I brag about this a lot in America – the first democratic republic of the world was established – if we want to view it like that. Of course, it wasn't a completely democratic republic, but it looked much more like one than it had done previously.

That text was simply sitting in a cupboard at Scheltema en Holkema,[†]

[†] Scheltema en Holkema: a large bookshop in Amsterdam.

in a splendid edition with a facsimile of the old text, a legible rewrite of it and a translation of that rather bureaucratic seventeenth-century officialese. I can read it now but then I still found that old Dutch fairly difficult. The right fragments were not too difficult to find, because the text states somewhere in capital letters: DOEN TE WETENE, 'we make known', and after this the announcement follows that we are giving up our allegiance to the Spanish throne.

With this, though, the curious notion arises that I, who displayed anarchistic behaviour in the sixties, thus now become an undeniable monarchist. Because who was extolled as the new leader? Our Prince of Orange,[†] as he is called in the text. So I have become a royalist after all. But I am certain that Willem's function at the time was a bit different from that of our current queen.

After the two fragments from the Acte van Verlatinghe the orchestra takes things up again and in the first part does not do much more than hammer. The hammering of the carpenters at the ships in Amsterdam harbour – BANG BANG BANG BANG – carries on for twenty-five minutes.

When we have crossed the 'i's and dotted the 't's as far as the revolution is concerned, the chorus immediately takes over the hammering, even though the first revolutionary text also sounds fairly 'hammered'. The chorus sings a virtually complete explanation of the actions you need to carry out to build a ship. At a particular moment – for those of you interested in mysticism, at the golden section – the one and only protagonist of the first part at last appears on stage: our friend Gorlaeus. Shortly before this is one of the few moments where you hear semiquavers. Gorlaeus is, as it were, conjured up, the mind out of the flesh, by very quick frenzied cor anglais, cor anglais with synthesizers and later by a tam-tam.

Gorlaeus explains his particle theory. It wasn't so easy to decipher the texts from the British Museum, because I received a copy which had been printed the wrong way round, black paper and white letters – for some profound reason which escapes me. In addition, the text was in Latin. An expert did me a good translation of the fragments dealing with matter and with the fact that, ultimately, everything consists of indivisible particles. Gorlaeus was the first to say this in the history of the world except, of course, Democritus and his followers – the Greeks have always done everything better than us.

In the meantime, I had set the Witsen text and those from the Acte van Verlatinghe, but I thought that Gorlaeus in modern Dutch was not really appropriate for the first part which I was, after all, visualising in 1620. So I then encountered the curious problem that after the translation of the Latin into Dutch, I again had to call in specialist help in sixteenth- and seventeenth-century Dutch, because in my piece I wanted Gorlaeus to

[†]Willem I, Prince of Orange (1533-1584) is the ancestor of a branch of the Dutch royal family.

sing as he would have talked in the cafes in Leiden in 1605-1606 where, under the influence (I hope) of the local beer, he had stood and proclaimed his theories – risking being knocked down in the process to. At the Institute for Dutch at Utrecht University, the modern translation of Gorlaeus was translated back into the language of around 1600.

When Gorlaeus has finished talking, the explanation of the shipbuilding has also finished. The piece ends in the reverse order, as far as the music is concerned, with a 'hammered' list of all the ships carpenter's tools. The last blow of the piece falls on the word 'bijl' [axe]. And in Witsen's book, too, this was the last thing on the list.

The final structure of the texts emerges, to an extent, while I'm composing. In general, I first establish in detail what I will and what I won't use, but in the case of the ship texts I still moved things around and drew arrows to things I had omitted. I have studied the Gorlaeus text closely to produce a coherent whole from it. In general, the texts are easily fitted to the music.

Toccata in E flat

Something very different preceded all this. I would never have been able to write such a large work had I not made a precise description of the musical form in advance. There are people who go about it differently. They have a vague, global idea when they start to write and then see what happens.

I often hear writers saying: in the third chapter a secondary character appears and he turns out to be very important in the final chapter. Actually this happens in music as well. There is a mysterious person in the whole *Materie*: J. S. Bach. Not all of you know that Bach often set his own name to music. That's four notes but you must bear in mind that a B in old German was B flat and H was B natural. This is how it sounds:

These four notes play an important part in the whole piece, like a sort of guardian angel, but in part 1 Bach is structurally present. When I knew about the hammering I knew immediately that this was a musical metaphor for a particular musical form, namely the toccata. The toccata was developed both in Italy and the Netherlands in the sixteenth century by organists and harpsichordists such as Frescobaldi and Sweelinck and lived on to the beginning of the twentieth century. People such as Prokofiev wrote toccatas – hammering piano pieces.

I then had the idea of looking at one of Bach's pieces from the *Well-Tempered Clavier* (and I have had a look in this book much more often than once – I study it nearly every day): the prelude in E flat from part one, which is actually a toccata with a ricercare. The piece is quick until, at a given moment, a slower part appears. This is the ricercare or the motet – these terms are interchangeable. It is actually an imitation of a choir piece. So Bach imitates a choir piece on the keyboard. Later he combines those two ideas, the slow notes of the chorus and the quick notes of the beginning. It is very strange that he does this because this particular form, the toccata and ricercare, was already obsolete in Bach's time. But for Sweelinck in 1610 (Gorlaeus's time), for example, it was a very current, interesting, modern avant-garde form. Bach must have thought: "I am going to compose a toccata with a ricercare; I'll use an archaic form for once and I'll do it better than Frescobaldi ever did." That was certainly the task he set himself, because he was a vain creature. So I oriented myself towards someone who himself used an archaic form. I reverted to 1620 with someone who, in 1720, also reverted to it. This seemed to me to be a good idea.

Put simply, it's like this: a Bach prelude consists of a number of moments and you can multiply them by a number such that you get units from which – if you use the same number of them as Bach – you get a duration of twenty-five minutes. It's a bit arithmetical of course, but as a composer, you are always counting. Bach was always counting too.

The orchestral introduction is the first bit of the Bach, the bit played quickly. In *De Materie* there are no less than 144 large hammer-beat chords for the whole orchestra. Still without the chorus. No singing. There aren't continually new, interesting chords – no, just these 144 beats. You have to imagine it as a gigantic magnified toccata-playing hammer. The rhythm is not regular, but ranges from very slow to very quick, an accelerando.

At the moment Bach begins his motet, the chorus starts with the Acte van Verlatinghe. Bach's motet, a stately four-part imitation, uses as its theme 'L'homme armé'.

Bach does it like this:

We know this melody because it had already been used in the fifteenth century as a cantus firmus for settings of the mass by Netherlanders. So it was already an archaic theme for Bach. During the singing of the text you sometimes hear a hammer beat in the orchestra, one note. That is the complete version of the melody 'L'homme armé', but in a very slow tempo, spread over the entire length of the chorale.

Now and then, a trumpet plays precisely what Bach writes at the corresponding moment in the piece and this highlights another exception to the rule that the quaver is the quickest note:

The place where Bach combines the long notes with the quick ones of the beginning is where I start the texts about shipbuilding. Here, for the first time, chorus and orchestra develop their hammering together.

"Volght nu, hoe men de scheepsdelen te zamen zet." ["Now follows how one puts together the parts of a ship."]

[*De Materie* part 1 is played.]

Hadewijch: part 2 of *De Materie*

Nijmegen, 1997

Lecture at the Catholic University Nijmegen, 9 April 1997.

The best way of learning a language is to fall in love with someone who doesn't speak your own language. At the beginning it isn't necessary at all, but at a given moment, the medium of language does turn out to be useful after all.

When you get your teeth into a subject you love, it often transpires subsequently that this is the only way of acquiring some small insight into a particular period of history. You cannot actually demand of a person that he gets to know a lot about history in one human lifetime – and I'm only talking about western history. But we have to do what we can and love is a good line of approach.

When I was about thirty, I was amazed at the music of a French composer who, I learned, had died in 1377: Guillaume de Machaut. This music is astonishingly beautiful and my love for it strongly motivated me to get to know more about what happened in the fourteenth century. I still have the feeling that I understand what inspired those people which, of course, is actually nonsense. But it is the case that I understand what inspired Machaut to make innovations in music. That really is quite something, and I suspect that it helps one to acquire some insight into that world, up to and including the methods of transport which those people had at their disposal at that time. That is actually imagination again, but that is not a bad thing. At the end of the day, I am not a historian, but a composer who sometimes dives into history to make it real and to make connections which create some sense of ownership.

This also applies to the first part of *De Materie*. Amsterdam 1620 is a metaphor for Amsterdam 1968, even though the work was written twenty years after that. So it is all a stage more complicated, as is more often the case with games. There are all kinds of laws and rules which you don't abide by. When you play Gooseboard you run the risk of falling into the pit (although you can perhaps get round this by shouting loudly: "This is an exception!"). You have to deal continually with exceptions to the exceptions to the rules. This is all part of the game.

There is a point to games. If a game is a good one, then you learn a lot about the world, circumstances and perhaps also about history.

My father thought it was elegant to see history not as a line but as a circle around you, so that you focus now and again on a particular point in history. Later I regarded this as an un-Marxist outlook, but now I have some sympathy for it.

The four subjects of *De Materie* are somewhat arbitrary and are very much products of their time. I could just as easily have chosen four other subjects. They have nearly all been part of the historic culture of the Netherlands. Part 3's Mondrian boogie woogie is close to me; it is not historical, but simply my own life.[78] I too sat at the piano trying things out. The order of the four parts is not chronological; the chronology is set out in school books. The character of a piece determines its place in the work. So *Hadewijch* is typically a second movement, the slow movement of the symphony. After a display of faster music, it is time for something more peaceful, then have a bit of a giggle and, to conclude, the finale: make sure you catch the last train.

For a long time I had planned to do something with Reims Cathedral and also with Hadewijch, but I didn't know that it would become the same piece. It often happens that things ultimately fall into place. People say: "Oh, those crazy artists", but it has nothing to do with that. It is the arbitrariness that you also encounter in nature. Every scientist will tell you that nothing works in nature. Those things we think are so beautiful are actually one huge rubbish heap, quite apart from the fact that everyone consumes everyone else all day long. And we can't eat turkey at Christmas? Come, come.

Doubtless I encountered Hadewijch at school but I had totally forgotten about it. The reason I included her in *De Materie* was that shortly before, I acquired a copy of the *Book of Visions*.

The work had been finished for a long time and had even been performed and *still* I had to battle with the fact that no one knew who this woman was, certainly not beyond our borders. Flanders is a happy exception to this, where she is far better known than in the Netherlands. It is wonderful now that, in the last year or two, everyone has heard of Hildegard von Bingen. She was just in fashion. Suddenly specific knowledge appears all around you, if you can still call that knowledge. Now, when I speak about Hadewijch, I have to say that she is a sort of Hildegard von Bingen – very stupid and, moreover, untrue, because there is as much as one hundred years between them – and even if time did elapse very slowly in the Middle Ages, a hundred years must have made a bit of a difference. Furthermore, there are no indications that Hadewijch had heard of Hildegard. I prefer to compare her to a troubadour, a *trouvère*, a *Minnesänger*.

---

[78] See the chapter on *De Stijl*, p. 214.

I often have to think about an observation made by an actor in the seventies. As you know, at that time we were all strict Marxists. In Eindhoven there was a group which was very high up in political theatre: Proloog. You really had to be strict to get into it. I liked them. Rik Hancké, a good-looking Flemish boy, played Christ, Frieda Pittoors started off there and also the Royaards boys. One of them said once in a lively discussion: "Emotion and passion are both nonsensical; the whole business of being in love is just an invention of the troubadours." I always found this to be striking and it is even true.

Hadewijch belonged to a group of women poets. They were probably well born – distinguished maidens who most likely had had a good education. In contrast to the Benedictine Hildegard, these women had, to a certain extent, a worldly outlook. We must assume that these groups of wandering women had taken the vow of chastity and that they sung both of courtly love and divine love.

The essence of my choice to set one of Hadewijch's Visions to music is that these two elements – courtly love and divine love – are not in conflict with one another. This is essential for the culture of the Middle Ages in general, but in Hadewijch's case, this is really driven home. The seventh vision, which I have set in its entirety to music, is an account of a development from physicality to spirituality by way of a few meetings which very much resemble erotic encounters. The 'he' who is the main character in the text was not written with a capital letter at the time, but is clearly interchangeable: a human being and a divine being. It is all mixed up and it is for every reader to decide how to interpret it. I regard this combination of religious or mystic ecstasy and eroticism not as a contradiction but, in essence, as the expression of the same sort of feeling. I suspect – or rather I hope – that this applied to Hadewijch too. Of the actual erotic experiences we know little, of course, and we must let our imagination come into play a bit. In my opinion, the vow of chastity had more to do with a vow of loyalty than celibacy. I suspect that actual physical love at that time was more usual and natural; arguably it occurred more often than it does nowadays in a yuppie society such as, for example, New York or a provincial town in America. That life is much more Victorian than the life Hadewijch led. If you give a woman a compliment in America these days, you risk being taken to court for sexual harassment.

This starting point – of not regarding religious ecstasy and eroticism as contradictions – later (in fact when the work was five years old) turned out to fit in well with my interest in irony. In my view, irony means that everything always carries its contradiction within itself. Something is always something else. Gradually I realised that that is what keeps the four parts of *De Materie* together. It is also an explanation of the fact that all the parts use historical models, as does the music.

This connection has only become clear to me in the past year.

As I have already said, the seventh vision is the central text in Hadewijch. The numbering of the visions is not Hadewijch's. Publishers later assigned numbers to them on the basis of time and place, but the texts really just run on. According to the numbering system there are fourteen visions. The seventh begins with 'Early one morning in Whitsuntide'. In that central vision, the line from the earthly (close to the ground) to the sublime (the spiritual) is strongest. Because of this contrast between very low and very high, I opted for this vision.

REIMS CATHEDRAL

I have superimposed the structure of Reims Cathedral which, in itself, has nothing to do with Hadewijch, on the text of the seventh vision. The cathedral was built at around the same time. When she was wandering round with those ladies, the lads, the 'freemasons', were busy building. The high point of the gothic was about 1270. Machaut was a canon at Reims for thirty years in the following century.

It is still astonishing. There was no electricity, yet they managed to construct buildings such as this.

Reims is my favourite cathedral because it radiates a certain symmetry. Beauvais is much larger, but it has collapsed three times. It was too large; their technique was inadequate to achieve what they wanted. Just like Pisa, also a miracle of beauty. Everything there was square, but they went and built a round tower and it was already crooked after two metres. Then you have to make a decision. You can stop there and start again, but the Italians said no, we're going to build a leaning tower. They did correct it, but it went wrong again. There is a second kink in it resulting from the second correction. But they knew immediately that it would always remain crooked. This solution is much more pleasing than just keeping on getting bigger. We've got nothing on them.

Reims Cathedral is more or less the biggest possible. If you want to know more about dimensions in a cathedral, as I did at the time, you end up in a dazzling world. How had they ever been able to establish how long a wall should be and where the next pillar should come? At that time, there were different 'feet' in circulation: Cologne 'feet', Roman 'feet'. Just try and work that one out. There is a wonderful book about Chartres Cathedral by John James.[79] He discovered which measures were employed there. Because the building of a cathedral took so long, new master build-

[79] John James, Chartres. The Masons who built a legend (London: Routledge & Kegan Paul, 1982).

ers arrived with other measures and other ideas. It is for this reason that it is so difficult to analyse precisely what they did. That has now been worked out exactly in Chartres. Each window has been measured and James knows what the measures were in each generation. He discovered this by examining the builders' initials in the cathedral.

The combination of mysteriousness and ordinariness in cathedral construction – "just make sure the mortar is ready" – I really like.

As far as the work is concerned, it is good to know that many ratios within the cathedral building are based upon root numbers. If you take the smallest roofed area, and call that 1, then the next is the square root of 2, then the square root of 3. The largest part of the roof, above the golden section of the whole cathedral, is the square root of 5. This is striking, because the golden section is a root five formula.[80]

These things interested me because I was curious about the ratios. They are expressed as small, but very precise, numbers. The freemasons knew all these numbers; they had discussions about them with the bishops. These were very important proportions for them. For example, they had a little movable machine which, on the bottom, told you what the square root of 3 was, if up above it was the square root of 2. These root numbers are not used in my musical notation itself but certainly in the compositional proportions within the piece.

What really captivated me about James' book was the rigorous investigation of those few people. You can be very grateful to them. It was an incentive for me to deal seriously with my subject.

HEAVEN AND EARTH

I pictured Hadewijch walking through the cathedral to the altar. This is audible, for example, in the clock-like chords at every pillar she passes. Just as most cathedrals, Reims is made up of a rectangle (4) and a circle, a divine form, with which I associate the figure 3. So, Hadewijch's walk from the entrance to the high altar is a move from earth to heaven.

I made it difficult for myself because, after *De Materie* part 1, I could only get her singing with difficulty. So it is not surprising that I needed a long orchestral introduction in order to create that sublime atmosphere.

Firstly, I wrote long canons with three-part chords. I thought: at the labyrinth, at the third pillar, she can start singing. That didn't work, nor half way through the labyrinth either. Only at the end of the labyrinth does she start singing. The labyrinth was on the floor, but was removed in the nineteenth century. It is still visible on this old picture.

---

[80] Namely: $\frac{1}{2}(\sqrt{5}-1)$

During a lecture on *Hadewijch*, Louis Andriessen showed
the plan of Reims Cathedral. Photo: Gerrit Serné

CANTUS FIRMUS

The cantus firmus in *Hadewijch* is a ballad-like melody, consisting of 7 x
4 crotchets:

In principle, this melody is repeated for each section, but you have very
quick and very slow repetitions. As usual, I have permitted many exceptions to the rules I make for myself, and I can't remember most of them any
more. Systematics – and you can pass this on – can be a great support.
They are the stakes with which you move forward. Of course it does happen that you get stuck every other minute and that you don't know what
you have to do. This is always unexpected and you have to accept it with
a certain amount of cheerfulness. I often go back to a sort of base element
of the work. You take responsibility for it, as it were. In this case, for example, this applies to three-part chords.

The slowest musical expression of the cantus firmus is to be heard in the uppermost notes of the clock-like chords which you hear at the points when she passes a pillar in the imagination. This cantus firmus is not meant to be detected because the time spans are much too widespread. The chords become increasingly thinner as she moves from earthliness to heavenliness. Initially they are very large, with many high and low notes, but at the end there is just one gong in the middle register.

Because Hadewijch begins to sing so late on, I became pressed for time as regards the distribution of the text. This is one of the technical problems which every composer has to deal with. I solved it by moving the texts together. In the beginning, I had thought that Hadewijch should be split into a choir of angels, into five different Hadewijchs, as many as there are chapels round the altar. I didn't do this. When Hadewijch draws close to the inner sanctum of the cathedral, you hear *a capella* voices. This point is the centre of the circle on the golden section of the entire cathedral and thus of the work. It is also the only moment in *De Materie* which is nine-part: an eight-part chord and the melody. The choir has started singing earlier and takes over a part of the text. Thank goodness that turned out to work well with certain words which occur at the same time. I call that pure grace. Hadewijch describes the meeting with 'him'. Finally, only Hadewijch's voice remains as a thin line. She disappears as it were in the circle.

'He' appears first in the form of an eagle; the chorus recounts the entire story. After that, he appears in the form of a child, and finally as a young man. Jacques Kruithof is a Netherlands specialist in Middle Dutch. He helped me when I was thinking about the piece. He explained, word for word, the old text which I used because in it there are very ordinary words that have a completely different meaning and he also did a translation which appeared in the programme. I have made grateful use of an article on Hadewijch by H. C. ten Berge in which he discusses Christian number symbolism. For example, 28 stands for Mary. You can fiddle around with these holy numbers. Precisely because they are so holy, you may add or subtract one; 28 is too holy to use. It's like not standing on the alter in a church.

The ballad is the model for the cantus firmus melody, because this form is often used by the troubadours. The simplest ballad form is an alternation between verse and refrain, in the pattern a-b-a-c-a-d-a-e, but it is also possible that more than one element is repeated.

The rhythms of the cantus firmus are based on the rhyme schemes of the troubadours. I had a long book[81] on these rhyme schemes, in which

---

[81] Hendrik van der Werf, *The chansons of the troubadours and trouvères. A study of the melodies and their relation to the poems* (Epe: Hooigberg, 1972).

each rhyme is indicated by a letter of the alphabet. There were approximately twenty variations which were applied very strictly. I have translated the letters of the rhyme schemes into numbers. In the beginning, I transformed the rhyme-scheme a-b-a-b (for example the rhyming words *groot* [large] – *lief* [dear] – *dood* [dead] – *dief* [thief]) into 4-8-4-8. That is the scheme for the first time that the cantus firmus sounds. It begins with a breve, the second note lasts for eight crotchets, and the third for four. There are always little groups of four letters because many ballads consist of four line stanzas. Sometimes I follow an entire poem.

The totals per stanza are also important. I wanted each time to use the same number of crotchets but to sub-divide them differently. In this way, you almost arrive at a magic square; it contains numbers which produce the same sum, in whichever direction you add them up.

Both the melody and the rhythms show an irregular regularity. I think the chromatic outcome of the melody is particularly good. I now see that it is B-A-C-H again, but in reverse order.

I am trying to succeed in giving an account of the work without too many technical details. I am trying to avoid harping on about chords, although that is what ultimately inspires you and what you are actually doing the whole time. The accounts of the cathedral and the cantus firmus are just trimmings.

THE FIGURE THREE

I spoke before (see p. 192) about that one chord:

In the first part, these four notes can be heard nearly always at the same time and, moreover, in the company of four other notes. These were eight-part chords.

In the second part the figure 3 becomes the central number. This has to do with the divine subject of *Hadewijch*. In contrast to part 1, the piece is in 3/4 time and the beat is divided in three, into triplets. These triplets are a fraction quicker than the quavers in part 1. I have already told you about this quickening of the pulse. Moreover, the cantus firmus is often accompanied by two other notes, so that the harmony in this piece, unlike part 1, is nearly always three-part.

Whilst I was writing *De Materie*, I acquired a sort of Eckermann[82] in the

---

[82] Johann Peter Eckermann wrote down his many conversations with Goethe and published them in *Gespräche mit Goethe* [*Conversations with Goethe*], (1835).

person of Alcedo Coenen. He was a young musicologist who kept track of a number of things I chose *not* to do. He also wrote the programme book for *De Materie*. It struck him that there was a second in every chord. He was right and there must have been a reason for it of which I was unaware. I thought: "Now I'll get you!" and for the following three days I went on composing *Hadewijch*; I was already on the fifth or sixth minute. Then there comes a page of chords exclusively without seconds with 'For Alcedo' written next to it. But those diminished thirds are certainly a lot uglier.

The notes which I just played are these:

For three-part chords you must omit one of them. You can put that fourth and that second the other way round too, and then you get this:

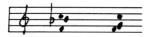

The second chord is a completely different chord, but it also consists of a fourth and a second. That's fine in this piece. I'm often discussing this with students. How do you analyse particular chords? what have they to do with one another? have they got *anything* to do with one another?

You can turn the thing around, then you get these:

It is difficult to hear the difference. The whole piece has actually been composed with these four chords. It is only at the golden section that you hear the 1-2-3-4 chord sound in its full glory, as though it is announcing the *a capella* section.

THE HOLIEST MOMENT

As I already said, *Hadewijch* was written in 3/4 time and the beat is divided into three. After the place where there is *a capella* singing – when the piece becomes increasingly higher and more spiritual – the harp begins to play crotchets. Here, 3/4 time becomes 4/4 time, although you would actually expect it to be exactly the other way round. These are fine exceptions, great exceptions to great rules. Moreover, the tempo is slowed with 3/4. That is not accidental either.

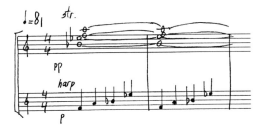

Of course, you had heard those four notes in the harp before. They are that fourth and that second. Those first three look suspiciously like three other terribly good notes in music history:[83]

Ennio Morricone, *Once upon a time in the West*

As we are talking about references, I know another one:

It is a piece by Bach, of which there are several versions, with very beautiful themes.

The whole piece is actually in F minor. You would expect it to begin in that key, but the nice thing about tonality is that the key is only established at the very end. Only then is it right. A famous example is Wagner's *Tristan und Isolde* (1857-1859). When people heard the first page, they

---

[83] In the chapter on *Rosa*, p. 242, Louis Andriessen elaborates on the music of Ennio Morricone.

thought it was atonal, because the key was not established in it. We now know that it is much more straightforward than that. The key is established at the end; it has always been so. *Tristan* ends simply in B major. At the end of *Hadewijch*, when the music has completed its ascension, it ends in F minor.

The major third in a minor key frequently occurred from the seventeenth century onwards, specifically at the conclusion. It was an invention of the Italian opera composers and is called a *tièrce de Picardie*, as you learn from the theory books (even though Picardie is in Northern France). It was one of the numerous elegant details in Italian opera around 1680. Another famous one which you learn in your schoolbooks is the Neapolitan Sixth; you have perhaps heard of this one too. The interesting thing – these technical things are quite diverting, even though they explain *nothing* about what is good and not good about a piece – is that the notes of Hadewijch's intimate final song:

are the same notes which begin the following part, *De Stijl*, but much quicker and a whole tone higher:

I had already completed *De Stijl* and so I could work with it. But I thought it was gruesome and ironic to connect the holiest moment of *Hadewijch* with a 'common' theme.

The transition from part 1 to part 2 links both of these parts rhythmically. That is to say: at the end of part 1, there are a few signals, a sort of chiming. These rhythms are already in the tempo which becomes important in *Hadewijch*.

The relationship between part 2 and part 3 is a melodic one and between the third and fourth parts there is a harmonic relationship. The final chord of part 3:

is precisely the same as the chord which begins part 4, even as regards timbre.

The quantifiable properties of the music are called 'parameters': melody, harmony (which is, however, not always present) rhythm, dynamic and colour. I think these last two are already slightly second-rate, but melody, harmony and rhythm are well thought of by composers and so are therefore your sole means.

It was only later that I realised that the three relationships which I have of course constructed myself are in three different parameters, namely: rhythm, melody and harmony. That is a little gift.

De Stijl: part 3 of
De Materie

Nijmegen, 1997

Lecture at the Catholic University Nijmegen, 16 April 1997.

DE STIJL

The third part of *De Materie* is entitled *De Stijl* [*The Style*] and is about Mondrian. If you were thinking of a symphony, this part should be a scherzo. So it should be a cheerful piece, but there is not much cheerful about it. As you know, the Dutchman, generally subjected to miserable weather conditions, has little reason to be cheerful. And certainly not when he ventures out of doors. The closer we get to summer, the worse the weather gets. This happens only in the Netherlands.

Mondrian also suffered from the miseries the climate, of course, but this is unrelated to his work. When I visited Expo '70 in Japan in 1970, they showed a film by John Fernhout called *Sky over Holland*. It's considered to be a rather kitsch film and continually draws parallels between the Dutch landscape and painting. Personally, I rather liked it, but the people around me found it extraordinarily tasteless. From an aeroplane you saw the splendid meadows and tulip fields, nice straight lines that faded into a Mondrian painting dating from the period I'm going to discuss. You could see from the film that he did those paintings because of that landscape, with all its rectangles and squares.

I also remember a friend of mine, a very good sculptress, who has been living abroad for years, in Peru as well as in New York now and then. I asked her if she'd never felt like going back to the Netherlands. "Go back?" she said; "To all those green handkerchiefs?" And I thought it was a nice description of that same landscape Fernhout had filmed so brilliantly, like a gigantic Mondrian.

To sum up – although analogies between art and geography are endless – I must admit that I, too, plead guilty to drawing the same parallels. I once took an American recording company executive to Marken.[†] It was on a November afternoon so it really couldn't have been much worse. But even so, you park your car and walk through the small town to the harbour. I took her up onto the dike. When you are standing there, with the

---

[†] A traditional Dutch island village off the coast of the IJsselmeer and perennial tourist attraction.

mainland on the other side of the water, you actually see nothing at all – but it is an extraordinarily intense nothing. There is an enormous sky with a terrifying cloud bank, very grey and aggressive, with a fierce wind which continually blows in your face and an inhospitable, angry, equally grey sea. It is actually all one colour. That's why there is so much grey in Mondrian's paintings. And that's what made this man world-famous: he did a grey painting in 1921. Right in the middle there's a sort of frayed horizon, with just one of those little towers far, far away. Someone who knows about paintings knows that late Rothko's have these frayed edges at the sides. That's what it most resembled. I said to my friend: "Now you understand better why my music is like it is," and naturally I thought I was being very profound. It had something to do with a combination of aggression and coolness, the passion of severity. You are allowed to make a comparison like that once in your lifetime. And of course, I was in love with her.

KAALSLAG

It was not until 1985 that my long-standing love for Mondrian was able to take artistic shape. In this case, the shape was, more than usual, deter-mined by practical considerations. The line-up of *De Stijl* and therefore of *De Materie* is connected to the fact that, around 1983, I was asked to compose a piece for Kaalslag [Demolition], a project involving two ensem-bles I had established: Hoketus and De Volharding. It was a weird and wonderful collection of people. At the time, the Volharding musicians were jazz musicians, all about forty, who could also read music very well and the Hoketus gang were going on thirty, but definitely pop musicians. A completely different breed. What they had in common, though, was a left-wing political orientation and an enormous devotion to all sorts of fantastic music.

The idea for Kaalslag emanated from a large demonstration against nuclear weapons in The Hague in 1983. About one hundred thousand people had assembled on the Malieveld and these two orchestras had per-formed, sometimes separately and sometimes together, with a repertoire of militant songs. They also played one of my pieces which has the politically correct title *Workers Union*. It can more or less be improvised. And wasn't there a commotion – because while it's one thing to have a high opinion of the progressive sector (which I do in any event), the piece was far too progressive. People found it too ugly and too modern. And what's more, I wasn't there.

The collaboration between the two orchestras, however, went down well and thus the idea was born of doing a big project which was to be called Kaalslag, because everything had to be different. It fitted in well with plans I already had at that time to establish the Terrifying Orchestra of the Twenty-first Century. To my delight, Ivo van Hove, the newly ap-

From left to right: Louis Andriessen, Cees van Zeeland, Cornelis de Bondt,
Willem van Manen. Photo: Josje Janse

pointed artistic co-director of the Holland Festival, came up to me a few weeks ago. An intelligent man with good plans. He asked me if I couldn't at last get moving with that Terrifying Orchestra of the Twenty-first Century. If it all works out, you can expect a large-scale premiere with the Terrifying Orchestra. I'll suggest arranging *The Rite of Spring* for this orchestra – and a piece by Frank Zappa, but he is dead now. Perhaps it's wacky enough to tempt Steve Reich. That's the direction, anyway – an orchestra that rigorously and vociferously breaks with the division between 'high' and 'low' art, to the chagrin of those of the conservative mind-set.

Kaalslag already had something do with that, because the instrumental line-up consisted of a fairly large group of winds, basses, keyboards and percussion. When they asked me to write a piece, I immediately said I'd like to do it. I had already formulated a plan to compose a piece about the twenties, about the avant-garde of that time. Mondrian was part of it, although I was thinking initially about Paul van Ostaijen's poem about the film star Asta Nielsen. Because I wanted to use texts too, I asked for four singers. They had to be jazz or cabaret singers, no Bianca Castafiore.[84] Later, this was expanded to include a female dancer / speaker; she sort of raps although the dancing and the speech are not directly connected. It certainly originates from the same source as the boogie woogie which plays an important part in this piece. Rappers have no historical consciousness but there is certainly a historical background. One of the inventors of boogie woogie, Clarence 'Pinetop' Smith, used to talk about boogie woogie as he played it – in fact, a sort of rap.

No sooner said than done. The piece emerged with ups and downs. Aside from the enormous technical problems (there was no money at all) I particularly remember Josje Janse's photos. She wanted to photograph the composers who had written for Kaalslag, along with a few other people, in a demolition-like situation. We went off to a demolition site where a few mechanical excavators were still lying around and we were photographed amongst all that junk. It was actually quite appropriate because, in order to write new music you first have to scrap the old. We thought that that sounded sufficiently polemic to let ourselves be photographed on a mechanical excavator. Cornelis de Bondt in particular managed to make himself look very serious and menacing.

In the score, you won't find a part for 'piano', but there *is* a part for Gerard Bouwhuis. When Gerard sits at the piano, you hear something completely different. That is characteristic of jazz music. In jazz, and also in Baroque music too, a performer only plays music he wrote himself. This can be his own composition, partly improvised, or can be music by some-

---

[84] Bianca Castafiore is the opera singer in the comic strip *Kuifje* [*Tintin*] by Hergé.

one else that he has made his own, so that you hear the player more than you do the piece itself. In my opinion this is essential to the production of music. The great chasm between classical music and so-called light music is to do with this. Pop music often comes over convincingly because you get the impression – mistakenly – that the performers are doing their own thing. With classical music you know that the performer hasn't thought up those things but has learnt them – like a sort of monkey who runs round with a hat. I'm the first to admit that it's much more complicated than that. There are excellent musicians who have really steeped themselves in their material. They have identified themselves with Mozart to such an extent that what you hear could well sound like Mozart's own playing. With Netherlands Baroque musicians in particular, you often hear that, in a manner of speaking, they 'become' Bach. A good example of this is Gustav Leonhardt. That's why, when Straub, the German film maker, was making a film about Bach, he got Leonhardt rather than an actor to play Bach. That was a smart move because it turned out to be a very interesting film.

Boogie woogie

Choosing Kaalslag was important in deciding that the central subject should be Mondrian and De Stijl. We know a few things about this man. We know what he had in his collection of gramophone records which is fairly unusual in the case of an artist who has been dead a long time. We know that he had musical interests, that he liked dancing and also that his last two paintings, painted in New York, have musical titles. These titles became very important for my piece. As you know, he painted *Broadway boogie woogie* in 1942/3 and he died while he was working on *Victory boogie woogie* (1944). These are paintings with lots of small squares filled in with many more colours than in the more contained paintings of the thirties.

Boogie woogie is one of the few jazz styles which I had got to grips with pretty well as a boy of about fourteen. There was a gramophone record at home – perhaps my brother had brought it back from America – by two black boogie woogie pianists who played boogie woogie on two pianos. This record, by Pete Johnson and Albert Ammons, was called *8 To The Bar*. It made a deep impression on me and a cousin of mine with whom I often played piano duets. We tried to imitate them as well as we could on one piano. It sounds a bit like Stravinsky, who wrote music in a certain genre and then put in odd, wrong notes. Johnson and Ammons were quite strict and precise and it 'swung' marvellously but now and again it went a bit wrong, especially in the middle voices.

Another inventor of the genre – you could call him the Anton Webern of boogie woogie –is Jimmy Yancey. He played around 1930 in the bars of Chicago, but the recordings only became known much later on. Yancey made approximately thirty recordings and I have them all. He was rediscovered when he was working as a ball-boy on a golf course in Chicago. The piano was an inexpensive way of having music in a cafe in the twenties and thirties. Boogie woogie was intended as entertainment, and especially as dance music, for the whites in the big cities.

In ragtime and stride the left hand went like this:

In boogie woogie, the left hand stays in one register:

There are a great many different ones.

Note that the left hand no longer jumps around, but rather travels in small intervals like a train. The sound of the train is, moreover, very important in the black music of America, certainly in the first half of the twentieth century. It's a symbol for the road to freedom. A different train symbol which you often hear in boogie woogie, and in singing too, is the whistle:

Another explanation for this change in the left hand is that, with this hefty rumble, they were reacting to the subway. These guys were playing in underground bars and would be shaking on their stools as the train passed by. Perhaps the length of the pieces can also be explained by the regularity with which this din drowned out the piano, although the influence of the dancers seems more likely to me here. At that time you could hire girls to dance with you for fifty cents or a dollar. There were deals between these girls and the pianists as to how long they would play. All these factors affect the structure and form of boogie woogie.

Boogie woogie originated from the blues, a vocal form with guitar accompaniment, with a fairly simple formal structure consisting of twelve bars of four beats each – so, 48 beats. Remember that; we'll be coming back to it. That chord sequence is constantly repeated until, for example, the dancer gives the pianist a signal to stop. The form is a-a-a-a; the best word for it is variation form. The right hand plays variations over this simple sequence, whilst the bass (the left hand), always remains the same. A form like this has existed in classical music for a long time and is called the passacaglia, a mysterious Italian word. Boogie woogie is actually a passacaglia too, although a true passacaglia really has a fixed theme. From approximately 1600 onwards, this form was widely used and there are famous examples of it, from the fiendish *La Follia* by Corelli to others in contemporary music. Bach wrote one for organ, with a theme which has become famous:

Webern wrote his Passacaglia for orchestra in 1908. Usually, the passacaglia is in triple time and at the end of it you hear all the voices at once.

MONDRIAN

When I had decided that the new piece would be about Mondrian and that it should be a passacaglia, it was as good as done. As simple as that.

And with that, Paul van Ostaijen was out of the picture. Asta Nielsen, the film star about whom he had written a poem, remained involved for a while longer. Perhaps she was the reason that there are four female voices in the piece. The decision to take Mondrian himself as the subject probably had something to do with the fact that, as a boy, I lived round the corner from the Gemeentemuseum in The Hague. There were a lot of early Mondrians there, symbolistic and expressionistic works which actually are not his most beautiful paintings. What interested me is how, in the space of about ten years, this man made the transition to purely abstract paintings such as the *Composition with red, yellow and blue* from 1927. How someone can do this – achieve this – is astonishing. For six months I read everything about Mondrian that I could find in order to discover what was going on in the head of such a man.

At the beginning I had the idea that it had been a process of rationalisation, that he had gradually wanted to divorce himself from that Blavatsky-like oddness and had, for this reason, started to work with numbers. But as I studied the sources, I found I was mistaken. It proved to be exactly the other way round. It was precisely because of his study of anthroposophy and what preceded it – the theosophy of Madame Blavatsky – that he came to abstract painting. I regard this as an absolutely remarkable development because the paintings themselves suggest that he used his intellect. And that is the case, of course, but his is a peculiar, artistic intellect which apparently does not simply work with symbolist relationships and numbers. Intuitive processes are also at work.

Recently I spoke with a student about this contradiction. Is it in deed a contradiction or are intellect and intuition somehow connected? How do you explain Rembrandt's way of working? He is busy painting a white hat and this is very painstaking work in which his technique stands him in very good stead. All of a sudden, he sees that he needs to add a touch more black in the bottom left hand corner. He dabs on a smudge of black and continues with the white hat. Whilst he is painting the white hat, rational processes are much more to the fore, but it is the stroke of genius which makes him decide to interrupt his work for that black smudge which turns the painting into a masterpiece. Those are conundrums indeed. But we have to promise one another that we will keep on working to solve these conundrums, in so far as it is possible.

PRINCIPLES OF VISUAL MATHEMATICS

In addition to the secret teachings of Madame Blavatsky, Mondrian also had in his library books by Rudolf Steiner, the founder of anthroposophy. There were quite a few obscurantist philosophers around at that time. Mondrian's bible was a book by Mathieu Schoenmaekers, *Beginselen der Beeldende Wiskunde* [*Principles of Visual Mathematics*], a masterly title. I have used it with grateful thanks. I imagine Mondrian devouring the book, underlining everything as religious fanatics and communists do. Here, he hoped to find the solutions to all the problems regarding the relationship between aesthetics and science. But alas, Schoenmaekers did not solve the problems, even though he had very passionate disciples. The only thing that was important to me was what Schoenmaekers had meant to Mondrian. The influence of this philosopher is constantly revealed, even in Mondrian's style of writing. It was very difficult for me to find a copy of *The Principles of Visual Mathematics*. I read it with some care because it is not easy, especially as far as his style is concerned. A few things strike you, for example, his excessive use of inverted commas.

Formerly, many snack bars used to make up plastic signs, dimly lit in weird, watery colours, with letters that slid into little rails, advertising everything they had on offer. I remember a sign like that, advertising: 'sandwiches', including inverted commas – so, not entirely real sandwiches even though they looked like real ones. Schoenmaekers writes like this. Practically everything is in inverted commas and he is just as lavish with italics. He seems to want to emphasise *everything* and, in so doing, has a preference for words which mean precious little, such as 'universal'.

In such situations, composers tend to make a bee-line for the octatonic scale. It has no beginning, middle or end; it goes from nothing to nothing. In the Netherlands, octatonicism was in fashion for quite a time, between 1940 and 1960 (give or take), under the inspirational leadership of Henk Badings.[85] This annoying disease went hand in hand with great pretentiousness.

Schoenmaekers hangs all sorts of philosophical theories on something resembling geometry. His theory of the perfect straight line became very important to Mondrian. Schoenmaekers first explains that a cross is unsatisfactory. One of the many illustrations in his explanation is 'the cross figure'.

First, he explains what is not the perfect line. He goes on:

> The perfect straight line is 'the' perfect line.
> Why?
> Because it alone, as a line, is perfection of the first order. Its ray, too, the perfect, never-ending ray, is perfection of the first order.

The term 'explanation' does not seem to be appropriate here by any stretch of the imagination. He goes on to discusses the cross figure as follows – this naturally has a lot to do with his religious background.

---

[85] In 1955, in a letter to his cousin Wim Witteman, Louis Andriessen wrote: "I am now going to play a three-movement piece with the titles: 'Peace–War–Peace'. That Peace is a bit of harping on with E-B flat-E flat chords and that War some nice thumping around on that Badings scale." Source: Lidy van Marissing, 'Composer Louis Andriessen: "I often talk to Bach"', *de Volkskrant*, 9 April 1969.

The figure which objectifies the concept of the pair of perfections of the first order, is the figure of the perfect right-angledness or, to put it another way, the cross-figure. This is the figure which represents ray-and-line, distilled to perfection of the first order. It characterises the relationship between the perfections of the first order as a perfect right-angled relationship, a 'cross' relationship. This figure is essentially 'open'.

I don't believe that Schoenmaekers' contribution to science was terribly important, but Mondrian's work springs, without any doubt, from this form of abstract thinking. From his own articles, Mondrian does not in fact emerge as an particularly original thinker. I was especially surprised by his articles on music which he wrote for the periodical De Stijl. He had fairly progressive views: Debussy was all right and he listened to a lot of jazz. Just like everyone else, he was shocked by the Futurists and the Bruitists who showed up with strange proto-electronic machines (which probably created a frightful racket). Mondrian kept abreast of it all.

Mondrian also knew Schoenmaekers personally. They met in Laren when they were both living there. Schoenmaekers sat there, surrounded by female admirers in long white gowns and sandals. Mondrian visited him at his house and even lived with him during the First World War. Later on, he criticised him too.

Schoenmaekers was, furthermore, a lapsed seminarian. He moved from Limburg to Amsterdam and later to Laren. He gave speeches on metaphysics to the circle of artists in Laren. I would have liked to have met this man. I reckon guys like him are still wandering round, at Oibibio[86] nowadays, with The Celestine Prophecy[87] in their rucksacks.

If you want to know more about life in Laren, the artists' village, and about all those eccentrics, you can get help from the book which Lien Heyting wrote about it. At that time, I went on a pilgrimage myself to look for Mondrian's 1915 atelier, because it appears in the second text which I use for De Stijl.

THE DANCING MADONNA

That second text consists of reminiscences of Mondrian and is spoken by a choreographer friend of mine, Beppie Blankert.

We decided to visualise Schoenmaekers' T-figure. Earlier, I had attempted to express this T in music but that was a dead end. A visual artist joined us and, after some consideration, we decided to make the T with a laser. The speaker walks backwards through the audience towards the conductor. Raising her arm, she blocks the laser beam which therefore increases in

---

[86] Oibibio was Ronald-Jan Heijn's New Age Emporium on the Prins Hendrikkade in Amsterdam. At the end of the nineties, the centre became defunct.
[87] The Celestine Prophecy by James Redfield was a best-seller in Oibibio circles.

length. When she reaches the conductor, she removes her hand and then, aided by two little mirrors, the entire T appears in a blue-white laser beam – diagonally, by the way because, as you know, diagonals were very strictly forbidden by Mondrian. This was the cause of his quarrel with Van Doesburg and the rift with De Stijl. You couldn't have green either, and this was sufficient reason for Bob Wilson, the director of *De Materie*, to project a nasty shade of green on to the backdrop during part 3.

Dancer and choreographer Beppie Blankert makes Schoenmaekers' cross figure appear by means of a laser. Photo: Tony Thijs

When the T is complete, the speaker grips the microphone and begins to relate, rhythmically and in sync with the music, reminiscences of Mondrian. As I've already said, the piece is related to rap. In any event, it has nothing at all to do with *Sprechgesang* [speech-song] that the Austrian composer Schoenberg was using around 1915. Mahler, Beethoven, Schumann – that was Schoenberg's little world, but once in a while he picked up something that was happening in real life, for example in the cabarets. He did think it was pretty interesting, those crazy girls with tent dresses and cigarette holders and thought: I'd like to do something with that. This became the song cycle *Pierrot lunaire* – it's always done by the wrong singers in the wrong way but that's another story. The piece refers to the world of cabaret in a melancholy, Romantic way. There is absolutely no further connection other than that – this is just Schoenberg's wishful thinking.

Rap is the complete opposite. Jimmy Yancey was that cabaret girl. He played something new on the piano (he probably gave it the name boogie woogie himself) and explained, in rhythm, how to dance it. "Hey, let's dance boogie woogie. Gankadankadang." You could regard this as the roots of rap. And so it is, itself, street music and not something related to street music. That is a very big difference. However, I think that any rapper would regard all this as nonsense, because rap is political and you really can't say that of Yancey.

Rhythmic speaking is an African-American tradition with its origins in the church. In black congregations in America, and I speak from personal experience, the minister just starts speaking normally but as he progresses, he becomes increasingly rhythmic. Musicians join in, they do a bit of drumming. Almost imperceptibly, it becomes music and ultimately everyone starts to dance. This tradition has influenced secular music too, just as in Europe sacred music in Bach's and Mozart's time had a considerable influence on secular music.

The text which Beppie Blankert raps was written by the widow of the composer Van Domselaer. They lived in another village with eccentric people, Bergen, but were often in Laren. Van Domselaer was also part of De Stijl. He wrote vaguely neo-Classical piano pieces which are rather nice. He died long ago but his widow once wrote down her memories of Mondrian for the literary journal *Maatstaf*. From these reminiscences it emerged that Mondrian loved dancing (which he did in Laren), preferably with young girls. Foxtrot, ragtime, Charleston – he knew them all. In photographs, you can really see that he was a stiff person, so he wasn't a great dancer. In his black suit he always looked like a minister. The artists in Laren called him the dancing madonna.

Mondrian's peculiar love for wildness coupled with his innate sobriety is reflected in my piece *De Stijl* in the boogie woogie which is a passacaglia. The boogie woogie functions as a model on various levels and you can hear boogie woogie as well. The funky bass-guitar-like bass line is not only literally, but also stylistically, completely 'eighties':

Just as in the boogie woogie and Bach's passacaglia, this theme determines the structure of the entire piece. It consists of eight bars in 3/4 time
and six bars in 4/4. In part 1 of *De Materie*, the figure 4 was central, in
Hadewijch (part 2) it was 3. In combining four and three, *De Stijl* forms a
transition to the large seven of the last part.

The division of a multiple of twelve (8 x 3 + 6 x 4) is a reference to the
left hand of the boogie woogie players or the blues musicians. This formula
continues throughout the entire piece. This gives me freedom because, in
this structure, you can conceal all sorts of things very well. It is, as it were,
a grid that you can cover up so that you can't hear it any more.

COMPOSITION WITH RED, YELLOW AND BLUE

In conclusion, I'd like to say a few things about the sound of the piece.
Mondrian's *Composition with red, yellow and blue* plays an important part
here.

A few things strike you about this painting. It is from the period in
which the black lines keep on going, right through the painting, to the
very outside. In earlier works, the black lines often stop before the painting
does.

Most striking, of course, are the five elements of colour: red, yellow,
blue, the black lines and the various shades of grey. In the piece they are
divided between five instrumental groups. Trumpets and voices are red;
saxophones yellow, blue trombones. The black lines form the bass. Grey is
the surprise element in the piece – I'll come onto that.

These relationships between colours and instrument groups should be
taken with a substantial pinch of salt because I allocated sounds to colours
quite arbitrarily. It is true to say that these five groups stay together through
the whole piece with a few hybrids (mixed colours in the instrumentation). This is to do with the division in five elements. I keep fairly strictly
to the system which came about as a result. I don't much care for direct
analogies. What concerns me is the idea of structure, time and relationships.

An essential aspect of the whole piece is that these various elements all
have their own tempo. That is because of Bach. The entire piece is actually a sort of chorale fantasy. That is an element of imitation, not of
Mondrian's christosophical side, as Schoenmaekers called his view of the
world, but of his (Mondrian's) Calvinist side. The singing is in general fairly
slow. The fastest element is the saxophones; they play quick semiquavers
for nearly the entire piece. The bass is actually a combination of different
values and has no fixed pulse. It is a sort of little Buddha. The trombones,
which you hear only at certain moments, are the slowest with those heavy
6/4 notes. The grey is, as far as tempo is concerned, comparable with the

saxophones. In essence therefore, there are three different tempi.

The percussion plays the role of a diplomat but ideologically (if you can use that word) it belongs with the bass and mostly has similar rhythms to it. But percussion has a magical quality and can adapt to anything because it has many missing parameters. The pitch is often indeterminate and consequently, the harmony too, and so it can fit in easily with all sorts of instruments.

The way in which I have used the painting is comparable with an anamorphosis. That is a painting or a drawing which you can only understand properly from a particular angle or perspective. An anamorphosis which we all know is the sign for a bicycle on the cycle path. If you stand above it (watch out you're not run over) then it looks like a weird, elongated bicycle. But if you are cycling, then in the distance you see a drawing of a proper bicycle. It is an old mannerist painting technique from the Italian Renaissance. You see a sort of little horn and, from a certain angle, it turns out to be a very beautiful madonna. They thought up the craziest things in those days.

When I resolve to talk for a short time, all sorts of peculiar twists and turns often crop up in the story. But that is good too. I imagine that amassing knowledge goes hand in hand with mysterious powers which we know too little about. I often think that I understand what someone is talking about because I understand how he uses his hands, for example. The way someone rolls a cigarette is also totally relevant. We must certainly not avoid knowledge of an intuitive and emotional type, but such knowledge is difficult to express in scientific terms. It works the other way round too: someone else finds a gesture annoying and so thinks that man's theories are no good. Explain that in philosophical terms. It's not so easy; let's just skip it.

Analogies between different artistic disciplines are also difficult to substantiate. You won't catch me saying that I was inspired by Mondrian and that's why I wrote *De Stijl*. I have a certain aversion to artists who randomly take up a project because they have been 'inspired' by something else. They are treading on very thin ice and it's then that you often see people making enormous gaffes. If you are involved with different disciplines – mathematics, for example, or visual art or architecture – it is easier to avoid analogies. It is safer to apply specific, more or less abstract, structural elements from that other discipline. Fortunately, people often say that the piece sounds nothing like Mondrian. From this we can derive a wonderful fact: evidently people have an idea how Mondrian should sound in music. All the same, I can really see that.

In *De Stijl* I have not tried to translate Mondrian's work into music. For reasons of safety (it's also a question of taking responsibility) I simply measured the perimeter of the painting and translated this into crotchets – just as idiotic, of course, but at least you can talk about it and there is no flaw in the argument. The perimeter measures 2400 mm. It must be clear from the text that I also was inspired by Mondrian.

The number of crotchets in the piece is equal to the number of millimetres round the circumference of the painting. The resulting number coincidentally matched the disco tempo which I wanted to use and also the length of time the piece was to last, twenty-five minutes. Then I 'read' the painting from top to bottom and from left to right. I converted the visual information I encountered into my own Mondrian. It looks like this:

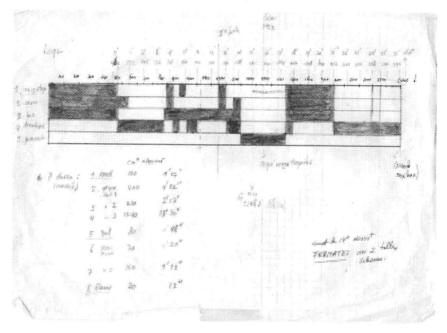

These five horizontal rows are the five colour elements and instrument groups. Where it's black, instruments are playing. Where it's white, then there is no playing. It begins with a lot of information, that's the red block; then the blue appears which comes back later as a sort of coda (like a tail). As I have already said, this is the slowest group; as far as I am concerned, these trombones represent the strict, Calvinist Mondrian. He had a great love for the straight line and valued Bach in particular as someone who tightened up rhythm. He infinitely prefers this to nineteenth-century music.

In the drawing you also see that the lowest line, the grey, only sounds in one place. That is the boogie woogie accompaniment of the rapper, on a piano that does not belong with the orchestra. In a live performance, that boogie woogie playing comes as a total surprise. The piano is behind the audience and commands attention, because it is from here that the speaker begins to move with that laser. A habit has grown up of de-tuning the piano so that it sounds more like a piano in a bar – that actually sounds pretty good. I remember that once they forgot to do it and it was really difficult to find someone who could de-tune the piano in time.

Mondrian, anti-Romantic and anti-naturalistic as he was, wanted to see the *Composition with red, yellow and blue* as a flat object. But using one's imagination, one can really see depth – see it as prison bars, or a window-frame beyond which a misty landscape lies. Even in a painting like this, there is a sense of space or, at any rate, the suggestion of space.

In music, people have attempted to suggest space by placing a group of trumpets in one corner and the strings in another. Then you had spacious music. One can't deny that it produced an effect but I suspect that music in itself is an abstract language. Music with long sustained chords or notes awakens the suggestion that it is further away than music that is played very fast and staccato. That also has to do with the acoustic space. It wasn't a coincidence that the masses written for the cathedrals in the four-teenth and fifteenth centuries have so many sustained consonances be-cause then they completely fill the entire space. You can catch very fast violin playing much better if you sit very close to it. In *De Stijl*, space is suggested by the vocal parts being much slower than the bass under them or the saxophones. I regard the saxophones as closer and the voices as further away. Even on the piano, you can suggest distance by making one voice play a slower melody than the others.

That brings me to a solemn word in conclusion. The true spirit of the piece is, of course, Bach. You often hear the B-A-C-H motif, but I regard the piece not only as a passacaglia but as a chorale fantasy as well. In Bach's organ pieces you generally have a quick section with the occasional very slow chorale melody. The quick music in the orchestra with slow vocal parts in *De Stijl* refer to Bach's chorale fantasies.

Vondervotteimittiss? [88]
I think we should go and listen to the piece.

[88] From Edgar Allan Poe, *The Devil in the Belfry*.

De Materie: part 4

Nijmegen, 1997

Lecture at the Catholic University Nijmegen, 23 April 1997.

If you want to give a good lecture, they tell you that you must first say what you are going to say, then say it, and in conclusion say what you have said. A wonderful system.

Yesterday evening I was in Paradiso[†] watching a semi-staged performance of a piece by Igor Stravinsky, a composer I admire; it was *The Soldier's Tale*. This is a theatre piece for very small forces, which he wrote with a Swiss poet, Ramuz, in 1916. He could not leave Switzerland because of the war and passed the time by writing a 'small theatre piece' with Ramuz (who, according to the annals, got drunk every day) which could be performed with a few friends. They could go on tour as a bunch of entertainers. This piece was *L'Histoire du soldat*. It was often performed at that time and, looking back, proved to be a masterpiece by a genius. Ramuz has got this piece alone to thank for the fact that he is still world famous and immortal. This is extremely embarrassing, especially when one realises that there was an extensive correspondence between the two men, and that later Ramuz wrote an open letter (in the form of a little book) complaining to Stravinsky that they never see each other any more. Ramuz may not have been such a great poet but – by letting the Swiss wine flow freely – he has, I suppose, earned his place in the annals of music theatre.

I have got on to this via how you construct a lecture – by doing the same thing three times. It links up well with what Stravinsky did, and not only in *L'Histoire*. In yesterday evening's performance the musical structure was very clear. The element of theatre was not present except in the person of one exceptionally effective actor, the seasoned performer Hans Dagelet. He looked like Stravinsky, with a beret on his head and a 1916-style moustache. The find of the evening for me was that the piece turned out not to be about the soldier but about the composer. There was a computer-animated video on a large screen with a lot of photographic material of Stravinsky. There was a princess in the story who turned out to

[†] See note on p. 97.

be Vera, his second wife and Stravinsky took the principal role in his own composition, which was very moving. Stravinsky, the émigré, can't find his way home – just like the soldier.

The reason I'm telling you this is because of the working method used by the visual artist who had made the video. He had used photos and film material of Stravinsky, conducting, walking, in all kinds of situations, and then had looped all this material. Later that evening, we were sitting around discussing the performance with a few colleagues when we were struck by the fact that the structure of the music comes to the fore so strongly. Stravinsky often uses material that you have heard already. This used to be called variable ostinato, an expression I'm not crazy about. It has also been called 'iteration'. In this respect, Stravinsky was the predecessor of repetitive music. It's a good way of dealing with material – the variations are short and remain close to the basic form. There are complex reasons for this which I can't put my finger on, but they are characteristic of the elements of music which are important to me, such as movement rather than language. Here lies one of the differences between Schoenberg and Stravinsky. I like to see the differences between these two composers as being the greatest contrast of the twentieth century, because that makes a lot of things very clear. The philosophers amongst you know that a number of fairly hefty books have been written specifically about this contrast. Poor Adorno, in particular, made things pretty difficult for himself because of the way he stuck his neck out on the subject.

Although this story may be valid in illustrating what inspires me in art and composition it is, I think, not directly applicable to the last part of *De Materie*.

CONCEPTUAL ART

Re-use of material has a long tradition in music. The oldest definition of this concept is variation. Repetition, staying close to your source, is also characteristic of pop music. All music which has an element of variation in it has its origin in dance. Now this is slowly becoming relevant to the last part of *De Materie*. The last part is (just as the other parts are) derived from a Classical form, but here (unlike the others) it is a dance form: the pavane.

The variation technique, which I have used here in the last part, has a lot to do with conceptual art. I regard the last part as the best example of a conceptual piece because, just like the first part, it is actually just one thing and that thing is connected to the director, Robert Wilson. I can tell you about this piece in two sentences. You can certainly listen to it if you want, but it is very close to the developments in visual art in the seventies. You don't need to take a close look at it – it's the concept which is important. The concept of part 4 is comparable with Ravel's *Bolero*, namely escalation. This is a concept of war; if you do someone a bad turn, he subsequently does you a bad turn, then you give him a punch and you get a punch back and in this way the situation becomes increasingly worse. We became re-acquainted with the word 'escalation' in the sixties because of the Vietnam War, which began with a small incident and ended with the *total destruction* of the Vietnamese people. In this war, the theory of escalation was vividly illustrated in practice. Ravel's *Bolero* is a historical example of escalation form, thus of conceptual art. It is not much more than a step-by-step increase. Some people draw interesting analogies with digital thinking but then you get McLuhan-like[89] nonsense. In Ravel's case, we see variation in the simplest possible form, namely a-a'-a''-a''' etc. The essence of these apostrophes is that something is always being added. You could almost take them literally. The piece gets continually louder and bigger.

In the section of the last part of *De Materie* which is directly comparable with this, the escalation does not happen in the dynamics but in the rhythm. This is different from tempo because, as you know, you can keep the same tempo and decrease the note values. The music then sounds quicker.

In the short second section of part 4, a sort of pumping movement begins – low-high-low-high – and the whole of this section is about this. You can compare it to breathing or to a pair of bellows. This movement escalates from very slow to slightly less slow. As is more often the case in *De Materie*, this movement is brought back to 3/4 at the critical moment, as the fastest tempo is reached. The tempo of the bellows is multiplied gradually to seven times the original speed. It is only a sub-section of the piece, not actually very relevant, but it is what you remember when you've listened to the piece, having simply forgotten all the literary references. Because, at the very moment that this movement, this breathing, is defined in crotchets, you hear singing for the first time and out of this, a climax develops.

'THE WONDER OF MUSIC' AND SCIENCE

For this part I have used two texts, of which the second is spoken and the first sung. The choice of Kloos and Madame Curie, the writers of the texts, is connected to the fact that I was still searching for a text when Robert Wilson got involved.

It all began with vague ideas about a piece in which musicology was central. I wanted to do something on 'the wonder of music' as it is called by second-rate writers. I looked for a text in which the miraculous and the scientific were both represented. Moreover, I had held a sort of vision of a great, late-Romantic exegesis for a long time. I decided to combine them and to concentrate on finding something from the late nineteenth century,

---

[89] In the sixties and seventies, Marshall McLuhan was very influential with his all-encompassing theories on the mass media.

(1880-90), preferably Dutch. Then I started to read, as you do when you're writing an opera or a vocal work. I remember that I had been occupied for a very long time with a Dutch composer, Alphons Diepenbrock, whom my father had admired and Mahler thought very gifted (for us, reason enough to listen to his work). I personally think he is much better than Matthijs Vermeulen, for example, but you can't pass that on, because it is not *bon ton* at all to say that.

Diepenbrock was a contemporary of Mahler and was deeply affected by late-Romanticism and by a decadent streak (which was, incidentally, much stronger in the poet Willem Kloos). I began searching Diepenbrock's works, because I had great sympathy for his music. I knew that his interests were wide-ranging – literary, too. He was a teacher of Latin and Greek in Den Bosch. He constantly referred to his music as too French for the Germans and too German for the French. At the time that would certainly have meant something but today it's more difficult to appreciate – although, to be mischievous, I assure you I can hear fairly quickly (with modern music too) if music comes from Germany, France or Italy. Diepenbrock was certainly somewhere in the middle. You could compare him with somebody like Zemlinsky, a good composer as a matter of fact (actually much better than Mahler whom I don't rate as highly).

So I had to look at Diepenbrock. Perhaps he had written a letter to that student with whom he fell in love. I knew about her from my father who knew Diepenbrock well. She was called Johanna Jongkind and when she went to study in Paris, Diepenbrock said to her – just imagine, around 1900 – "Try and hear some of the music of a young composer there who is writing brilliant, totally new music." He was talking about Debussy who, at that time, was completely unknown in the Netherlands. In short, Diepenbrock was an interesting man.

I started reading Diepenbrock's *Brieven en documenten* [*Letters and Documents*] in five volumes, but the volume describing the beginning of his relationship with Johanna Jongkind wasn't yet published. That wasn't too much of a problem because the donor of Diepenbrock's letters, although ninety, was (and is) still alive – Eduard Reeser, a brilliant man who lives in Bilthoven. I looked him up to ask him (very tactfully, of course – you have to earmark a whole day for that) if he could possibly see if he could find that letter to Johanna which contained everything about the meaning of life, beauty and death (all of which had to be included in *De Materie* too). Later on, he wrote a nice little letter saying that he hadn't been able to find what I was looking for. But of course it must have been there. However, the sixth volume is now out, so you can look it up yourselves.

Madame Curie

In the meantime, the then director of the Nederlandse Opera, Jan van

Vlijmen, had decided to produce *De Materie* and to ask Bob Wilson, the American minimalist / slow-motion-director, to direct it. That was a bit of a performance – lots of telephoning, journeys, off in a hurry to Hamburg, we'll skip over all that. At last, it came off. Wilson does occasionally do other people's works although he is first and foremost a director who does his own thing. He wanted to know how much was already finished and what he could still contribute to the work. I was able to tell him that I had finished the first three parts and that I was thinking about the last part. I told him what ideas I had, that I wanted a fusion of art and science (all rather ambitious and high-flown, but that is good, I think) and that I was looking at Diepenbrock's work. I remembered photographs of Diepenbrock with a strange hat on. I sent these to Wilson. Because he is visually oriented, you mustn't bombard him with complicated texts but rather with silly snapshots.

Wilson suggested various things, one of which was a collection of writings by Madame Curie. I read them and his idea turned out to be spot on, even though it was an exception to the rule that *De Materie* should take place within the culture of the Netherlands. Because I often actually go by rules and then make an exception to them, that in itself wasn't a problem.

In the CD version (as opposed to the performance) two somewhat longer fragments were cut because the structure of the piece did not relate to them.

The overall structure of the music in which Kloos appears is based on the sonnet – 4-4-3-3, according to the number of lines per stanza. Sonnet form was practised a lot at that time which is strange because it is a very Classical form (it fits in with the pavane and I'll come back to this later). It is only at the conclusion of this closed form, as it were *after* the music, that Madame Curie appears. It is a sort of coda, the music after the music.

She speaks texts from two different sources: fragments from her lecture to the Académie Française which are purely scientific texts, and fragments from a diary which she kept after her husband, Pierre Curie, was run over by a carriage while crossing the road in 1906 and died of his injuries. They had a very good marriage – they were crazy about each other – and moreover they were scientific colleagues. About ten years before they had, as you know, discovered radium and radioactivity, and thereby won the Nobel Prize. One of the texts relates to this. The diary is exceptionally moving as a result of its singular combination of the emotional side of the death of her husband and how the laboratory work was to proceed. You'll be able to read and hear this in the text at the end of the piece where the music is silent. On the CD, the text is spoken by an English actress. As the original text is in French (even though Sklodovska – Madame Curie – was a Polish scientist who went to study in Paris and became Pierre Curie's assistant there), to have it in Dutch would not make sense.

The text of Madame Curie's with which the piece ends is essentially unaccompanied. Those few chords which you still hear are four different phases of the 1-2-3-4 chord. It is a sort of summary of the entire *Materie*, both harmonically and melodically, because the top notes consist of B-A-C-H plus an added fifth note.

Recently, an ex-student wrote to me from America that he had been very impressed by a long, nervy, cerebral orchestral work by a German composer (a good composer in point of fact), Robert H. P. Platz. In that piece, for a large line-up with soloists and singing, there comes a moment when everything is still. Then you hear PPAAH, a very large chord, and then everything is still once more. Afterwards, they continue. That one chord was an entire orchestral piece, forming part of a cycle. In that one-second piece, all the notes that Platz uses in the entire piece sound at the same time. So that is also a kind of summary of the whole. It's a very good idea and it sounds good. Moreover, the score looks magnificent: a very big, white page with practically nothing on it.

Willem Kloos[†]

To a large extent, Curie's text at the end of the piece fulfilled the expectations I had had of Diepenbrock and a few others I had studied. Through the excellence of both Curie as a writer and the quality of the text itself, people were able to hear and see what inspired me to write the whole piece, all four parts of it. Through Kloos, something did linger on of the Netherlands late-Romanticism after all.

Scene from *De Materie* part 4, Robert Wilson, De Nederlandse Opera, 1989.
Photo: Jaap Pieper – Maria Austria Instituut

[†] Willem Kloos (1859-1938) was an Amsterdam 'poète maudit', leading figure of the Dutch literary 'Eighties Movement' which emerged in the 1880s. He worshipped Beauty in many sonnets.

I had already had the idea that a great pavane should unfold. This was something to do with my father; his *Pavane* for piano was in my mind when I decided to do something with sonnet form in this fourth part. We all know people like Dèr Mouw[†] and Kloos. Kloos had had my sympathy for years because he was always drunk and exceptionally unhappy. Moreover I think he's a very good poet. I like his extravagance. You could almost call him Wagnerian, although I think he's more like Baudelaire. He looks more like Baudelaire than Wagner, too, but he certainly knew Wagner's operas.[90]

I wanted to write a pavane with the structure of a sonnet, namely 4-4-3-3 – that is, two quatrains and two *terza rima*. Of the many sonnets that I read at that time, it was those by Dèr Mouw and Kloos which made a particular impression. In the end, I didn't take a whole sonnet, but four *terza rima* from my two favourite sonnets by Kloos.[††] The ecstatic words fit wonderfully well with Curie's writings: their theme – how love overcomes death – though very general, is no less profound for all that. This theme is perhaps at the heart of the last part. It was also a specific topic of the time in which the piece is set, as it was for the artist at the end of the nineteenth century.

The music is based on a complete sonnet; it is strictly constructed in a 4-4-3-3 relationship. Part 4 is thus itself divided into four parts.[91] In the first section, you only hear the high chords. Here a ♩ = 72. In the second section the low parts are added. The 'breathing movement' which then

---

[†] Johan Andreas Dèr Mouw (1863-1919) was a Dutch poet whose poems were published posthumously under the name of Adwaita (the Indian mystic name meaning 'twofoldness').

[90] Willem Kloos translated of *Der Ring des Nibelungen* into Dutch.

[††]
Droom-schoone dood en onsterfelijk verlangen,	*Dream of beautiful death and eternal desire,*
Pracht van te vatte' en te voele' in vaste armen, –	*Splendour of catching and feeling in steady arms, –*
Schoonheid, gedrukt aan 't luid-bewogen harte, –	*Beauty, pressed to the loudly pounding heart, –*
Pracht van elkaar al vlammende te omvangen,	*Splendour of holding each other in a fiery embrace,*
Zaligheid doende in sprakeloos erbarmen,	*Blessedness released in wordless compassion,*
Zaligheid zelve in de opvlucht aller smarte.	*Blessedness itself in the lifting of all pain.*
O, lust! Daar over mij de branding slaat,	*O, desire! the billow break over me,*
Bij 't doffe bruisen der ontroerde baren,	*By the dark spray of the thrilled waves.*
Te zien hoe 't Leven om mij heen vergaat, –	*To see how Life perishes around me, –*
Maar Liefde niet, en midden in het staren	*But not Love, and while staring*
Op 't rustig stralen van uw klaar gelaat,	*At the quiet glow of your open face*
Vereend met u, ter eeuwigheid te varen…	*United with you, journeying with you to eternity…*

(Transl. Tim Coleman)

[91] Alcedo Coenen described the four sections of part 4 in the programme as follows: (i) the first seventy bars, characterised by sustained chords; (ii) the following seventy bars, characterised by alternating instrumental chords (so-called hoquets), with a long crescendo to a climax; (iii) fifty bars, beginning with a drastic slowing of the tempo (from 72 to 54; see also the ratio 4:3; the choir sings four terza rima from sonnets by Willem Kloos); (iv) the last part, characterised by dragging chords and with a lecture by Mme. Curie about her scientific work and her deceased husband.

emerges escalates, as I said earlier, step by step up to that seven so you ultimately end up at seven crotchets – but it takes twenty minutes to get there.

The golden section plays a role throughout, including part 4 as I have established subsequently. It is magical. The golden section of the piece lies just after the second quatrain. This is not the climax but the start of the singing of Kloos' *terza rima*. At first only the men sing. At the start of the short fourth section (the last *terza rima* of the sonnet structure), the women also sing. This division has to do with the fact that in *De Stijl* only women's voices appear and is one of the many ways in which the four parts of *De Materie* are related. There are all sorts of balances between the parts before and after the interval, for example in speaking and singing, men and women.

ROBERT WILSON

I knew Robert Wilson's work sufficiently well and admired it greatly. He became famous in the Netherlands in the mid-seventies with *Deafman Glance*, a wordless theatrical performance. Later he made *Einstein on the Beach*, a seven-hour performance with music by Philip Glass. Common to both Wilson and Glass is their preference for the repetitive, for minimal art. Wilson developed slow motion theatre. This was not only to do with what was happening in visual art in America, with monochrome paintings, conceptual art, landscape and Zero. At that time, the Americans were influenced more than the Netherlanders by non-western art. One visit to the Noh theatre in Japan makes it clear how much someone like Wilson has picked up from it. In Tokyo, in 1970, I attended a Noh theatre performance and I thought it was truly fantastic. Nothing happens for a while. Someone is unhappy – and that more or less takes up the same amount of time as one act of a Wagner opera. It is nothing like Wagner because no tension is created. Then someone is walking towards you (you think) but you don't see him walking. He's just standing there, and when you pay attention to the musicians for a while, he's shifted a little. Later I realise that he's moving downstage on a sort of skate-board. This man can be the princess, for example – she can be played by a grey-haired old man in the Noh theatre. There are two or three Noh plays in which the Emperor appears and he's played by a very small child. That is the sort of theatre I like because everything is so different. It is the other side of reality. As you know, realism is as quiet as the grave, and we must keep our distance. The Noh theatre people have understood that for a thousand years or more. Since the fifteenth century nothing has changed in it and that, too, is really to be valued.

Bob Wilson makes something David Lynch-like from it.[92] It is very much

---

[92] David Lynch, film maker, known for *Blue Velvet*, *Twin Peaks* and *Lost Highway*. His films often suggest a mysterious, oppressive tension which does not need any justification in the plot.

linked to our western culture but actually very different. I knew I would give him enormous pleasure with very little. 'Less is more' became my motto.

PAVANE

Finally, I will return to the pavane, because for me it is very personal. And so we are back where we began, with the dance. As a little boy, I played a piano piece by my father, the *Pavane*. He wrote it for his eldest daughter (thus my eldest sister), so that she could choreograph it. It is a beautiful, solemn little dance and what is striking is that it is fairly chromatic and modernist, especially for my father in the thirties. This is because he was influenced by the composer Pijper at that time.

First eight bars of the Pavane by Hendrik Andriessen

A stately dance like this was at that time (and previously) in fashion in France. You probably know Ravel's *Pavane pour une infante défunte* and Fauré also wrote one for orchestra. The pavane had actually died out three hundred years earlier; it was originally a sixteenth-century dance which had been very popular in France and Spain. Luckily there is a book about dance at that time: *Orchésographie*.[93] It is the first scholarly book on dancing and appeared in France in 1589. If you are interested in the material, it is a treat to read. It is also useful for musicians because it not only includes the steps but also the notes and the melody. If you want to know more about Stravinsky's *Agon*, you must get these little books – there is another by Mersenne – because they were lying on his desk as he was composing it. And the pavane is described extensively. The pavane would usually be followed by a somewhat quicker dance in three. Of course, this combination of four and three fitted well into the overall structure of *De Materie*.

[93] Thoinot Arbeau, *Orchésographie* (Langres, 1589).

Such happy synthesis is proof for me that the piece is well constructed. Moreover, the sonnet and the pavane are at a tangent, which I find very good. Odd combinations of controllable things can come together, but if you really try to control everything, then nothing turns out right. I believe that nature is constructed in such a way that, in reality, nothing works. Why is an oak an oak and a beech a beech? There is bound to be someone who can explain it.

Later on, my father orchestrated his *Pavane*. Somehow or other, the fourth part connects with this (and the ghost of Diepenbrock is in there, shuffling around). I think that the fact that the *Pavane* resembles Pijper is also an interesting aspect. Quite why Pijper had a greater influence on my father at that time than Diepenbrock, I do not know, but perhaps there is a connection. Perhaps you could only become a good composer in the Netherlands if you first learned everything by Diepenbrock and then as much as possible by Pijper; you couldn't do any more in the time you had. Suffice it to say, it resulted in a very beautiful piano piece.

You will notice that part 4 of *De Materie* unfolds via references to the piano piece by my father.
The construction of the pavane can be compared with Wilson's way of working. The escalation grows exponentially:

Eventually it does become a pavane, but also a very large slow-breathing protozoa (earlier I used a pair of bellows as a metaphor). It is a high-low motion, and you can regard the 'high' as the breathing in. This movement is the long 7 in which the figures 3 and 4 from the first three parts come together. The strange – I could almost say the dialectical – thing about the 7/4 bar is that here it doesn't sound like a 7/4 bar.

It divides into two, you will agree. If you compose in 7/4, with the 'high' in the first bar on the first beat and the 'low' in the second bar, the whole thing swings round over seven beats and falls back again. And so a heavy-breathing monster appears and stretches itself over fourteen beats. These beats are tremendously slow; there are 54 in a minute and so each is longer than a second.

At the climax, the melody of the pavane and the B-A-C-H motif come together in one big, mechanical movement which has a very dramatic effect.

Once I set this 'breathing movement machine' in motion, an interesting technical problem arose. It has to do with voice leading. I'll look strange trying to explain this, but I'll have a go nevertheless.

If you have more than one note at the same time, all the parts can go their own way: the upper voice, the bass and the middle voice. This is called voice leading and it becomes interesting when you pass from one group of notes to the next group of notes. Many composers think that voice leading is not so important; they search for a beautiful chord and another beautiful chord and then do not worry about the relationship between the individual notes of the two chords. This is because, around 1880, Debussy hit upon the idea of repeating the same chord but a tone higher. He produced some very beautiful, new chords and got an enormous kick out of it. Here's an example:

He thought this chord would do (it was very modern at the time). With this, voice leading had actually disappeared. That chord was comparable to one note, in which the upper partials were suggested.

With the 'breathing mechanism' , however, the uppermost note of the low chord is linked to the lowest note of the high chord. Just listen:

You actually hear this:

and not the uppermost notes of the high chords. Because actually it is:

It was only when the chords were placed further apart that I noticed that the voice leading was like this and did not lie with the two uppermost notes. And so I had a double problem: I had to keep an eye on the basses and the uppermost note of the uppermost chord. It was very difficult to link everything together in a beautiful way.

When I heard the piece again recently, it struck me that the dramatic quality of the development of that very simple section lies to a large extent in the voice leading between the two chords, more so than in the intervals in the chord (an important observation before you go off and become composers yourselves).

Actually I am quoting Quincy Jones. In the eighties he was known as a producer of a fair number of top pop musicians but us older ones know him as a trumpeter and especially an arranger for all sorts of big bands in the fifties and sixties. I remember an interview with a laid-back Quincy Jones, in which he, in his marvellous bass voice, speaking of Madonna and others, said: "The real secret of music is counterpoint." But he didn't mean that. He probably meant voice leading.

Rosa, a Horse Drama

June 1998

Lecture for composition students at the Royal Conservatoire in The Hague in De IJsbreker, Amsterdam, June 1998.

PETER GREENAWAY

Rosa is the first opera I made with Peter Greenaway. After *De Materie*, De Nederlandse Opera asked if I would like to think about writing another work for the Muziektheater. At the same time, I heard that Greenaway wanted to create operas and I got a commission from British television to mark Mozart's bicentenary year; this was Annette Morreau's[†] plan. Six composers were each invited to make a video about Mozart. I said I would like to do one and that I would like Peter Greenaway to look after the pictures. And so, in 1991, our collaboration began with the film M *is for Man, Music, Mozart*.

I think that, in Greenaway's films, I recognise something of my own work, namely the combination of intellectual material and vulgar directness.

I had got to know his work during my memorable trip to London for a performance of *De Staat [The Republic]* by the London Sinfonietta in 1982. In those three days everything happened. On the first day I rang Michael Nyman, whom I had met once before. He had to go to the premiere of a film for which he had composed the music and invited me to go along. He was fairly laconic about it. It turned out to be *The Draughtsman's Contract* by Peter Greenaway who was not so well known at that time. I was completely knocked sideways by the film. On my second day in London I was present on the only occasion that orchestral works by Frank Zappa were played – by Kent Nagano and the London Symphony Orchestra. The performance of *De Staat* on the third day was certainly not the best I have heard. Orchestral musicians can sight read well but, once again, this turned out to be insufficient and, in any case, the concerts are always worse than the first time they sight read it.

[†] Annette Morreau, founder Director of the Arts Council's Contemporary Music Network, introduced Louis Andriessen to Peter Greenaway in 1989 on the occasion of her TV series 'Not Mozart' commissioned by the BBC for the Mozart bicentenary in 1991. Composers were invited to choose directors for an 'alternative homage' to Mozart: M *is for Man, Music and Mozart* was the result.

Not entirely to my surprise, Greenaway popped up in Amsterdam one month after my conversation with Annette Morreau. Over lunch we discussed the film. He explained his ideas to me. I'd already said to him that I saw the film as an exercise for an opera.

With conductor Reinbert de Leeuw and librettist / director Peter Greenaway during a rehearsal for *Rosa, a Horse Drama*. Photo: Hans van den Boogaard

Greenaway also knew of me before this meeting (around 1980 I was still playing in the group Hoketus). After my three-day trip to London in 1982, I asked Michael Nyman to write a piece for Hoketus because we were planning a tour in Great Britain. Its title was *Think slow, act fast* and I thought the piece was very good but the musicians thought it was too simple. Hoketus stemmed from, amongst other things, criticism of the slicker elements of American minimalist music. The gulf between the improvisers, the more rigid people in the group, and those oriented towards pop was noticeable at the time and eventually, it was one of the reasons the group disbanded.

The tour was fairly successful. I was still playing the piano with Hoketus at the time and Michael was at most of the concerts. It seemed that Greenaway was at the first concert in London, in the Round House, a trendy venue at the time. He was very well informed and had already made films about composers, such as John Cage and Robert Ashley. He has good ears. His choice of Michael Nyman for *The Draughtsman's Contract* was not bad at all. Nyman wrote a brilliant score, based on Purcell.

He hadn't written anything for a few years at that time, and so Greenaway rescued him as a composer.

Nyman didn't have too much experience with films. He had a problem with the fact that Greenaway did not always use all the music he had composed, but this is what happens when you write for films. You've written a wonderful symphony and then, bit by bit, it gets chucked into the waste-paper basket. I knew that Greenaway was flirting with other composers and I had also seen two films on which he had worked with other composers, for example Wim Mertens and Glenn Branca in *The Belly of an Architect*. Perhaps Greenaway saw in me his new film composer but that was not what I had in mind. I don't like music through speakers. I wanted to write operas, the good thing about operas being that the composer is more important. I didn't quite put it like that to Greenaway but he understood it very clearly. This was certainly apparent when we were working on *Rosa*; he had the greatest respect for the score.

COMPOSING FOR VOICE

In the last few years, I've noticed that I have been more interested in non-musical elements, such as images and text, than in harmony, melody, rhythm and other parameters. Doubtless there is a profound reason for this which escapes me. Since the generation of serialist composers in the late fifties, non-musical elements have been vastly under-rated. Oddly enough, the reason for this lies with this first generation – Boulez, Nono, Stockhausen – even though they engaged themselves with vocal music. It is true that they thought in a revolutionary way, but they composed in the tradition of the Second Viennese School and they were all vocal composers. These days we realise that leaps of major sevenths and minor ninths in Webern's vocal parts spring originally from the idea that these intervals are the most expressive ones. It was not until the generation of Boulez and Stockhausen that this was distilled into twelve equal intervals in the octave. By doing this, they removed the tonal tension, a very negative step, I think. Ever since (from 1959 to today) the voice has been written for in purely instrumental terms, something that I think is stupid, naïve, and very constraining in an unhelpful way.

Two weeks ago, for example, I was in Manchester at the ISCM festival. I went to a lot of concerts there, but not one note was sung. No one dares to write for voice these days. (Fortunately there are exceptions; on the day before I arrived, a great song cycle by Harrison Birtwistle was premiered which was a huge success.) Almost all the pieces at the festival were linked to narrative elements as regards mood, title and subtitle. In the main, we heard gloomy pieces in Mahlerian and Wagnerian idioms. I was very surprised that the human voice had been so neglected. I see it as a form of fear. I don't really know why, but it has something to do with the fear of letting yourself be seen. There is no art to notating a few ninths and sevenths; the result is too drab and grey for me. If there is singing, then you really have to make choices as regards certain intervals. You must dare to take risks in your musical language.

I really love music from a completely different quarter, in which the voice is also used as an instrument. Berio composes very well for voice and I have been a great lover of be-bop, jazz and the scat vocals since my early youth. Ella Fitzgerald was already singing like this in the early fifties. I have been strongly influenced by Les Double Six, who were later called The Swingle Singers, and The Four Freshman in America, who really sounded like four trombones. (Somewhat unnecessarily, they actually made a recording with four trombones).

This way of singing was a way out of the problem which twelve-note music had caused. Even today it is clear that popular music, in the use of the voice, has a head start over classically-oriented music. Singing is essential in pop music, just as are non-musical elements such as clothing, lighting and movement.

ACCESSIBILITY

All this is important because I am trying to make it clear why I write all those accessible, not to say, populist scores. Moreover, in *Rosa*, accessibility was, for me, a subject in itself.

Until I wrote *De Materie* there was a sort of split in my work. On the one side, there were the 'official' works, long pieces for large ensemble which were profound and interesting and in which I used high-tech serial techniques. Until I was forty, I wrote, in addition, 'instant' music for the theatre, film, puppet theatre and newly-established crazy theatre groups who did operas with a lot of dialogue and also a lot of singing – eight-part singing for eight amateurs, with very complicated chords. I thus took risks which serious composers were not expected to take (we're now talking about the seventies). There was an odd discrepancy: the composition of important large-scale works for the concert hall cost me about ten times as much time as the pieces for theatre groups. I took my work as a composer very seriously, but it was never intended to be difficult or burdensome.

In *De Materie*, I tried for the first time to bring these two sides together – I don't mean these types of music but my way of working. I wanted to combine the rigid formulae with an intuitive way of writing. It's a lot more complicated than that, of course, but in *De Materie*, it worked to a certain extent so, ever since, I have not worried about this discrepancy. Personally I can't really distinguish any more between whether I am dealing with 'theatre pieces' or 'concert pieces'. I do, of course, make a distinction between music which is more difficult, and that which is easier, to listen to but I'm not entirely certain if this has to do with the way you compose it.

As Stockhausen said when he was here in 1982: "Serialism is in my blood." He can write a complex serial work intuitively – it's completely improvised but it sounds, or feels, structurally very strict. (This strictness could probably be confirmed by an analysis). That is the secret of beauty: it reveals itself through laws of which we are unaware.

A CONSPIRACY AGAINST COMPOSERS

Greenaway's first suggestion for an opera later became a film. I didn't like the structure. There were too many dialogues which forced me in the direction of an old-fashioned *verismo* opera. The film, *The Baby of Mâcon*, takes place at the court of the Medicis and is very shocking. The script is not entirely impossible for an opera. I made a counter-suggestion: why not do *Mâcon* as a sort of *Matthew Passion*, as the fourteen Stations of the Cross – a very stark *tableau vivant* like frescos by Giotto. But according to Greenaway, Giotto was too Christian.

With the help of De Nederlandse Opera – or, more precisely, Pierre Audi – we finally got a result. Greenaway came up with two projects, one of which immediately spoke to me. He suggested writing twelve operas which portray a conspiracy against composers. Between Webern and John Lennon, ten composers have already been shot dead, and one of those was the film composer Juan Manuel de Rosa. You can find the other victims in the programme for *Rosa*. If we ever get round to doing the other eleven operas, I would very much like to begin with Corntopia Felixchange, the lesbian singer.

The idea of the twelve murders was so good that, for a moment, I even thought that Webern and Lennon were dreamed up. Masterly. This way of playing with history, reality and imagination is essential in twentieth-century art and is the only thing I find really interesting. When are things real, and when are they an illusion of reality? The musical ideology of *Rosa* should be summarised as a game of double meanings.

The story of *Rosa* is very simple and completely incomprehensible. That is very amusing. Don't try and grasp every sentence, because that is out of the question. There are a couple of singers who have three or more different roles and fortunately this makes the chance of identifying with any character very small.

Juan Manuel de Rosa is an avant-garde composer who, one fine day, forgets the avant-garde and becomes famous as a composer of cowboy film music. He has a twisted relationship to money. His fiancée or wife or girlfriend (it's not completely clear which) is well born. The story takes place somewhere in Latin America. Rosa lives in an empty abattoir where he composes his film music. I do not believe that Rosa was a terrific composer. At one point, he plays a little melody by Brahms with one finger on the piano. He thinks that he's playing something special but in the opera it's clear that it's not very impressive.

Rosa is a bad guy. He is completely uninteresting as a person and wholly unreliable. It becomes clear fairly quickly that he is not very nice to his girlfriend. He pays more attention to, and derives more pleasure from, his horse which he uses to give free reign to his machismo and illusions of power. You can ascribe all sorts of symbolic meanings to the horse if you want.

Esmeralda, the well-born girl, appears to love him. This part of the opera is certainly criticised, from a gender perspective, as not being very enlightened. Why does she love him? Is she really that stupid? There are always people in the hall who conclude from this that Greenaway is a woman-hater. That's going a bit far. The singer who sings the role of Esmeralda (a grotesque caricature of an affectionate girl) also plays the blonde woman at the beginning who has something to do with the murder investigation. There is constant talk of doubles, the story within a story being the simplest form of this. Everything is made complicated in a very non-psychological way which I find very good.

At a certain moment, Rosa becomes afraid he is being pursued. There are two gigolos who later turn out to be cowboys. Are they Esmeralda's brothers? Whatever the case, from the moment he's so horrible to his girl-friend, they follow him. You see this on the film screens above the stage (there are more than ten screens which are pushed up and down). In the films you see the actors and the singers who are standing on the stage. When the cowboys murder Rosa, then everything becomes really compli-cated. The girl marries the 'body', body and girl are both put on the horse and then the horse is killed. And *then* another woman appears – the detec-tive inspector who is going to investigate who murdered Rosa and why.

Rosa is murdered because it has to be clear that we are watching a cowboy film story. That is what I found most important about the whole project – it's not about Rosa, but about film, especially westerns, and about parody. This last subject is very interesting, but not really appropriate for a discussion. The slightest explanation can be deadly.

Rosa was Greenaway's debut as a theatre director. So, in a way, he con-cealed himself behind all those film screens which is very interesting. The story of *Rosa* is subordinated to the fiction which Greenaway constructed around it. His original libretto was actually about the question of why you should write an opera. It is full of excursions around the characters, the audience and the hall, by which means he totally alienates the piece from the psychological drama. He continually flirts with the culture of Ameri-can westerns and I really feel comfortable with that.

COWBOY FILMS

When I was ten we often went to see cowboy films and I got to know about heroes such as Roy Rogers and Gene Autry. I have been following the development of the western for a long time until, at a particular moment, I felt had reached a high-point in my love for American cowboy films. This high point is important for *Rosa*. One day, a leftish, intelligent, Italian director (Sergio Leone) said to his friend, the composer Morricone: "I am going to make a spoof American cowboy film. Could you write a parody of American cowboy music?" Later, Leone's films came to be known as spaghetti westerns. You must see the third film that he made, *Once upon a time in the West*, at least once in your life. This three-hour masterpiece, the definitive end to cowboy films, is interesting for composers, because music plays the principal role.

Morricone started out as an avant-garde composer. In the sixties in Rome, there were two groups in new music. 'Musica Elettronica Viva' can be compared to what later in New York was called 'downtown' and consisted chiefly of American composers living in Rome, like Frédéric Rzewski and Alvin Curran. The 'uptown' avant-garde music in Italy centred around the group 'Nuova Consonanza', led by Mario Bertoncini. One of the members of this group was Morricone, a composer and performer. He started writing the music for Leone films because Sergio Leone himself was an avant-garde playwright.

Morricone wrote the perfect parody of cowboy film music at least it was a parody to begin with, but now the poor wretch doesn't do anything else. So remember: if you start doing something ironic, just ensure that the irony is taken seriously.

I think, however, that Morricone must have known precisely what he was doing. He has written more in one year than all of us put together have written in our entire lives, and in the meantime he has become immensely rich.

These may appear to be just amusing anecdotes but funnily enough, they are now very relevant to music – because of this sort of thing, you can understand why music is like it is.

REALITY

There are many different ways in which film images can illustrate a relationship with what is 'really' happening on stage. For example, in the beginning the 'second singer' (who later becomes Esmeralda), is singing about being in an opera. One of the things you can do is let balls roll into the orchestra pit from the back wall of the stage. As she starts to sing about this, you can see it happening. Greenaway combines the real balls with a film of rolling balls which is projected onto the large front screen. During the rehearsals, the balls really ended up in the pit, but a solution to this was found.

Actually, Greenaway wanted to cast a real horse in the leading part. During the overture, this horse does appear on stage but in the rest of the performance it's replaced by an imitation horse. There are many reasons for this, of which animal rights is not even the most important. Having a horse as a diva is fairly demanding. For example, you would need to have a stable in the building, because you couldn't keep on transporting the horse. Every so-many hours the straw would have to be changed and so you would have to employ people full-time to do it. Not a problem in the Carré Circus but the Muziektheater is not equipped for it. Another concern would be that an animal could, at the most unexpected moments, react violently to everything that's happening around it. Now, you could give a horse a shot, of course, so that it's less nervous on stage – that would be OK, it often happens and it doesn't bother the horse. But the difficulty would be that a horse in that state wouldn't want to walk. For all these reasons it was decided to make a masterly, perfect model.

After the performance the office of De Nederlandse Opera had several phone calls from people who had made bets on whether the horse was real or not. The telephonist really entered into the spirit of the performance – she told callers that it was not a real horse, but an Amsterdam police horse.

I saw how they made the horse in the opera workshop. It was a real high-tech Robocop. In the flies of the theatre were four or five technicians who made the horse move – the four legs, tail and the head all moved independently of one another.

This fitted in excellently with the Tom & Jerry quality of the whole work. A discussion on the political incorrectness of Rosa and *Rosa* started. In this sort of discussion, the man and the work are lumped together for the sake of convenience. A work of art cannot be politically incorrect; at the very outside the characters can. But this discussion did indeed take place and it would be best not to dwell on it. All the misunderstandings proved, yet again, that you have to put clear quotation marks round everything you do. Evidently this is still necessary. The non-ironic use of violence or sexual violence is exclusive to the film culture. It must be very clear that *Rosa* is criticising this culture totally. The violence in *Rosa* is theatre; it has more to do with cartoons than with the world around us. I have never heard anyone complaining that Tom & Jerry are politically incorrect, but they are, constantly.

Hout [Wood]

Greenaway and I have always worked fairly independently of each other. In the script there were moderately detailed instructions as to the production. I had asked him at the outset not to write anything which needed to have a relationship between the action and the singing. Greenaway never needed to synchronise with the music like in a cartoon. But as he is very musical, the tempo of the images was often in harmony with the character of the music.

Because the text was about the making of films, I wanted to make an opera which was as long as a film: ninety minutes. The text was not initially divided into the twelve scenes of which *Rosa* now consists. I think that was my idea and I subsequently asked Greenaway to give some sort of indication of the length of each scene which I kept to, apart from a few small alterations. The overture is much longer than he had in mind, for a very simple and banal reason which is that Greenaway was pretty slow with his scripts. Because I hate rushed jobs, I started work on the overture as soon as he had given me the first text.

At the same time, André Hebbelinck, a concert organiser in Antwerp, asked me for a new piece. I said I was busy writing something that was to be the overture of a new opera; he thought it would be good to programme it. Later, André Hebbelinck became the artistic director of the Matinee op de Vrije Zaterdag in Amsterdam and, for its one thousandth matinee, in 1997, he programmed the *Trilogy of the Last Day*.

At a later date, it is difficult to reconstruct the order in which different ideas in a piece finally slot into the right place. Earlier, I had written *Hout* for Paul Koek and LOOS. The melody from *Hout* can be found in the overture *Rosa*, but in the piece for André Hebbelinck all of *Hout* was included. It is a four-part canon in unison for tenor sax, marimba, guitar and percussion. It begins with a very clear motif:

This is also the beginning of the Phrygian scale which has a long tradition of being associated with death. Oddly enough, it is only in the Christian world that the Phrygian scale begins with a minor second. The Greeks started from the top:

This is the Phrygian scale the Greeks knew. Stravinsky knew it too and in his *Cantata* he uses that part of the Phrygian scale because he'd studied his books very carefully. Or Craft had.[94] Possibly.

I rewrote the piece *Hout* for the overture of *Rosa*. The entire four-part canon from the Antwerp version returns in the overture, but in an im-

---

[94] The conductor Robert Craft was Stravinsky's assistant for years and published their conversations in many volumes.

proved form. Of the canon, I only kept the melody in the tenor sax which I arranged once again. *Hout* is only for tenor sax, whereas in *Rosa* I had four saxophones. They take over from each other and sometimes double each other so that the melody has a certain colour during the playing. There is no point in writing a tenor saxophone concerto if you have three saxophonists sitting there that you can use. The canon refers to the pursuit of Rosa by the two cowboys.

In film, the chase has a rich tradition and this is also true of film music. A few years ago, a grand master in this genre, John Williams, was guest composer at the summer course in Tanglewood where I was also lecturing. John Williams wrote the music for *E.T.* – you don't have to feel embarrassed in the world of modern music if you don't know him because he doesn't write 'our sort of music'. He felt out of place at Tanglewood. He writes tonal music and there were all these young composers, very serious-minded and academically trained. He assumed that they held him in contempt because of what he did and that they would find him totally uninteresting because of his commercial activities. This was the case, but with a few happy exceptions.

He was not completely at ease, therefore, but spoke honestly and openly about his work. He proved to be very inspirational for certain composers who had initially had contempt for him and said things that you would never hear from anyone else. I enjoyed his enthusiasm for solving funny small details, such as car chases.

Brahms

Fairly quickly there was another spirit in the opera. In the very early sketches you find:

This sounds like a children's song but it is one of the waltzes for piano duet by Brahms (opus 39, no. 2, 1865). This little melody is the leitmotiv for the whole opera. I used this piece because it refers to a childhood memory. It has a meaning for me that goes far beyond the quality of the melody. I did not choose it because I needed to have sentimental pieces in an opera, but because I knew it so well and it nestled deep in my heart. Why do you compose what you compose? From the age of ten to twelve, I shared a room with my sister Cilia who was eight years older than me. She had the habit of humming in bed, with her head buried in the pillow, before she went to sleep. I had of course been in bed for a long time before she came to bed but I heard that song I don't know how often, say three thousand times. It is a totally different song from all the other songs in my life. And at last I had the chance to get rid of it and forget it completely. That is one of the reasons why I compose: to get rid of other music.

VULGARITY

Things which seem easy are in general the most difficult. This applies to music too. You know how highly I esteem Ravel for this reason. "Yes, of course", you think as you hear his music, but we know – and this is true of Ravel and others – how difficult it is to write music and have everyone think 'Yes, of course', but which doesn't sound like Andrew Lloyd Webber. Anyone who has ears in his head knows the difference between the simplicity of Ravel and the simplicity of Andrew Lloyd Webber. Ravel, just like Stravinsky, can create something very simple in a complex way. Lloyd Webber does the opposite; his music seems to be brilliant and luxurious, but it comes about easily.

Rosa contains refinements in composition which are not obvious when you hear it for the first time. I will continue to talk about this. In addition, I shall give an example of the way in which material is transformed in *Rosa*. Compositional refinements have almost always appeared to be the exclusive right of the modernistic, complex composers. Because twenty years ago, I myself was a modernistic, complex composer, I know very well how you can organise pitch and other parameters. So even in the music of *Rosa*, which sounds vulgar and stupid – or is about vulgarity and stupidity – you find serialist techniques and other cerebral treatments of musical material.

Moreover the vulgar has a certain attraction for me. Sometimes, obligations put me in situations – surrounded by chic people – in which I have the wrong clothes, the wrong ideas and the wrong behaviour and suddenly I become intensely aware of all the things I can't do. Then I am happy that I can leave the building and write vulgar operas. I can imagine that you'd want to write in a very refined way if you come from the slums.

OVERTURE AND RAP

Music for the theatre creates some extra difficulties for the conductor. All sorts of elastic elements in the score, such as tempo and the precise length of a pause, must ultimately fit with what is happening on the stage. In the case of *Rosa*, there were, in addition, approximately fourteen film screens to take into account. There are signs in the conductor's score which relate to the films shown on the screens.

After the opera has ended, the actress and rock 'n' roll singer Phyllis Blanford raps a long, complicated alphabet, in which she narrates the story of the opera once again. She did it for the first time at the dress rehearsal. There was applause, the curtain came down, people began to talk and to get up – and then she began to rap. The situation was very embarrassing and awkward, but also very ironic. Greenaway came up, grinning, and we agreed that it was good. You can use something like that as a joke but as this rap lasts a good twenty minutes, then the fun is soon over and the embarrassment remains.

The overture of *Rosa* is not a real overture, of course, because it is not a real opera. Towards the end of it, the chorus sings a few texts which Greenaway had already sent me.

When I again began to fret about when the libretto was going to arrive, he said, as if innocently: "Oh, so you want everything in the order of the piece." "Exactly," I said.

I never did get that text. I merely got an amusing book about all the things that can happen when you are at the opera watching an opera. I more or less distilled a libretto myself from that book.

In the meantime, I only had a year to complete the rest of the opera and moreover, because the overture had ended up longer than planned, I had to steal time from other scenes. I had to make up time on all fronts and this is an interesting way of dealing with time. The pursuit, the *chase* in *Rosa* is an important subject and appears in the guise of an old musical form, the canon.

If there is some suggestion of an actual plot in *Rosa*, it doesn't really begin until scene 3 when the horse comes down. Scenes 1 and 2 merely describe bizarre things which take place on the floor of the stage, like the balls which end up in the orchestra pit. This did not discourage me from beginning, in scene 1, with the sort of music you hear when an opera is *really* beginning.

Scenes 1 and 2 have the same tempo as the overture. At the end of scene 1, I get the chorus – flying in the face of normal dramatic rules – to sing fortissimo high B flats and Cs.

COMPOSERS OF COWBOY FILM MUSIC

Scene 2 contains the first real aria. The blonde singer sings a list of data, followed by a run-down of drinks and various bodily fluids.

October 13. Blood.
October 14. Coffee and Blood.
15. Beer. Debauchery.
Saturday 16. Milk, Debauchery, Coffee, Tears.
Sunday 17. Debauchery and Debauchery.
Miss Monday

Funnily enough, I interpreted this last wrongly. I understood it in the sense of 'Miss World', but suspect that it means 'Monday is missing'. In her second song, when she is singing about Rosa and the hundreds of ways she slept with him, you hear for the first time a rhythm in the orchestra which composers of cowboy film music like to use when there are horses galloping past on the screen.

The scene ends with a sort of fanfare. These are, of course, the four notes from *Hout*, but this signal later proves to be the dénouement of the opera – the most dramatic moment in the last scene, the text being "The dead man was a composer".

In scene 3, Rosa's black mare descends from the rafters of the theatre. Greenaway asked me to write 'heavenly music' for this scene. It is a descent into hell. For the first time you hear the tuned temple blocks, the two isolated notes of which are a distant metaphor for the clatter of hooves in westerns.

SCENE 4

In *Rosa* everything begins (fairly late on in the piece) when Esmeralda, the main character, sings for the first time. She begins to complain about that guy, her fiancé Manuel de Rosa. I wanted to create an objective musical situation for this moment, by which I mean: don't simply trust your ears, or follow the musical logic of that moment but, rather, make something out of completely independent musical material.

I have simply taken a three-part harmonised melody, the sort of material associated with Esmeralda – simple diatonic – the core of which consists of four notes which we know from a lot of Stravinsky pieces.

I decided to adapt this melody, immediately after the first phrase. I'll play it very slowly:

These are very quick triplets. You hear a sort of relationship to the original chords. There are fifteen different chords which sound almost the same.

This has to do with the fact that a diatonic interval is always being com-bined with a chromatic one. Intervals of the major scale, such as a major second and a major third, are diatonic. Sevenths and ninths are more chromatic in character. This is the principle which results in this part of *Rosa* sounding as it does. There is always a ninth or a seventh (always major) combined with a fifth or a fourth. Afterwards there turned out to be some thirds in there too, which actually surprised me.

This part took me a day to write; in the opera it just lasts two seconds. You can turn out entire arias in an hour if you use what Stockhausen called 'pre-formed material' but that is something completely different from writ-ing down good chords. You want to write those as precisely as possible. Sometimes when you are writing, it helps if you think that you can use things later in a different way, but I wasn't thinking about that at that moment.

These difficult, chromatic Schoenberg harmonies are for me a sort of therapy, I would almost say; I just concentrate on one thing. For many composers that's the only thing. They sit there focused, thinking about how they can put things together and keep themselves out of the mire which surrounds them, and with which one has to deal with when one composes. The best way of working is to look for different methods which are not opposed to each other. In the end, you just have to do what comes into your head and see what happens.

I feel a strange responsibility, even for details which appear to be very unimportant. If you give a lot of attention to a particular thing, it becomes more important to you than other things. This does not always coincide with the opinion of others. There are countless examples of composers and writers who work very intensively on what they take to be their master-piece but become immortal because of some small thing which they turned out in a couple of days, and which they themselves don't regard as impor-tant – little touches of genius that reflect the quality of immortality, some-thing transcendental which goes far beyond historical meaning.

The writer I am thinking about is Eduard Douwes Dekker, a civil serv-ant who was working in Indonesia around 1850. He wrote a lot of things: political documents, literature, short stories, memories of his youth. He fiercely criticised the way in which Netherlands administrators dealt with the local Indonesian population. Within the space of three weeks he wrote a particularly strange pamphlet attacking Netherlands politics, which made him famous and immortal far beyond the borders: *Max Havelaar*. The book is *Ulysses*-like in form. The chapters differ greatly as regards their structure. All sorts of literary forms are used next to each other – poems, plays, a sermon, political speeches. This made Multatuli [as Douwes Dekker called himself] famous, but he would have preferred the government to listen to him.

Pieces on which we work the hardest are, therefore, not always our best pieces. But we have a duty to surround all our work with highly-organised material, the pillars that can support all the stuff between them. It should be possible to think of them as contrasting material.

Back to Esmeralda again. I still cannot really appreciate the quick movement of the fifteen chords. During the performance I thought when we arrived at this passage: "There we have the little Schoenberg again; let's just get onto the real melodies." Happily, the melody of this part is just as simple as the melody that Esmeralda sung before it.

And all this to make a short story long.

In *Rosa* there are a couple of cynical arias; duets sung by the two gigolos who later appear as cowboys (and then as priests who marry the body and Esmeralda, and then as detectives in the murder investigation). They always appear together and also always sing together, because they are like God who, Janus-faced, always speaks in two voices in Stravinsky.

At the end of the fourth scene there is a tutti during which a very frightening picture appears. One side of the floor moves slowly upwards and you see about twenty people lying on it, like corpses. Later in the piece, Greenaway does precisely the opposite. The floor goes up and you see the underside of the floor (very difficult to do). These technical *tours de force* are important dramatic elements; they contribute a certain character.

Rosa, scene 4: The floor tilts. Photo: Deen van Meer

SCENE 5

In the fifth scene Rosa appears for the first time. His musical entry is rather trite. The serious notes which I have just described are a good introduction to this. His song (with triplets) comes straight from the Italian jukeboxes which I heard in cafes when I was studying there at the beginning of the sixties. This, for me, is a metaphor for the erotic. Everyone must find his own metaphors, just as Stravinsky, Ravel and Nabokov cultivated theirs. The actual subject matter is less important than what you do with it and your attitude to it.

At the end of the fifth scene, the bad things which Rosa does are screamed out hard and loud, GA GA. The last chords are:

You think – that's BANG BANG, but it is also:

The D flat and the G in the bass can be exchanged because I have the brains of a jazz pianist. This diminished fifth in the bass simply means the dominant seventh chord *and* the flattened second which is the same thing in jazz. In place of G7, you can also play D flat7 as the dominant of C major. So when I was writing it, I thought: "This is actually a cadence in C major."

SCENE 6

That C major thus also appears at the beginning of scene 6:

This is undeniably C major. The left hand is doubled by tuned temple blocks. That is a metaphor for horse riding music in American westerns. Subsequently Rosa goes and plays the piano. When all is said and done, he is a composer. That becomes this Brahms waltz:

From this we can see that he is not a good composer, because as soon as he touches the piano, he plays a melody by somebody else. The notes of the polka which he then sings are the same as those in Esmeralda's lament in scene 7.

Rosa is believed to have lived in Latin America. Here, for the first time, a *latin* element is audible. In the orchestra, you hear:

A Spanish dance which closely resembles the polka was an important factor in the emigration of salon music to America in the years following 1800. The aria is a commentary on the polka because the 2/4 bar is alternated with 5/8. Each time there is a small extra beat. Rosa begins with a melody, the origin of which I have forgotten. It is a sort of Japanese mode which appeared earlier in the opera.

It is simple; everyone can write it. I still think the high E is a good choice, because it is unexpected in that context which is a sort of G minor. And for the real connoisseurs, in the guitar there is the theme from *Hout*, Rosa's most important motif.

SCENE 7

In the meantime, Esmeralda realises that Rosa is bad and not interested in her. The orchestra plays a long introduction to create the mood which I wanted for her:

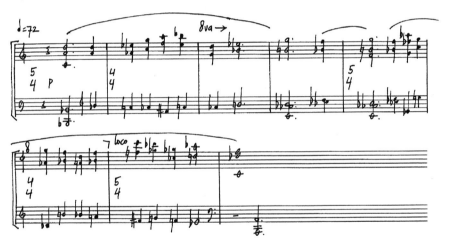

The melody is repeated later a semitone higher. This is often an effective technique but this caused me problems because I wanted to have three oboes to play this painful section. Here, they need the high a, which you can't expect of an oboe. I phoned the oboist in question and asked how this could be solved. Did I need a *musette*, a smaller French oboe? He said: "We'll see, I'll bring the *musette* to the rehearsal." And then of course it's really great when he shows us that he can play the high a impeccably. The amount of difficulty it takes to produce this note typifies the sound that I had in mind – a bit of pain.

Even if you know the work well it is difficult to hear that this melody (which is later sung by Esmeralda), is the same as the Japanese one you have just heard Rosa sing.

You can't hear this if you don't know it; you need to study the score for this. The same applies to the three-part setting of Esmeralda's song (see above).

The chords were rich enough to help me later. I didn't use them again in the piece, but the principle on which the combination of intervals is based helped me to find the thirteen chords in *Tao*, where I was a bit freer in my choice of intervals. The beginning of *Tao* was new for me, because two of the thirteen chords are simple triads: six-four chords.

In Rosa's big aria which ends the scene, he enjoys – for the first and last time in the opera – the triumph of the world-famous film composer and you hear this clearly in the music.

Esmeralda (Marie Angel) and Rosa (Lyndon Terracini) on his horse.
Photo: Deen van Meer

SCENE 8

The following scene, the eighth, is a very 'straight down the line' – I should almost say Andriessen-like – canon which is directly connected to the overture, where *Hout* already popped up. I had already used the melody of this canon in the overture because, in the libretto, a chase had been planned: the two cowboys go out on their horses to murder Rosa. (Greenaway suggested that they do that because they are Esmeralda's brothers and she had complained in letters to their mother that Rosa is such a bad guy.)

The canon in scene 8 is a part of the canon in *Hout*, now two-part with two identical line-ups: tenor sax, piano and guitar. I did more or less the same as I did in *Hout*, organising differences in the entries of the second voice. There are entries on the third, fourth, sixth and seventh semiquavers. What you *can* hear is that the entry of the second voice is lagging behind slightly, so the distance between the two voices is always different.

For the film composer, the canon – the pursuit, the 'chase' – is important. There is an older word for it – 'catch' – which I think is better, because here it is about catching Rosa. Greenaway shot the film for this in Colorado which has all the scenic clichés of the cowboy film. When the rehearsals were at an advanced stage he telephoned me to tell me that the film did not fit the canon in scene 8. He wanted me to lose a few seconds. Now, seconds are rather difficult to select when the tempo is ♩ = 100. I had done a beautiful cut when I was called again a week later. They had all the same found a solution. Cut the cuts: you can still do that too.

So, *Hout* is a large canon, in which the entry of the second voice always changes by a semiquaver. At the end the canon becomes unison. In scene 8, bass notes are added towards the end. Finally, when the three shots in the script ring out, there are three beats rest. It is clear, especially in this last detail, that *Rosa* is a greatly exaggerated Tom & Jerry score.

SCENE 9

The murder has been committed and the body has been found. Immediately – and even this sometimes happens in Tom & Jerry films – the following scene begins with a wonderful homophonic chorus. Bach is a master of this and I think that we sometimes have to show that we have learned something from this composer. The chorus begins with slow note values and the orchestra accompanies it playing material reminiscent of *Hout*.

Scene 9 is one of the longest in the opera and is one of my favourites because the daring, serious musical material and the 'vulgar' material are strongly contrasted and confronted with each other. Here, the only genuine *latin* music appears. The characteristic thing of this genre is not the harmony, nor the melody, nor the instrumentation; just as in all pop music, the percussion is the defining element. This is one of the things that I have learned from *Rosa* and it can be clearly heard in scene 9.

Somewhere between these fragments of *latin* music there is a moment when the opera begins again, fairly unexpectedly. You hear the same chord and the same melody (the first notes of *Hout*) and there are long pauses. Nothing happens. It is a sort of memory, a *déjà vu*. You are a bit stoned and you are trying very hard to concentrate. I do this in *Vermeer* too; it's theatrical. It is here to reflect a small part of Greenaway's script. The murder investigation is now in full swing, with all the appropriate organisational things. The cowboys have now become Alcan and Lully (a sort of Thompson and Thomson from Tintin) who are helping with the investigation. Suddenly they stop. They walk towards the front of the stage and look at the audience. I thought that was a very defiant image and wanted to use it. Then you have to explain to the director that the 'petrification' of the music is because of his instruction about the two cowboys coming to the front. It works very well. Subsequently everything carries on – nothing has happened.

Scene 9 also contains the wedding. A priest comes and peculiar people appear and disappear very quickly. It seems as though they are letting Esmeralda marry the corpse. Later, the horse becomes very important because, after they are married, she is stuffed into the horse and Rosa's corpse is put onto the horse. Musically, the wedding itself is very different from what you would expect in an opera. It is a toccata for orchestra with very simple semiquavers which are continually repeated. A short while later, the cowboys arrive and they bellow the three-note waltz motif through the wedding toccata. The wedding is a well organised gradual escalation of the one idea which begins and ends with two quotations from toccatas. It begins in this way:

This is Prokofiev's famous Toccata. When I was young, you couldn't go to a single piano recital without this piece being played (or Bartók's *Allegro barbaro*, which is also never played any more). So the first quotation is Prokofiev.

The closing quotation is a toccata actually entitled Sonata but known as Toccata because many notes are repeated.

It is the Sonata in D minor by Scarlatti. Just like Stravinsky, Scarlatti is one of my heroes who, when writing, always reflected a certain musical tradition or convention.

The wedding music is a good example of the combination of a fairly rigid structure and intuition. A solemn moment such as this can take shape in so many different ways in opera. It is precisely in the limited form of an orchestral passage that passion can find its expressive space. For the most part, it is not so much ironic, but maintains a certain distance between these two quotes. Actually, that has nothing to do with quoting, because the Scarlatti and the Prokofiev form an integral part of the strict, aggressive structure of the toccata. I just needed two pieces and these two happen to be part of my musical baggage. If I think about toccatas, I only know three; in addition to the two mentioned above, there is this one too:

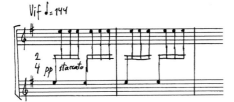

Maurice Ravel, *Tombeau de Couperin*, last movement

but I couldn't use that – it would be blasphemy.

SCENE 10

Scene 10 is a great duet between the two people, one on and one in the horse – Rosa's dead body and Esmeralda who was stuffed in the horse after she was violated by the cowboys. They sing a wonderful duet together. But – a question that Greenaway put on the agenda – how can a corpse sing? I saw two possibilities; either he sings in a crazy falsetto or he has two voices. But because I used the latter for the cowboys, I began to think about the possibilities of falsetto. So at that point, we started searching for a baritone who could sing falsetto well. We found him: Lyndon Terracini.

I won't burden you with the fact that all the motifs I use are based on the four notes from which everything stems. What I find beautiful is the moment after the duet. For the first time it is completely still. On the CD you hear something in the silence which makes you think it's going to rain; during the performance it does rain. Now I know how they make rain in a theatre.

SCENE 11

In scene 11, the penultimate scene, everything has calmed down a bit. It begins with a small aria from Rosa on the horse, interrupted by the chorus. Now he is alone. This scene begins with the Brahms melody on a mouth organ:

This is a symbol of the loneliness in cowboy films but, more important, it is a homage to Ennio Morricone. His masterpiece, *Once upon a Time in the West*, has a very dramatic dénouement (after three hours or so). In the first quarter of an hour of the film, nothing happens at all. There are scenes of a railroad station at an over-hot midday, but there is nothing to see. After a quarter of an hour, a man turns out to be sitting there with a fly on his lip.

The most important 'character' in this film is the mouth organ played by Charles Bronson, a fantastic actor. The Bronson-character is going to avenge his brother's murder and plays the mouth organ during the whole film; he is so angry that he can't speak any more. After three hours you realise why he plays the mouth organ and doesn't speak. He only plays three notes but they are precisely the three right notes. It is very difficult to write three hours of film music with three notes on the mouth organ. Just like my three notes in *Rosa*. Mine are not as good, but they do come from Brahms.

Scene 12

The important thing about the last scene is that it reverts to an important tempo: 66. This is related to earlier tempi in the first part. The entire scene is written as a funeral march, in this rhythm:

The *marche funèbre* needs its own tempo, ♩ = 66. The other tempi in *Rosa* were also chosen carefully, even though the listener won't notice. Just as Bach did in his Passions, I gave each scene in *Rosa* its own tempo before I began to write. I have also tried to use as little musical material as possible in each scene, although I haven't been entirely consistent in that.

I decided to lessen the tempo gradually after the canon, after the murder. The murder investigation is accompanied by a big ritenuto, not regular but exponential, so that ultimately we end up at the tempo of this last funeral march.

In an earlier plan of Greenaway's, Esmeralda was going to be burnt on stage. After many discussions, which I was not party to, Greenaway decided to suggest, through film images, that the cowboys, having burnt the horse, also burn Esmeralda. I will try and persuade him to do it live once. It's very complicated in terms of what you need to arrange in the way of firemen, quite apart from anything else. Not that we will burn a real actress every evening, but it still remains a problem.

I have two tempi in scene 12. The second tempo is ♩ = 100. This comes from the overture and scenes 1 and 2 and in the first instance, from *Hout*. You will hear that the bass line of the funeral march recurs in this faster tempo; then it looks like a sort of Bartók. This is a metaphor (for me) of the strange syncopated rhythm which is the actual tempo of the funeral march. In another tempo you have to write it down strangely so you can let it sound like the *bom bom bombom* of the funeral march.

Another important detail at the end of the opera is that, in determining the pitches, I took account of the limitations of the trumpets:

I thought I shouldn't make the parts too crazy, so that they don't have to go higher than E flat. These days, very good trumpeters play fortissimo up to the E flat (except if they have to play the following day) but you shouldn't really write for them higher than C sharp.

I went up to E flat which, in fact, wasn't a problem. It was quite the highest and loudest thing in the orchestra – I hadn't yet reached those pitches in the entire opera, so there were many reasons for doing it. With this in mind, I had to think hard about how I would work up to this pitch during the preceding two minutes' music. To get to B flat minor, I had to ensure that it appeared as a completely fresh and new idea in the opera. You can imagine what a problem that was: how do I get to B flat minor as surprisingly, beautifully and wonderfully as possible. For weeks before I got to that point, I avoided all B flats and Fs. These things are very important.

The music ends with a very dramatic version of the four note motif. Here I call it 'Rachmaninov'. I think that, at the last moment in the opera, you mustn't be too timid: you can finish off unashamedly.

Now you know everything.

Trilogy of the Last Day

Amsterdam, 1997 / Apeldoorn, 1999

Combination of a lecture for composition students at the Royal Conservatoire of The Hague, held in De IJsbreker in Amsterdam (September 1997), a lecture for the International Young Composers Meeting in De Gigant in Apeldoorn (February 1999) and interviews by Mirjam Zegers in 1997 and 1999.

The *Trilogy of the Last Day* is a three-part work for large ensemble which lasts for about an hour. The three parts are independent of each other and can be performed separately. But first I want to discuss two things about the trilogy in its entirety: the subject matter and the relative lengths of the three parts.

The subject matter proved to be very suitable in helping me to find sympathetic forms for the work.

'Death' as a subject sounds very pretentious, ambitious and profound and it is all of these. When you are over fifty, you begin to realise how short life is. I don't want to say that you are in a hurry; that is always bad. But life turns out to be shorter than you think. When you are twenty, you can't imagine how long ten years is. Perhaps you can if you are very wise and sad. Don't think about it too much, it isn't good for you. Just bear in mind that, when you are twenty, you don't understand these sorts of things. I certainly know it now. It is a fraction of a second – that's the problem.

In the *Trilogy*, I was not concerned with lamenting the fact that we all die; that this is very sad and that we must try and become immortal. That is more for artists who want to become famous. The sentimental side of lost love didn't concern me either, but I was interested in the way in which artists through the centuries dealt with death in their work.

LUCEBERT AND LAO TZE

The idea for this whole piece came from a poem by Lucebert[†] which I used for the first part of the *Trilogy*. Lucebert died while I was writing this first part, which is about death. He was one of the first generation post-war

---

[†] Lucebert is the pseudonym of the Dutch experimental poet and artist L. J. Swaanswijk (1924-1994), leading figure of the 'Vijftigers' (the group of experimental Dutch poets in the 1950s).

avant-garde artists, like Cage and Feldman in America. He doesn't have a great deal of affinity with these composers, but there are all sorts of links to be made between the different cultures in western countries after the war. The influence of the war was greater than we realise nowadays. Everything that happened after 1945 (in Russia, the Netherlands or America) has a direct relation to the Second World War. But that is another subject on which I shall speak some other time.

Lucebert and his friends listened to Ornette Coleman, Charlie Parker and Miles Davies (those sorts of heroes) more than they listened to Schoenberg and Webern, who at that time were not yet known in the Netherlands. That only came later, half way through the fifties, the era of late be-bop and more chromaticism in jazz. The Vijftigers also wrote a lot about jazz, especially in their poetry, and they experimented with abstract poetry. They can be loosely compared to Beckett, but Beckett was too chic for them; they were more worldly. Early Lucebert is very cryptic, later he became more accessible.

It soon became clear that I would use, in addition to Lucebert's text, other texts on death, texts written from different points of view and from different cultures. In the first part, I also use an old song from Brabant. In the second part, *Tao*, my interest in China and Japan come together. I certainly know now that these countries have about as much to do with each other as, say, Amsterdam and St. Petersburg but, for a long time, both of them were, to me, a long way away. On a visit here, the first thing that a Japanese man would recognise would be the similarities between European cultures because of the sharp contrast with his own world. In 1970, I went to a Gagaku[†] performance in Japan with Toru Takemitsu. This not only influenced this piece, but also *De Tijd* [*Time*], especially as regards the choice of instruments. In *Tao*, chapter 51 of the *Tao Te Tsjing* is sung in Chinese by a female chorus. In addition to this, we hear a Japanese poem about a man who is sitting sharpening his knife. The poem is sinister (he is not just sharpening his knife, of course) but also absurd. I believe he was sitting there sharpening it for seventy-three years.

I wrote the text for the third part myself, based on a text from the encyclopaedia, of which more later.

THE BEST COSTUME

I am not able to write larger works without knowing how long they will be. I form a picture in my mind of certain details before I put one note on paper. This can be seen in the drawings which I always do in advance. Firstly, I draw a house on paper.

The bigger proportions determine, to a large extent, the arch-like form

---

[†] Music of the Japanese court.

of the piece. I don't understand how other people just decide one day to write a long symphony and simply begin. You could say that I was a strange bureaucrat, but I am just doing what I want. If, all of a sudden, I improvise something which becomes much too long, I can decide to include it precisely like that after all. This is what makes composing interesting. Beethoven is a good example. Without thinking about an absolute duration, he puts things in a very adventurous form.

I like to limit my thinking about a piece to a certain time-frame, because I then feel much freer than I do when I am *really* free to do what I like. You can compare it to a police officer who likes wearing a uniform. Some uniforms make you smaller and more stupid; others, like those of the actor who is playing the king or the emperor, make you much bigger. The idea of wearing a costume (that is a better word) is typical of composing. You feel as if you have to behave extraordinarily, otherwise the piece can never be a good piece. We must try and find our best costume when we are composing. It can be a very crazy costume, or a worn-out old jacket; it depends on the piece you want to write.

The Latin word 'componere' also means: 'to put yourself together'. It is not only 'putting together', but 'putting yourself together' too. In Dutch this meaning is still used whenever someone is screaming the place down because something bad has happened: pull yourself together. This has to do with the uniform, the costume: be sociable, behave well.

That costume is certainly very important as far as the *Trilogy* is concerned, I think, because of the subject matter. One thing I cannot emphasise too much: I do not want to express my fear of death or anything like that. I think we all have a fear of dying, but you cannot ask music to deal with a subject such as this. I think music is too good for that. The death of a loved one is so unbearable that you can't burden music with it. I will be the first to throw a stone at the composer who writes an Anne Frank Cantata. There are things you should not do.

RELATIVE LENGTHS

There are various ways of thinking about the length of a piece. There is, of course, a difference between the *real time* length and the psychological length of a piece. I am constantly trying to find the relationship between the two, so that you can combine them. Take a small aria by Bach. As the composer knows, that sense of eternity must be achieved in three minutes,.

When I write larger pieces I decide the 'clock-time' fairly quickly – the number of minutes the piece will last. As far as an eight-minute piece is concerned, the relationship between the psychological length and actual length is not really on the agenda, but that relationship becomes problematic in the longer works.

De Materie [*Matter*] (1984-1989) is about things which you can touch. For this reason it was immediately clear to me that it had to have an even number as its magic number. The piece is in four parts, each lasting twenty-five minutes. That was the length of a side of an LP but I chose that length primarily because the number 25 lends itself well to a simple game with numbers:

$$4 \times 25 = 100$$
$$100 = 10 \times 10$$
$$10 = 1 + 2 + 3 + 4$$

This last series of numbers forms the basis of the central chord in *De Materie*, which consists of intervals of 1, 2, 3 and 4 notes.[95]

You don't only determine the *real time* length. In *The Last Day* there are some pauses. These cause a number of problems. In general, I count a fermata as double its value. A *poco ritenuto* is worse, because you can't measure it any more. *Hadewijch*, the second part of *De Materie*, lasts twenty-five minutes if you count precisely. Slow music always has the tendency to get slower. The conductor Reinbert de Leeuw, who likes the piece a lot, added many ritenutos, which means that the piece lasts longer on the CD. This does not really change one's perception of the piece; afterwards, the listener will remember the four pieces as being about the same length.

As far as I was concerned, the relative lengths between the three parts of the *Trilogy* had to be very different from those in *De Materie*. I wanted to write a non-symmetrical three-part work. In addition to relationships between the parts, I also had to deal with the length of the whole. I had something between fifty and sixty minutes in mind and wanted to have a diabolical, macabre dance at the end – and a scherzo like that can last a maximum of twelve minutes. This enabled me to establish the length of the other two parts.

The drawing (the house) soon looked rather like this:

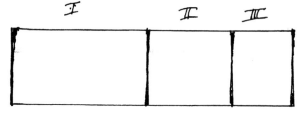

The vertical line relates to the amount of activity and the time is shown horizontally. I tried to discover the ratio between these three lengths. After

---

[95] See *De Materie*, introduction, p. 187 ff.

some calculating, it was clear to me that it was twice the ratio 3:2. Very talented mathematicians will discover that, for the whole trilogy, this ratio comes down to 9:6:4. I'll summarise it a bit because this choice can be very complex. It took me a few months with a calculator.[96]

I had an image in my mind of an accordion that had been pressed against a wall. It is not out of the question that this compression has to do with films of car safety tests in which you see cars driving at speeds of 100 km/h into a thick stone wall. The figures sitting in them look amazingly like people. Not only externally – they also have a heart and a liver to enable the examiners to collect as much data as possible. And all this so that they can get you out of a car alive. The most sensible conclusion would be that you'd never get into a car again but that does not, alas, make your life safe. Then you'd have a train accident or a roof tile would fall on your head. Pascal, the French philosopher, once said: "All the misery in the world is derived from the fact that people cannot stay at home." He's right, of course: it is best to stay at home. But if you can't, then go for a short stroll but try and get home as soon as possible.

My friend Jeroen, who had an anthroposophical upbringing, said that strict anthroposophists subscribe to the theory that anything which moves faster than 70 km/h must be resisted because it is inhuman. Bikes are fine and horse riding is acceptable too. I don't think that we will ever experience a world in which this is put into practice, but I do think that this theory contains a profound truth.

When I had worked out the outline, I was nearly done. I was satisfied with the lengths I had chosen for the three parts and I had found the subjects and the texts for the three parts fairly quickly. Sixty minutes' music for large ensemble and voice is a lot of work, but I had already had a vision for a fourth part. This was to be a sort of odyssey, about a boy who travels the world and experiences all kinds of adventures, 'De Reis van Sint-Brandaan' [St Brendan's journey]. This part should be as long as the entire trilogy. I doubt if I will ever write it, but that's irrelevant.

If I did write it, the entire trilogy would become the first part of a two-part work and that is the reason why there are different singers for the whole of the trilogy. In the first part you hear four men's voices, the second part is a small piano concerto with four women's voices and in the third part, children sing. At the end of the trilogy, the whole family is present. In the fourth part, all the voices should come together. Not until I was com-

---

[96] Or as Louis Andriessen said on another occasion: "I will not burden you with all the different ways in which I have tried to achieve a logical, but beautiful ratio. I think that it did not take me more than one or two mornings" – from which one concludes that Louis Andriessen works only one morning per month at the very most.

posing the first part did I decide that a solo child's voice should be included, and then only because I knew that a children's choir would be singing in the third part.

EIGHTEENTH-CENTURY ANARCHISM

The *Trilogy* is actually an attempt to gain access to the nineteenth century. From Stravinsky to Steve Reich, from the gamelan to Miles Davis and Stan Kenton, this is all part of my musical language. But one thing is clear; I almost completely shied away from the nineteenth century. I must admit that I thought a few bars of Tchaikovsky were nice, and certainly Rimsky-Korsakov (a sort of proto-Stravinsky). I also think Chopin and Mendelssohn are terrifically good but everything after 1900 is a closed book to me. Everyone tries to convince me that I must listen to Bruckner or Mahler but that doesn't help. I have not the slightest idea what that music is about.

Now that I've reached sixty, it is time to enter the nineteenth century. I won't succeed from this side of history, so I am trying to approach the period from the other side. I really like the old Johann Sebastian Bach, and his sons now provide me with access to the nineteenth century. One of the most important elements to emerge in their day was the development section which you encounter in the first movement of a sonata or Classical symphony. After various musical ideas – contrasting ideas as regards tempo and dynamics – have been presented in the exposition, they are developed in surprising modulations. That is particularly relevant for someone who, in the last twenty years, has occupied himself with non-developing forms and so-called minimalism. I find the Classical sonata form too rigid and completely uninteresting, especially because of that stupid recapitulation. Late Beethoven is a case apart (and I must say that I found the little diamonds by Schumann which Charles Rosen played here last week very good), but what attracted me in particular was the freedom in the early, irregular forms of Carl Philipp Emanuel Bach. This period is more anarchistic than that of the strict Classicists.

I find the development section in early Classical music very interesting. Through greater freedom in the rhythmical structure, composers at the time could combine different time values and modulations. There is more chromaticism in the development sections than the expositions. This has interested me since I wrote the string quartet, *Facing Death*, for the Kronos Quartet. It uses the same subject matter throughout. *Facing Death* is actually a development without exposition or recapitulation. Those are just superfluous conventions, just like the wigs they wore at that time. Imagine: people like Mozart always wore wigs. Like everyone did.

At the beginning, no-one knew what they were doing and we are in such a period again. We do not know what we are doing, and so we must hack a path through the jungle of musical possibilities. You must establish your own situation. Grab your machete and hack yourself a path. Don't feel as though you know what you are doing – that is totally the wrong feeling.

In concrete terms, this meant that for the trilogy I chose development form (especially for the first part, but for *Dancing on the bones* too). In so doing, all sorts of interesting pitfalls appeared in my path such as, for example, writing conventional tonal music. These days, many composers fall into this trap. In a sense, there is nothing wrong with using tonal music but you must be able to assimilate it into your own musical language. Otherwise, how far can you narrate something which hasn't yet been spoken?

I remember the premiere of a work by Penderecki in Donaueschingen. Firstly, you heard the sounds that were fashionable and hip at that time – chchchwwkihvoechchchchcgggggh – for a while and then the entire string orchestra settled into an octave D together. Everyone was shocked by the first octave to appear for ages in avant-garde music (we were living in a strange world). Previously, Penderecki had written a piece entitled *8'37''*, which was scarcely performed in Poland. He tried again with *Threnody pour les victimes de Hiroshima*.[97] This piece became world famous, even though it was the same piece. It was an important piece at that time. Music like that was certainly not being written in Poland in 1960. After that first octave, the first tonal music soon sounded again.

These days, writing triads is not problematic, but you soon run the risk of ruminating on something which others have done better. If you, as a composer, think about dramatic tension, leading notes, harmonic rhythm or other elements which are linked to development form, you can easily get too close to existing music. Ultimately, composing with tonal material turns out to be just as difficult as composing with spectra.

---

[97] Penderecki changed the title on the initiative of Roman Jasinski of Polish Radio, who took the piece to the UNESCO Rostrum of Composers in May 1961.

The Last Day

Amsterdam, 1997 / Apeldoorn, 1999

The piece must creak as if the lid of a nineteenth-century coffin were slowly opening.

Lucebert's text, 'Het laatste avondmaal' ['The Last Supper'], is an extremely dramatic, pessimistic and aggressive poem. This last supper seems to take place one evening during the Second World War, just after another mass grave has been filled. Lucebert suggests the lighting in an old painting, "lush brown twilight falls on her hair", but "closed eyes peering through the lashes at charred bread". There is talk of "the last glimpse of sunset glow", which a bit later appears to be coming from a completely different film.

> The huge grave is closed
> the last sand strewn over the sand trampled
> and meantime the last slide taken
> red slide day which coloured the last day
> so red the heavens
> seemed filled with blood filled with sweat and blood
> (translated from the Dutch by Nicoline Gatehouse)

Lucebert's text [98] explains the Expressionist approach in the music, as in the last five minutes.

There are two versions of the first part. The original version, for a group of four new music ensembles, was premiered in the Festival of Ensembles in Amsterdam in 1996. During the concert I immediately noticed that there was too much doubling, so I cleaned it up. The definitive version, first performed by the Ensemble Modern, has a thinned-out instrumentation.

Failed unison

For part 1 I also did a drawing first:

---

[98] Lucebert, *Van de roerloze woelgeest* [*Of the motionless turbulant spirit*], (Amsterdam: De Bezige Bij, 1993).

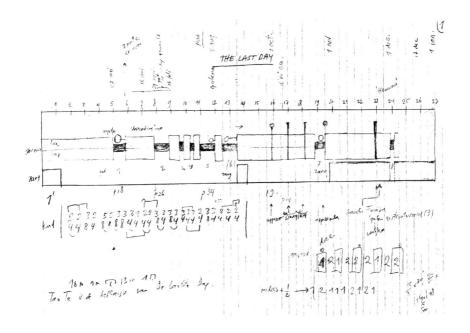

The large blocks in the middle are important in how I conceived the piece. These blocks indicate passages for the whole ensemble, emanating from the idea that there will always be two things happening. This sounds more interesting than it is because, mostly, the two things are very close together – like an a and an a': for example a melody which is generally accompanied by four-part chords, and the same melody (sometimes in octaves or transposed) with slightly different harmonies and a slightly different tempo. This means that the whole piece consists of canons at the unison.

This has to do with the large numbers of canons I have heard in my lifetime. I am not very good at counterpoint, but I like canons and imitations very much, especially at the unison. I like to regard counterpoint as failed unison.[99] I find the idea very interesting that, despite all efforts, it's not possible to bring the parts together. Bach's fugues are the magnificent result of a completely different endeavour. Moreover, this thought supports my conviction that the things that appear to be the easiest are in fact the most difficult.

If Johann Sebastian Bach had been sitting here – and this is quite possible, it would only have been a five-hour drive for him after all – he would have laughed and said: "Of course it is all about failed attempts at unison, but it is also very difficult to get them in unison."

[99] See also the chapter entitled 'The Utopian Unison' in Louis Andriessen / Elmer Schönberger, *The Apollonian Clockwork.*

This has been an important subject for me in the last ten years. In the seventies I also regarded unison as the expression of a political ideology. To an extent I still think it is, but now I see it as more philosophical. This has to do with the development of philosophical fashion. At the beginning of the eighties, someone confessed to me that he didn't know what post-modernism was. I said, I don't really know that well either, but I think that it means that Marx is out and Nietzsche is in. I still believe that that is a good description of what was going on.

Originally I saw unison as a political matter and I ascribed a Marxist interpretation to it. Now that I see failed unison more as something philosophical, I'd sooner think of Nietzsche. He often used the word 'irony' too. This seems to have something to do with the interest in dramatic irony shown by German Romantic philosophers immediately after Kant.

Dramatic irony was a term used in the time of people such as Schlegel and Fichte. The Romantic philosophers say that everything already has its antithesis in itself and there is no hope of a development which leads to a better situation. At the same time, Hegel developed his dialectic theory, which roughly says that two opposing positions – thesis and antithesis – lead to a higher unity – synthesis. Within that, I believe, lies the beginning of the discussion between the modern and post-modern ways of thinking.

BLACK HOLES

Everything has been easy up to now. You see that I have already drawn in a thick black line on the design because I had the idea (also on account of Lucebert's text), that there should be 'black holes' in the development of the canons – significant moments in the piece where it is more or less completely still. It is not totally still; real quietness is a bit nonsensical if it lasts too long, so there are small cloudlets of musical dust, small things which ensure that it is not completely motionless.

Cornelis de Bondt, a good friend and strict composer, once remarked that Stockhausen writes in a highly-organised way but always leaves some crumbs on the table. That is how I wanted to compose. I didn't actually dare to; for me, everything must always be nice and clean..

Then suddenly a boy starts singing a song. In the drawing he is represented by white circles. He only appears in the silences – but not always. The first time he shows up unexpectedly; you don't see him when you are sitting in the hall. The second time you expect him in the holes but he doesn't appear. This works very well; it is almost a theatrical element. The silences become more silent because the boy is not singing.

The texts (from an old ballad) which the boy sings were found by Francine Kersten in the P. J. Meertens Instituut which later became famous.[100] There were only two sources – a recording made in the thirties by an old woman in Brabant who certainly couldn't sing, and more or less the same text in an album of verses, written in the dialect spoken a few villages away. No one could remember the whole text. The ballad was sung in Brabant around 1880 and tells a strange story. A lady goes to the grave-yard with her maid to look for her father's skull. She wants to ask him what it is like in the hereafter. She takes the skull home with her, puts it on the table and then it begins to talk. It says: "I am not your father; I am a poor man. Please take me back to the graveyard. If you want to see your father, go into the next room; that's where he is sitting." She goes into the room and sees her father sitting, burning, in a chair with lots of flames and snakes surrounding him. A Hieronymus Bosch horror film on a Friday night. A nice little nineteenth-century folk song.

I thought the song very suitable for a little eight-year-old boy who sud-denly appears and begins to sing. The melody is my interpretation of the melody which the old woman sang. She sings it wrongly, with odd thirds, so I tried to correct it so that it would sound more like an old song.

The boy has four entries, his longest solo being in the middle of the piece; that is also the end of the text. The fourth entry, in the nineteenth minute (see drawing), is a sort of *reset*.

The composer Klas Torstensson used this word to refer to a new begin-ning in the middle of a piece. I think this is a good word for it. It makes me think of the recorder player turned conductor Frans Brueggen's sports cars. When he was still young and had wild hair, he often drove old MGs. He even had a manual for one of the oldest ones he had. No matter what the problem, the manual always started by saying "remove the unit". What-ever the trouble, first of all you had to remove the unit completely. I think those English guys in tweed jackets simply got on with it and spent their Saturdays happily tinkering. I don't believe that Frans ever got to this point.

The boy's *reset* consists of two lines from the beginning of the poem which I had not used earlier. It sounds as thought the whole story is starting again from the beginning.

One thing you should know about the thick line is that the boy's long solo, half way through the thirteenth minute, is the middle of the piece; that is the sign for the men to begin again. That is also a *reset*. The blocks underneath are the four men's voices.

SELF-TRANSPOSING CANON

The Last Day is written on an *unendliche Melodie*:

---

[100] The P. J. Meertensinstituut was immortalised by H. J. Voskuil in his cycle of novels *Het Bureau* [*The Office*].

The melody transposes itself and this makes composing very easy. You just continue. It is a reference to my beloved Johann Sebastian Bach, who also wrote a transposing canon in *Das musikalische Opfer* [*The Musical Offering*].[101] This melody shifts up a major second each time. It begins in C minor and after a few bars you are in D minor. So you get an endless canon.

The harmony is also pretty simple. If you do your best, composing is not so difficult (it should be fun, too). At the beginning, the melody is different, a descending hexachord:

This is the melody at the beginning. It is a descending hexachord which was used to write laments, requiems and *lyke wake dirges* in the Middle Ages. It is the Phrygian scale, already well-known to the Greeks who always defined scales from top to bottom and not the other way around as we do. So this scale is relevant.

At the beginning I harmonised these notes with parallel dominant seventh chords.

TWENTY-TWO CHORDS

Shortly afterwards I began to add 'wrong' notes. I generally changed the seventh. This happened throughout the opening chorus, where the men are singing:

---

[101] *Das musikalische Opfer* [*The Musical Offering*], Canones diversi super thema regium no. 5, with the motto: 'Ascendenteque Modulatione, ascendat Gloria Regis' ['May the King ascend in glory as the theme modulates and ascends'].

Then I lined up all the mistakes. To my great surprise there turned out to be as many as twenty-two different chords. I had thought there would have been about four or five. I transposed them all in such a way that the top note was C and, in so doing, they became abstract tonal material.

I found a few of them not characterful enough, number 10, for example, (you have certainly heard this chord before in musical history). Also, number 12 is not very distinct. But I do like the others.

I especially like number 4; this is my opera's, *De Materie's*, chord. There are also references to my earlier works in them which is where the OONG-KAH motif is important:

This is one of the fundamental motifs in *De Snelheid*. At Yale, they used to call me Mr Oong-Kah. But those references are actually not so important.

It was not until later that I discovered that chord 5 is about eighty years old. I listened to *The Rite of Spring*.

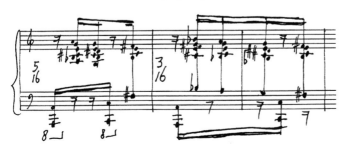

Here we see the Stravinskyan octatonic material which is in more than one chord.

I had discovered chord 6 when my brother used to play Milhaud's *La création du monde* and it ended with an added seventh:

When you are twelve, that is a very interesting, modern chord.

So all the chords have a special meaning to me. It is striking that I used chord 9 because there is an octave in it. I could use it though because, oddly enough, it is out of step in the series of chords – it sounds like a mistake. That is precisely why I chose these chords: they must sound like different personalities. In this company, chord 9 acquires some character again. Right notes sound wrong – that is to be valued. The others are fairly average. You can see that chord 7 is the inversion of chord 4. I don't actually use any inversions in the piece, but it is a good way of creating links in the material.

There are exceptions, but the system is: canons on two levels, mostly in two registers. The higher the register, the closer the chords; the lower the register, the wider they have to be.

From the twenty-two chords I made a series of the seventeen good ones and then arranged them in the way that you are familiar with from your harmony course at the Conservatoire.

It works very well; after a time you recognise a characteristic harmonic sound in the piece. Obviously I make mistakes if I choose to and I take things out so that it sounds the way I want it to.

STOLEN PROPERTY

In his metamorphoses, the graphic artist Escher did what I have done in this piece. For example, he gradually transforms birds into fishes. This sort of metamorphosis is the idea behind the continually transposing melody which forms the basis of the entire piece.

De Snelheid is also an Escher-like situation: you walk up a staircase and, from above, the staircase seems to be just as long as when you were standing below it. The tempo in the wood-blocks, with which it ends, is the opening tempo, even though it is notated in a tempo which is four times as fast. The time signature is the same, but the note values at the end are crotchets while at the beginning they are semiquavers.

The idea of canons at the unison, which I again stole from Bach, came from his choral fantasies for organ but it also refers to the choral fantasies in the Passions, in which he uses a melody in different tempi. He writes very fast music, for the orchestra for example, and now and again a very slow melody in another voice, for example a boy's chorus or in a different register on the organ .

In the *Trilogy*, you find (in addition to the canons) a lot of imitative writing, often at the unison. I write the combination of the different tempi partly by ear but, in general, I begin with numbers. Everyone should do what he wants in order to achieve the desired result. Mostly I decide to have a fast pulse, a quick semiquaver for example, and then I choose a series of numbers for the note values. The boy's song is very simple. I just use 1 and 2 (you might imagine that I would choose 5-5-5-5.) They can be regular or irregular, but a regular irregularity is also possible. The fast canon at the beginning of the piece, for example, is something like 7-8-8-7-8-8-7-8-8 as opposed to 7-7-7-7-7. It sounds fairly regular but it shifts. That is actually serial composition. In other works, I have often used a system of acceleration. Series become increasingly small, for example 8-8-7-7-6-6-5-5, but hyperbolic series are also possible, such as 8-8-8-8-8-7-7-7-7-6-6-6-5-3.

I think in steps, I could almost say digitally, not in a continuum of sound. So, when we have an accelerando or a diminuendo, I think stepwise. This has to do with an orientation towards the objective tempi of the Renaissance or Baroque, as opposed to the continuous ritardandi of the nineteenth century. If you are interested, I should tell you that the most important topic is rubato. Rubato means something totally different in ethnic music than it does to the music-theatre composer in the seventies. The literal meaning of the Italian word 'rubato' is 'stolen'. Stolen time. How did they do that stealing? In Baroque times, people did not steal real time, because in the following beat everything was back in its place. Stolen time was always given back within one beat, like Charlie Parker. A pattern of semiquavers in France in 1740:

sounds like this:

These were called 'notes inégales'. The first note in the beat is longer than the other three notes – the beat is always in time and you are free to divide the music inside the beat.

In piano playing from around 1830, real time was beginning to be stolen – this is what we now call rubato – but Chopin still played with a strict rhythm in the left hand and the melody in the right hand rubato.

A slowing of the melody in the right hand did not need to affect the rigid movement of the left hand:

Frédéric Chopin, Nocturne op. 15 no. 3

The arrows in the drawing which cut through the large block from the sixteenth minute onwards, are sort of quoted outbursts. These expressionistic tutti are references to late Romantic symphonic music. You also find a literal quotation here:

This is the opening of the last movement of Tchaikovsky's *Pathétique* Symphony. It is a sort of scream. You find this harmonic formula frequently in that period. I find it strange that no one has said to me: hey, Tchaikovsky, because it is obvious to me.

Tao

Amsterdam, 1997 / 1999

Tao begins with the fact that I got to know Jeanette[102] forty years ago. She had a copy of *Tao Te Ching* by the Chinese philosopher Lao Tzu in, with hindsight, a very good translation[103] and I stole that book from her then – 'borrowed' it and never returned it. That was not very serious, because she had the Upanishads and other magical original texts. As the Dutch say, in a peat bog you don't look at one lump of turf.

Since then, I have always loved that book. What pleases me about it is the paradox. The Tao is contemplative, and thus differs from the wisdom of Confucius which deemed it possible to change society. For me, the Tao's use of paradox is very close to the use of irony at the beginning of Romanticism. The paradoxes are often staggeringly simple in all their profundity, for example: great virtue is no virtue at all. That is why it is virtue.

Ethics and aesthetics are jumbled up. This is more or less where I stand when I am thinking about thinking and the poetry of life. For this reason I want to read Kierkegaard (he wrote a large tome on the subject).

Tao is the Way of Life, but you don't learn a lot directly from the text. Nothing is really clear. The writer starts off by saying Tao is not Tao. Moreover, it is very questionable whether this is actually the beginning, because the order is uncertain. Because of the form in which these texts are now available, the Tao does resemble a book but originally it was a collection of little planks fastened together with string. Doubtless that string did break, and it is very probable that some of the little planks were lost and that someone put them back together in a completely different order. The division into chapters was done much later. In most editions, the texts are presented in two parts, the first of which contains worldly wisdom and the second deals with the question of how to wage war, it is assumed.

Even though Lao Tzu himself has become a legend, very little is known about him. He was certainly no boring Indian guru, dispensing wisdom from a Rolls Royce.

---

[102] Jeanette Yanikian, whom he was later to marry.
[103] Lau-Tze [Lao Tzu], *Tau Teh Tsjing* [*Tao Te Ching*], introduced and translated by J. A. Blok (Deventer: Kluwer, 1956).

Tao, Tomoko Mukaiyama at the koto. Photo: Philip Mechanicus

There are a few good chapters on death and immortality and it was when I was looking at these that I suddenly saw that I could use Lao Tzu for a piece, namely as a part of the *Trilogy*.

TOMOKO MUKAIYAMA

In the meantime, I had composed a piece for Tomoko Mukaiyama, a virtuoso Japanese pianist. She plays in the way I love – distant and without the attitude "Hear how beautifully I am playing" that you encounter with many pianists. I found that she was closer to the Taoist culture than I was, even if it was only geographically. I decided to write a piece in which I would combine a text from the *Tao Te Ching* with a piano concerto for Tomoko. At that time I didn't yet know that she would sing, whisper, talk and play the koto. That only became clear at a much later stage, probably because of a piece by Martijn Padding, *Nederland Muziekland* [*Netherlands Music Land*] for soprano / actress Jannie Pranger and Tomoko, in which both women talk and scream at each other. I thought that was entirely appropriate for what I had in mind for the piece.

FUNERAL BELLS

Tao was a commission for the seventy-fifth anniversary of the festival of new music in Donaueschingen. I suspect that a certain amount of chromatic complexity in the material is connected to that fact. On the other hand, the chords are derived from the first part of the *Trilogy* and this has nothing at all to do with Donaueschingen. Although the three parts can be performed separately, I clearly see the first two parts as connected to each other.

It was clear to me, even in the early stages of planning, that Lao Tzu had very little in common with the macho strength of the first part. The spiritual, emotional level, guarantees that the two parts will be totally different. Then it is interesting, even amusing to create relationships on an abstract level between the harmony, the melody and the motifs. The *Trilogy* is very classical, if not romantic, in its *leitmotifs*. And with this you create memories of earlier moments. It is the most vulgar, but also the clearest, way of creating relationships.

There is one point in *De Materie* [*Matter*] at which I make use of a memory and I always thought that moment worked very well. For *De Materie* I wanted to write four works that were completely independent of each other; in the case of the *Trilogy*, I did think more consciously about some sense of cohesion. The point I mean is the great outburst at the end of part 3, *De Stijl* [*The Style*]. If you only know *De Stijl*, then it is an odd occurrence. But seen in the context of the entire *Materie*, it turns out to be a fairly emotional recollection of *Hadewijch*, part 2 of *De Materie*.

The rhythm does not belong in *De Stijl* either, it comes from *Hadewijch*.
The funny thing about this example is that I first composed the recollec-
tion and only then the occurrence itself, because I still had to compose
Hadewijch. But I knew at the time that I would use that rhythm in *Hadewijch*.

In the *Trilogy*, funeral bells are an important recurring motif. At the end
of *The Last Day*, the men sing:

In the two following parts, this motif is important. In this, the writing of this
Trilogy differs very little from the writing of an opera in 1880; it is one large
form. Within the larger whole there are smaller, more or less independent
forms. In earlier times, you see long works that are purely compilations of
smaller pieces, like the Passions and *The Well-Tempered Clavier*. In my cupboard, I have a book by some German professor or other (written about
1910 or so) which sets out the connections between the preludes and the
fugues in *The Well-Tempered Clavier* – an unfathomably profound work, of
which, say, ninety per cent is wishful thinking. In some sections, a connection is evident, but my view of the entire thing is diametrically opposed to
his. The dazzling singularity of this piece is that there simply are no connections and in most cases a prelude is completely independent of its fugue.
There are a few exceptions. I believe that Bach's aim was to write the most
kaleidoscopic book possible, a demonstration of genres and of everything
he could do. The peculiar need for a German Romantic to make connections like this is typically nineteenth-century, I believe, and completely
wrong.
    I find the ideas on form of the early avant-gardists much more interest-
ing. They talked about music which, ideologically and philosophically, is a
fragment of a larger whole which doesn't exist. When the piece begins, it
sounds as if it has been going for a while. This 'moment form', the open or
endless form, was very important in the sixties. This idea became so widespread that *every* piece you finished was an *Ausschnitt* [excerpt], part of a
larger whole.
    Unity remains a complicated topic. In the nineteenth century, it was
very characteristic to interpret a symphony as a whole. That was fairly new

at the time. Mozart and his contemporaries did not think at all about achieving unity, except in the key. All the minuets are interchangeable, just like the finales. So you could use the finale of the Jupiter symphony in C major as the finale of the G minor symphony. The only reason Mozart would complain about this would be because of the key, which was very important to him. The strings sound very different in G minor, and that is a good reason never to accept this.

CANONS AND HOQUETS

In *Tao*, just as in *The Last Day*, I use hoquet techniques. *Tao* begins with canons in the strings with each musician playing a note in turn. These complementary melodies have to sound other-worldly; I wanted to make the sound slightly silvery and sandy through the use of background noises. I thought a lot about it, but could not come up with an elegant solution. I still have the kazoos (used a lot in country and western music) which I bought in a little shop in Princeton where I was living at the time. I also had a telephone conversation with the flautist Eleonore Pameijer about putting cigarette paper between the keys of the flutes. Suddenly, I abandoned it all as being rather childish.

A remnant of that idea lies in the fact that each note in the strings is accentuated by other instruments – not only normal instruments such as the piano but also by a bowed cowbell. I first experimented with cowbells with Peppie Wiersma, a percussionist in Amsterdam. What luck – she turned out to be a virtuoso in this technique because, wherever the piece is played, most people get absolutely no sound out of the cowbell. When they realise how difficult it is, then they go home to practise or try another cowbell, so it all comes out all right.

With Tomoko, too, I tried out various techniques on the koto. Initially, I thought that she would have to play with little sticks on the strings but nothing came of it. You can follow all this in the film which Frank Scheffer made about the genesis of *Tao*.[104] In it, you also see Tamoko's journey to Japan, where an aunt gives her the koto and explains how you play it.

A STRANGE, OLD, EXOTIC INSTRUMENT

The opening of the piece, a slow passage in the strings, can be compared to musical or emotional stillness. Then, at a given moment (just a bit too late, you think: now I know) something totally new begins in the oboes. The sound created sounds rather like an exotic instrument. I'm not saying that I am trying to express the Chinese spirit, but it does have

---

[104] Frank Scheffer, *Tao – The Road*, 1997, Allegri Film Amsterdam.

something non-European about it. This happens not only through the notes the oboes play but chiefly because the melody is doubled – rhythmically – with totally different, very high, notes on two piccolos, flute and solo violin. This is a fairly direct reference to the works of Claude Vivier,[†] who does a similar thing in *Bouchara* and *Zipangu*. He adds a second, bass-like, note to a simple melody. It is a sort of drone – like the sustained note which you hear on the bagpipes. It is nearly always a sort of tonic but you frequently hear a fifth too. Anyway, you can mess around with it. Vivier uses very high chords, according to a system of counted overtones which depends on the interval which appears between the note in the melody and the sustained note. They are very complex harmonies, sometimes in parallel chords, sometimes a different chord per note. And this produces a very idiosyncratic sound – Messiaen-like but also very simple, as if played by some very strange, old instrument. Because all the instruments are playing the same rhythm, you think the sound is coming out of one instrument. It can also be a sort of colouring of the singing voice. I thought it sounded so novel that I put it into *Tao* as a sort of second motif in addition to the small hoquets in the strings. In the four-part chords I have used tonal harmonies based on thirds. One of the chords, for example, was not much more than a dominant seventh chord.

In the last part, that Vivier-sound recurs. There are a few sections which refer to children's songs, and where you hear strange, high chords. I do that in *Vermeer*, too, using melodies on which Sweelinck wrote variations.

COMPANIONS OF LIFE AND DEATH

After the oboes, four female voices sing the Lao Tzu text. The texts tells of thirteen companions in life and thirteen companions in death and recounts what you must do in order to remain invulnerable to death. There is talk of someone on whom death has no grip and who can resist all dangerous things – the rhinoceros, the tiger, the sword and also temptation. It is a very relevant, but totally unfathomable, text.

The sinologist, Burchard Mansvelt Beck,[††] made lists for me of all the Chinese characters of which the text consists, then the meaning of those characters, and then the transcription of the Chinese in the western alphabet. This 'pinyin' script is used these days in newspapers too. In place of Tse Tung, they write Ze Dong. The system is a bit strange, but very logical. In my list, there was also a rendition of each character as a Dutchman would pronounce it and the meaning of the word. Of course, I have referred to other translations. Not that all that helped, but I like knowing what I am doing.

[†] Claude Vivier (1948-1983) was a Canadian composer.
[††] Burchard Mansvelt Beck is Professor of Chinese Languages and Cultures at Leiden University.

The funny thing about Chinese is that the meaning of a word is dependent on its emphasis. Differences in emphasis are not only possible as regards dynamic, as we know it, but also in pitch. Little glissandi upwards and downwards cause differences in meaning – which is irritating if you want to set the text to music. Happily, Mansvelt Beck was able to tell me that, in Chinese opera, they don't take any notice of this. You can do what you like as regards melody, and the meaning is divined from the context.

A SPIDER FROM HEAVEN

Suddenly Tomoko begins to play the piano (GANG GANG). Her solo, with those ruthless fingers on the piano, I have always associated with a magical animal which lowers itself from above, conjured up by the music. The piece is performed 'horizontally'; suddenly a spider appears from the sky and lets itself drop on its own silken thread.

This entrance is very important and has therefore been placed at the reversed golden section. The music consists of contrasted material, music which is related to, or is in dialogue with, what is already happening at that time. We already know the chords from the beginning; they are displayed in the harp, the cellos and the double basses, but here they sound so totally different that you don't actually hear the similarity. From the series of twenty-two chords from part 1, I chose thirteen chords because of the two times thirteen companions in the text and, moreover, at that time I had not yet heard part 1. I reduced the four-part chords to two part chords. In the piano part, they develop almost exactly according to a serial pattern.

When the piano has descended so far that she has reached the orchestra, there is a climax. The musical meeting evidently has an enormous influence on both parties. At this point, the tubular bells sound the two-note, later three-note motif which, to an extent, carries on the death motif. For the premiere in the Netherlands, René Jonker arrived with two real church bells. That sounded tremendous.

You can compare it to the death motif in *Carmen*:

After this climax, the orchestra takes over the piano's material. The pianist leaves the piano and moves slowly towards a koto on the floor. You still hear a piano, but it is in the orchestra. During the tolling of the bells, Tomoko drops down further; she arrives at ground level and goes to sit behind the koto. When the orchestra has stopped, she begins to play, during which she recites a short Japanese poem and later sings, about the man who is sharpening his knife. His clothes are falling apart, his hair becomes grey and he still sharpens his knife. It is a mysterious, very strong poem, with a combination of mortality and immortality comparable with that in Lao Tzu's texts.

A certain menace emanates from the words but the music does not react to it. The orchestra has already withdrawn and all attention is directed towards the koto and Tomoko. It struck various people that, in the entirety of the *Trilogy*, this was a sublime moment whether you understand Japanese or not. Perhaps it does indeed express what the piece is about, but don't ask me what it is.

GRID STRUCTURE

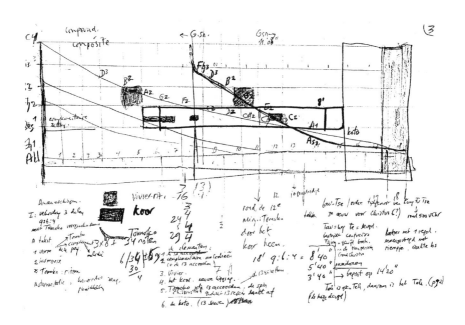

For *Tao* I also did a drawing first, but in the end the sound of the result deviated greatly from the drawing. The strings and the solo piano are, for example, silent much earlier than the drawing implies. Here, the supporting structures can be hidden; you don't compose them but they are there.

I call that a grid and it is related to montage; both are about discontinuity, but montage is shock-like and in a grid you let holes appear in a continuous movement. By leaving something out, there is room to bring something else to the fore.

When the pianist is silent, chorus and orchestra take over her task. An apotheotic entry follows in the chorus, very different from the first entries. The orchestra imitates the piano part in a sort of grin which is, at the same time, a cry for help. The bells operate as a sort of climax, but you have heard them shortly before in the chorus, which works well. You can argue about precisely where the climax is.

The downward line in the drawing is not actually for the piano but for the pianist – then the drawing is correct. Her part is a continuous whole, a piano part which develops into a koto part. First, with her hands, she plays descending lines on the piano, always small intervals. Everything is close together, at the very most half a metre, but the difference between the highest and lowest note sounds, I would say, much greater. After she has 'crossed' the orchestra, she descends further towards the koto. I did not compose the last minute of the drawing. It was already finished.

The last note of *Tao* is an F. At first, it hadn't struck me at all that *The Last Day* ends on an F as well. The preceding sounds are also so different that it doesn't register. Once I had established that similarity, I decided to let part 3 end on an F. And with that, one of the difficulties of musicology becomes clear, that is that a similarity which can be positively established by a good detective turns out to be based on coincidence.

Dramatic Music

Tao does not have the character of a development, like *The Last Day*. For one thing, there is no treatment of motifs, although there is talk of a dramatic development. This is caused by the contrast between the very independent solo part on the one hand and the chorus and orchestra on the other. Round about the golden section point, the drama comes to a climax albeit in the low register. In this respect, *Tao* strongly has the character of a development section although it doesn't sound anything like one.

Richard Strauss differentiated between dramatic music and symphonic music in his long introduction to the edition of Berlioz' *Treatise on Instrumentation* which he annotated. Evidently, at the end of the nineteenth century dramatic and symphonic music were also regarded in that way – as two sorts of music. It is an amusing contrast. Perhaps we are skating on thin ice, but I do believe that good theatre music has different laws from good symphonic music. In general, symphonic music is more contrapuntal than theatre music. It struck me that there is no counterpoint in film music, even though the first generation of film composers consisted of composers who had migrated from Eastern Europe and who were strongly orientated towards Bruckner and Mahler. They did have a thorough understanding of counterpoint but this appeared not to work for film. However, that would be a bit too much – film and music form their own counterpoint.

You could say that part 1 of the *Trilogy* is symphonic and part 2 dramatic.

As a theatrical presence, Tomoko had great influence on the nature of the piece. For example, it was clear to me that, as a koto-player, she had to sit on the ground, just as in Japan. That I stick to this is my own personal preference as the composer. If you want, you can take that into account, but I don't think it is necessary. After my death, it won't make any difference.

Odd situations occur when Tomoko is not available as the soloist. Her part includes a Japanese text, so I think it's a nice idea that the soloist has some affinity with that language. But the four singers sing in Chinese, and that is not much easier. Of course, they seldom sing in their mother tongue.

It is fairly unusual to indicate in the score ethnic characteristics of any of the musicians. I haven't done that in this case and therefore wrong solutions have been suggested. It is strictly forbidden to split Tomoko's part. If you do, you simply don't understand the piece. But whether it can be played by a Norwegian man, I am afraid the answer is yes.

Dancing on the bones

Amsterdam, 1997 / 1999

The third part of the *Trilogy* is a diabolical scherzo, based on Camille Saint-Saëns' 1874 *Danse macabre*. The title does make reference to this but it comes originally from a completely different quarter. When I wrote this piece, it still had the very hip title – *Brain Voltage*. *Dancing on the bones* is the title of a chapter in a book by a Canadian writer, Margaret Sweatman, whom I once met in Winnipeg. She gave me the book. It describes a marriage which , from the woman's point of view, is kaput . She is a lawyer and is increasingly doing her own thing. The very short chapter 'Dancing on the bones' is strong. It describes how, in the middle of the night, when her husband makes love to her, she suddenly feels her skeleton sitting there. She feels her bones dancing. I thought it was an impressive image and I asked her permission to use the title.

SCHERZO

Between 1890 and 1910 the fantastic scherzo for symphony orchestra was very fashionable. Most of these scherzos are now forgotten. I have always had great sympathy for them – they were all about writing a piece that went as fast as possible. Dukas' *Sorcerer's Apprentice* is, I think, the fastest; it is moreover notated three times as fast as it sounds.[105] Saint-Saëns' *Danse macabre* is never played any more, but it has an important meaning for me. If you have heard a piece like this continually from when you were six to when you were sixteen, you can't make an objective judgement at all. Everything you experience as a child has a meaning which cannot be compared with what you experience after you are twenty-one. Writers have known this for a long time. In art, such childhood reminiscences are relevant, assuming that you are trying to entertain your audience.

So I have always had a great love for this genre. The best thing an artist who greatly admires Cézanne can do is to try and paint in his style so that he can discover how Cézanne did it. This is, of course, only interesting if it is difficult at the same time, and writing a scherzo is certainly that. Hardly

---

[105] See the chapter on *De Snelheid* [*Velocity*] on p.175 ff.

anyone can do it any more. Robert Heppener[†] can, Tristan Keuris[††] could do everything and my brother Jurriaan could write them too.

You used to learn how to write scherzos at school; now, most people don't know the rules any more. Which rules do you have to comply with? No idea. A lot of knowledge has been lost – you notice this when you become older. Of course, there are ideological reasons as well why composers today would never want to write a piece like that.

De Snelheid was also to be a 'sparkling scherzo', but I think that the idea of writing a piece like that is even older. In the sixties, when I applied for a commission to write a short orchestral piece (which became *Anachronie I*), I added: "A short orchestral piece in the style of my father's Ricercare." That short, beautiful, sonata form-like orchestral piece was played quite frequently at that time. It's not a scherzo, but I imagine that I was already thinking about *The Sorcerer's Apprentice* at the time. I actually chose *Danse macabre* as my model, but as regards form they are much of a muchness. I could equally well have chosen Rimsky-Korsakov's *Capriccio espagnol* or *Scherzo fantastique* by Stravinsky, although the weakness of the Stravinsky piece lies in its slow trio. That is lazy. He was young, twenty-five, and evidently he was not up to letting this quick movement just continue. Dukas does, however; *The Sorcerer's Apprentice* is a one-part scherzo, except with a slow introduction and references to it at the end.

Encyclopaedic death

The text for the third part of *Trilogy* had to be precise, medical and clear, without the pretensions of an artist who is writing about death. After a few conversations with a doctor friend of mine, I decided to let the children explain what happens to the body when we die. I took hold of the encyclopaedia, looked up the word 'death' and translated the text into what an eight-year-old would say if he was explaining it to his seven-year-old sister. This is where the sentence "You don't shit and you don't piss any more" originated.

The children have to speak in their mother tongue, otherwise further alienation occurs, which is not important.

Danse macabre

Saint-Saëns called *Danse macabre* a 'poème symphonique' and gives as a tempo indication 'Mouvement modéré de Valse', a quick waltz in one, approximately $\downarrow$ = 69 i.e. the whole bar. The piece is light, French, parodic

---

[†] Robert Heppener (b. 1925) is a Dutch composer.
[††] Tristan Keuris (1946-1996) is a Dutch composer.

and ironic.

The first subject is fast:

This immediately brings me to the most important aspect of the piece, namely that the whole piece is written in quasi-sonata form. What I like about it is that the two subjects appear directly next to one another. There are no transitions and no modulations. The second subject, also in G minor, follows hard on the heels of the first and has a different rhythm:

There are two things about the first subject which are very sophisticated. If you really pay attention you will hear that every first beat is a different note. Moreover, that funny F minor, in G minor, is very strange as a second chord in a scherzo. This becomes important in the development of the chromaticism in the piece. It is a substitute for something which is a subdominant. We can discuss its true function. The A flat is certainly a reference to the Phrygian scale which has been linked with death for centuries.

Transitions are a very important topic. In *Danse macabre* they form a strong part of its structure. The reasons why I don't find some composers very good is that their transitions have pretensions to be a development in the structure of a piece. On the whole it doesn't work like that. The pedal point, for example, is often misused in transitions; as a movement from one point to another it is seldom functional in a development. I very much like the pedal point at the end of Saint-Saëns' development and how he combines the rhythms of the two themes, and shortly afterwards, in the main key, both melodies. The transition, with its long sustained D, chromaticism and stretti, has a double function – as a structural element and also as the introduction of the climax of the piece. Very good. A sort of dénouement. Then you hear what the whole piece is about.

The solo instrument in *Danse macabre*, the violin, is a response to the poem on which the whole piece is based. In it, the devil dances in the graveyard. He plays a violin with a scordatura [106] – the E string is re-tuned

---

[106] Scordatura: different tuning, where a string is tuned as an unusual note (in this case the notes G-D-A-E flat instead of G-D-A-E. This interval A-E flat was know for centuries as 'il diavolo in musica', the devil in music).

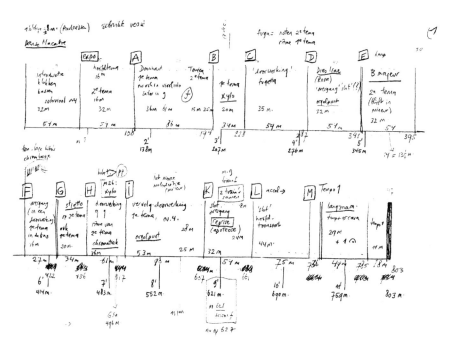

to E flat. Saint-Saëns almost continually uses open strings. All the skeletons rise from their graves and do a little dance. It starts, of course, in the middle of the night (you know that because of the twelve strokes of the clock with which the piece begins). Sometimes you have to be as vulgar as possible and Saint-Saëns knew it. At the end a cock crows and that is the sign for the skeletons to go back to their graves. Apart from the violin, the xylophone plays an important part. At that time, it was a fairly new instrument and was chiefly used for special effects. Of course, here are the rattling bones of the dancing skeletons, intended to fill children with terror. And it succeeded. I first heard the piece as a child and, after about fifty years after that first fright, I am using *Danse macabre* as a model for this scherzo and the xylophone at the same moments as Saint-Saëns.

BLOW-UP

I first counted the number of bars in *Danse macabre* and they are on the horizontal line in the above drawing. Under the horizontal line you find the minutes and the total number of bars. I had a duration of twelve minutes in mind for this part. Using the two recordings of the Saint-Saëns which I had, I found out that I had to multiply the length by 1.7. This makes life easy when you begin to compose. For the sake of keeping track, I used the division in rehearsal letters. In each part, the number of bars is equal to 1.7 times the number of bars in Saint-Saëns' piece. I also took over the time signature: 3/4 time with tempo indication ♩. = 69.

I listened to *Danse macabre* before I began to compose and I sought out useful things which I wanted to interpret. So I have used its two themes and related them to material from the other sections of the *Trilogy*, four-part harmonies for the most part. It is slightly more complex because in the important first subject I used the structure of a perfect fifth and the diminished fifth of Saint-Saëns' solo violin. Just as in *Danse macabre*, my second subject is slow whole-tone music.

The opening of *Dancing on the bones* is certainly the most direct reference to Saint-Saëns but I also follow his ideas on development, such as the stretto. At letter D in *Danse macabre*, you find a new melody which interested me because it sounds like the most important motif in *Rosa*. But here it has a completely different significance. It is a sort of third subject:

Real connoisseurs will recognise this melody:

It is the Gregorian song 'Dies irae', which is sung in the Catholic church in the Requiem Mass. This melody is about one thousand years old. These days you have to explain all this because it has disappeared from 'general knowledge'. Terrible.

I liked it because it is the most important motif in *Rosa*:

I thought: "I have heard that before." It was only later that I recognised the 'Dies irae'. So I was not sufficiently vulgar to use the melody myself.

At letter E, Saint-Saëns begins a section in B major which has already appeared long before letter A. I picked out the new instrumentation – clarinet and harp. So sometimes I take over the sound and not the pitch.

HAPPY ENDING

At the end of the piece, at the moment when Saint-Saëns combines his two themes, a children's chorus begins to bawl. They sing as if they were in a children's musical, and thus the entire *Trilogy* has a sort of happy ending. It doesn't become completely happy but the song has something optimistic about it.

The combination of these two themes is not the same as the entry of the children's chorus but the chorus was the strongest trump card I had in my hand. I am a gambler by nature and I have also played many games in my time. The game of cards is a very useful metaphor for a whole lot of things in life and also for music-making which, happily, we also call 'playing'. You come up against a card game in music now and again. Stravinsky was certainly in there (that's fine by me, of course): *Jeu de cartes* and the card game in *The Rake's Progress*. On a much higher level, playing is nothing more than 'adopting an attitude'. That's my definition of composition and, I'm gradually beginning to realise, probably my philosophy of life too. This bears a strong resemblance to an ironic attitude to life, tragic or not tragic.

I had to find Saint-Saëns' most important trump card in *Danse macabre*. Without doubt, it is the simultaneous return of the two themes, fortissimo. For me it was immediately settled that this moment had to coincide with the entrance of the children's chorus in my piece. Ravel's *Daphnis and Chloë* suite number 2 ends with a very quick dance with chorus.

Dancing on the bones sounds like an instrumental piece, not a vocal piece. You could perform it without chorus. Most of the sung notes are doubled in the orchestra. The second suite of *Daphnis* is also often performed without chorus. But I don't like *Dancing on the bones* without children – because then the emphasis would be closer to the model of the 'instrumental scherzo', which to me is merely the starting point.

Sometimes I let myself be led astray by things which I would normally avoid. *Danse macabre* is written for symphony orchestra, and that is thus here my model too. The *Trilogy* is written for large ensemble but in this part it sounds more like a symphony orchestra. The line-up in the strings is now 33222,[107] as it was in the performance by Ensemble Modern. The brass is doubled, there is some woodwind, but no bassoons except a double bassoon. There are two percussionists, two pianos, two synthesizers and a harp, two guitars and a bass guitar.

ELECTRONICS

These days, an important extension in the practical possibilities in composition has been realised, thanks to electronics. In the last fifty years, the synthesizer has become very important but electronics can also play an

---

[107] That is to say: 3 first violins, 3 second violins, 2 violas, 2 cellos, 2 double basses.

important part as regards the balance in an orchestra. Not especially in this piece, but certainly in others, the balance between the instruments is only possible because I know that there is a public address system in the auditorium and, rather more important, someone who knows how to operate it. I do not use amplification in order to make the sound louder but in order to achieve a refined balance by amplifying parts of the ensemble. Since the seventies, since *De Staat* [*The Republic*], I can – thanks to amplification – combine instruments that you would never have even considered combining.

I have to say that these things don't just happen. We composers just have to do the things we want to do. And so, in this case, we help the technicians to find new methods and to discover what is good for music. They need us. To an extent it is our duty to consider the practical sides of the performance, to change them and to improve them. Such as writing for bass guitar. When I was writing *De Staat* in 1976, I often listened to soul and other pop music – so that piece contains a fairly substantial bass guitar part. There was one guy who could more or less play it, even though he said it was impossible. I must admit that I did actually change two notes but, these days, there are at least twenty people who can play it. We have to start somewhere, then things actually change.

There is a famous example by old Bach. The great Toccata in F[108] starts like this:

and later, in the pedals, this solo:

Half way through the piece, he repeats the pedal solo in C. In so doing, at a given moment, he reaches high F.

Everyone knows that, in Bach's time, organ pedals went as high as C – there was no high F or E or D. He simply wrote it down; let's see what happens. And now all organs have a high F. Sometimes we have to help

---

[108] J. S. Bach, *Orgelwerke* [*Organ Works*], ed. Peters Band III.

history on.

This is not a plea for effect music. I warn you – if you are a good composer, you don't use effects.

Ensemble Modern has a full-time technician who is very important. He works during all the rehearsals and even during group rehearsals checking the balance which is, as a consequence, marvellous. He knows the score inside out. I dreamed of such technical possibilities when I was composing *De Staat* half way through the seventies. It took twenty years to get there. But it can happen that your dreams come true through hard work.

Writing to Vermeer

Radziejowice, 2000

Two lectures during the composition course in Radziejowice, Poland. Just as in the lectures on the Trilogy of the Last Day *in Apeldoorn, the audience consisted of young composers, theorists and musicologists. At a concert in the Centrum Nieuwe Muziek in Middelburg, Louis Andriessen spoke about the opera. Parts of this talk have been worked into the text (with thanks to the Centrum Nieuwe Muziek in Middelburg).*

To begin with, I would like to mention two subjects which are very important to me. The first, the crossing of the boundaries between high and low art, is not really under discussion in *Vermeer*, but has certainly kept me busy during the last thirty years. I show solidarity with people who are not hierarchical and who do not think that Boulez is better than Miles Davis.

The second subject, which certainly is important in *Vermeer*, is the human voice. These two subjects have a lot to do with one another.

In the Netherlands, the traditional hierarchy amongst the instruments has, to a certain extent, been removed. Many musicians around me, with classical 'bourgeois' instruments such as the violin, can play pop music and also hill-billy and Brian Ferneyhough.

Conversely, I have always used many instruments in my work which, from their birth, have been regarded as not good enough for 'real' music: saxophone, guitar, keyboards, bass guitar, whatever you like, as long as it is *dirty stuff*.

Much has changed in this field. When the English composer Cornelius Cardew, who was very important in the sixties, wanted to perform *Le Marteau sans maître* by Boulez at the beginning of the sixties, he couldn't find one guitar player who could play it. He decided to learn to play the guitar himself. After two years he could play this piece a bit. It is a notoriously difficult guitar part.

Now we are forty years on, and in Amsterdam you can easily find five or six guitar players who can play acoustic, as well as electric, guitar very well. In this they were helped by composers who wrote pieces for them and produced concerts in new venues, but it is predominantly the motivation and dedication of these musicians which we have to thank for this development.

The same problem is now emerging with singers. There are opera singers, oratorio singers, rock 'n' roll singers, pop singers, actors, and between all these tiny 'provinces' are huge barriers. I will devote the last twenty years of my life to demolishing them and I hope that you will help me. It is necessary in order to develop the new singing style which we need.

THE IMAGE OF THE COMPOSER

This is the first time I have given a somewhat longer lecture on *Vermeer*. Naturally I talked a lot to the press when the opera was performed – this was no doubt because I collaborated with a world-famous director. You have to explain continually why you have done what you have done. This isn't bad; you get used to it. When you speak to journalists, you should be aware that they like to hear bold statements, especially a provocative one-liner which always looks good in a newspaper. It's all a game you have to play. It is part of your life as a composer.

It is not only your music, but your behaviour in public too, which influences the image which people form of you. You can avoid all contact with people but then you have an image of being an awkward, inaccessible composer, and I think that is much more vain. These inaccessible, very interesting and withdrawn composers are, in the main, not the best ones although they often awaken high hopes in journalists. In this area we can learn a lot from people such as Bach, Stravinsky, Purcell and Mozart. When someone asked: "Why did you do that, Mr. Mozart?", he simply gave them an answer. In his letters you can read how amusing he could be. So I have my doubts about the existence of the famous genius that no one can find.

But it can be worse. I must warn you straight away about the other extreme, about those people who, during their careers, are always 'wheeler-dealing'. Musical history is, to an extent, shaped by composers who are not particularly good but who can talk very well, who write the right letters at the right moment to the right people and who have good media contacts.

I do rather prefer the crazy people who live in tiny houses in the forest. They compensate for a world which is completely Americanised. The ultimate form of late-capitalism means that the product itself is completely unimportant. The only important thing is that someone buys it. You must ram it down people's throats – or some other random aperture. No one thinks Coca-Cola tastes nice; you can't tell me that they do. But there are people who maintain that they think it is marvellous. They are proof of Coca-Cola's successful marketing. Good composers know this these days and use it as an argument for criticising accessible music.

There are also composers who move from the one group to the other. For the last twenty years in Poland you have had a very famous one, Górecki, who never shows up anywhere, scarcely composes and mostly gardens a lot. That is likeable, but he doesn't need to worry any more, after the world-wide success of his Third Symphony.

There isn't a lot of forest in the Netherlands, so the situation is pretty hopeless for me.

Of course the world is much more complicated than is suggested by a dichotomy such as this, but I like this sort of polemic or dialectic thinking. It requires distance and this can create the space to think about it.

This dichotomy is comparable to the difference between foxes and hedgehogs which the British philosopher Isaiah Berlin[109] described in an essay on Russian literature. The hedgehog has prickles and is nearly blind. He goes underground, always points straight ahead and tries to find his way in the same direction. The fox (and I am more like this) is always looking around him; he picks out something which he needs to work out, temporarily, before he continues in an unpredictable direction. The hedgehogs are not bad composers, however – just look at Schoenberg, Webern and Mahler.

MUSIC AND THEATRE

I am very aware of the fact that in *Vermeer* I also use material which has its vulgar side. What do I mean by vulgar? You can compare it to kitsch – material which is used too often and only works for masses of people who have no experience of listening. Music is then merely a recognisable background for images, dance or prayer. In general, we must accept that music is readily surrounded by other things. Music is at home in the disco, the church and the theatre.

As a composer you have continually to define your position – how far you go with what you could call unauthentic material. I am talking in the abstract but in composing it is very concrete. Two extremes are Brian Ferneyhough (for those of you who don't know him, his music sounds as though you are playing five pieces by Schoenberg at the same time with a few extra parts added) and Andrew Lloyd Webber (music which doesn't contain one original note). We can all choose where we stand in this room full of possibilities. Whilst I was writing *Vermeer*, I continually had the feeling that I had to manoeuvre like a fish in the current.

I am not the sort of composer who writes a piano concerto, a sonata and, from time to time, an opera. Someone like this can be a good composer but I have no confidence in opera composers without experience.

When I was fifteen I wrote music for a friend's puppet theatre. Since then I have always written a lot for theatre, film, dance and video. In the

---

[109] Isaiah Berlin, 'The hedgehog and the fox', in *Russian Thinkers* (1981).

sixties I wrote theatre pieces for the group Baal which lasted the whole evening. You could compare Baal to the work of the brilliant Polish direc-tor Grotowski. He created grotesque, absurd and very sharp theatre. For Baal, we mostly used old stories with a lot of singing (in up to eight parts) and a small orchestra, five or six people on the stage. Moreover, the stage was on the same level as the auditorium.

I believe that you learn much more from situations such as these than you do if you write for the symphony orchestra, simply by virtue of the fact that your audience is totally different. The audience is larger but also less familiar with music. This is a problem but also an advantage. These audi-ences have an interesting outlook on what music is. Composers know that music has its own musical meaning, but for ninety-five per cent of the people around us, music has, in the first place, all sorts of other meanings. It is important that you realise this. You must not suffer from it, but enjoy it, use it and make the best of it.

In the first opera which I did with Peter Greenaway, *Rosa*, accessibility was an important topic.[110] I didn't choose it simply because the main char-acter, Rosa, is a composer of cowboy film music, but with an eye to the audience which I could expect at this opera. It was clear that it would not consist of hard-core new music lovers, for the simple fact that some people would come because of Greenaway. I didn't need to get into their good books but I did want to make their expectations part of the composition. Moreover, that is precisely what Greenaway did in the first version of the libretto. He assimilated people from the general public into the libretto and described their thoughts.

The piece was loud, violent, shocking and terrifying and that was prob-ably the most significant reason why it could only be seen in Amsterdam. This city has a long liberal and a reasonably free-thinking tradition which is a great advantage as far as art is concerned. New York did consider *Rosa* but ultimately chose *Writing to Vermeer*.

The two operas are total opposites. Greenaway came to me with three suggestions, from which I chose Vermeer. He wanted to write a libretto around a peaceful, domestic situation. The text was to consist of fictitious letters to Vermeer from his wife Catharina Bolnes, his mother-in-law Maria Thins and the model, Saskia, whom Greenaway dreamed up.

I wanted to make a sort of companion piece to *Rosa*, comparable on some levels but also completely different. In Louis XVI's time, you had images on the mantelpiece which were known as companion pieces. On the left-hand side you would have, for example, a farmer's wife and on the right a herdsman – twin pictures representing opposites, male and female,

---

[110] See the chapter on *Rosa*, p. 242 ff.

black and white. The serenity of Vermeer was entirely appropriate. I wanted to write music of a dynamic tranquillity (these are the words that Stravinsky once used to describe the grand finales of his Greek ballets *Apollo* and *Orpheus*).

The film M *is for Man, Music, Mozart* retrospectively then became, in effect, a sort of overture to the two operas I created with Greenaway.

He thought that Vermeer as a subject would be more appropriate as a chamber opera, even though we had the enormous stage of the Amsterdam Opera at our disposal. But I chose that subject because I had a good idea about how to make the opera suitable for a larger stage, of which more later.

Before I talk about the piece I want to show you a few paintings so that you know what Vermeer was like and how important he is. But before I do that, let me tell you about the situation in the Netherlands at that time.

HISTORICAL BACKGROUND

In 1568 the Dutch began to fight the Spanish. Everything to the north of France belonged to the Spanish crown. There were various reasons for this fighting. The Netherlands had a certain tradition of emancipation of the lower and middle classes for which they sometimes needed to fight, but religious reasons were important as well. The Netherlanders were Protestant and the Spaniards Catholic. At the end of the sixteenth century we founded the first republic but peace was only achieved in 1648. From that moment on, the Netherlands became an independent country and that part which is now Flanders remained temporarily Spanish.

In Vermeer's time there was great economic growth and that is always good for art. But history follows its own patterns. Holland, surrounded by water on almost all sides, quickly became a coloniser and conquered large parts of the world. This made the country even richer.

As I have already said: art flourishes in a time of luxury. Most of the paintings from that time in Holland are paintings which people liked to have on their walls to show others how well people were doing, how beautiful their clothes were, how opulent and rich their lifestyle. There were a few painters who painted ordinary people (Jan Steen was very good at this). The genius Rembrandt is a case apart, but for me, Vermeer is the greatest of the period.

PAINTINGS

Vermeer (1632-1675) was fairly well known in Holland but always remained poor. During his lifetime he only painted thirty-four paintings. That is not a lot, even for a short lifetime – he died when he was forty-three.

Johannes Vermeer, *The Music Lesson*, circa 1662-1664, canvas, 74 x 64.5 cm. From the collection of Her Majesty Queen Elizabeth II. Photo: Christine Elkhuizen.

There was one man who collected Vermeer's paintings during his lifetime and he died in 1672. Thereafter, financially, it was, of course, a complete mess. The baker sometimes bought a painting because then at least he got something in exchange for his bread. Vermeer's debt to the baker ran to more than one thousand guilders, a fortune in those days.

At school we learned as children that Vermeer painted beautiful, domestic scenes. In the main he depicted young girls – servants who are performing simple daily tasks. A girl pouring out milk is the most boring subject you can imagine but he makes a masterpiece of it. Greenaway sees Vermeer as the inventor of photography because the scenes in his paintings only last a second in reality. The amazing thing is that he could capture a moment such as that in a painting which he worked on for a year. A concept like 'efficiency' did not exist in Vermeer's world at all. Efficiency is the enemy of art.

We also learned that Vermeer is famous for the unique colours, yellow and blue, which he used. These two colours cannot be found anywhere other than in a painting by Vermeer. Scientists have managed to discover to a large degree (ninety-five per cent) how he created these colours and which chemicals he used, but the last five per cent remains a secret.

Catharina (Susan Narucki) in *Writing to Vermeer*, Peter Greenaway,
De Nederlandse Opera, 1999/2000. Photo: Dean Golja.

The little street is one of the few paintings which Vermeer set outside.
Generally we find ourselves inside, where people read or write letters, give
them or receive them. The content of the letters is a rewarding subject for
our imagination. Of course they are about one of the most beautiful subjects of all – love. Music and love are old friends. In seventeenth-century
painting, there are many references to music as a symbol of love, as in *The
music lesson*. In this painting you see a girl sitting at a harpsichord, with her
back to the onlooker. Above the instrument hangs a mirror in which her
head is also visible. One of my discoveries is that, in the reflection, her
head is turned a quarter of a turn. She is looking towards the boy and
fantasising. We all do this; we are playing the piano but are looking out of
the corner of our eye to see if we are making an impression on the girl.

Why do I love Vermeer's paintings so much and why can't I stop looking at them? We do not understand why they are so beautiful, just like the
beginning of Mozart's G minor symphony. It looks very simple and it is
incomprehensible why this theme is so much more beautiful than all the
others. One of Vermeer's secrets which was only recently discovered can
perhaps explain something. Vermeer paints everything, very beautifully
and very precisely, with shadows but the human beings *have no shadows*.
My theory is that the people are not real. The women are sorts of angels.

Vermeer probably had a professional model because there are a few
girls in his paintings which you recognise again and again. The model

could, however, be one of his daughters – he had a lot of children. In the painting *The allegory of painting* the woman really looks like a model. It is clear that she is posing with the book and that trumpet (which are, of course, symbols) but it looks unnatural, even in the painting.

In musical language I like to confine myself strictly to the most important topic. Anyone who knows Vermeer's paintings will understand that a piece about Vermeer's women should at the very least be a homage to the beauty of the paintings. So you have to write the most beautiful music you can imagine.

With the *Woman in blue reading a letter* we are getting very close to the opera. The woman is pregnant and is reading a letter. At that time there was still a war with the Spanish – not in the country itself but at the borders. In the streets there was fighting between Catholics and Protestants. The letter in the painting could very well be a love-letter from a soldier to his pregnant wife. Moreover, we know that Vermeer's wife was almost constantly pregnant because she had many children.

In the opera, Vermeer is in The Hague, because he has been asked to inspect some paintings. The three women sent letters to him; obviously he wrote letters to them, too, but these are not included in the opera. The Woman in blue could be his wife who has received a letter from him about how things are going. I just don't know who painted it if he was in The Hague.

In good reproductions of his paintings, you can see that Vermeer's light blue and his dark blue come from the same source – fifty per cent of it consists of the same indigo combination, a colour which was pretty difficult to obtain in those days.

Why are the paintings so beautiful? Beauty is a strange subject. It would be stupid to judge the girls according to the usual criteria of the fashion magazines; that sort of beauty has very little to do with this. The girls are beautiful because they remain themselves and are not aware of the camera.

The great power in Vermeer's paintings is the tangible presence of a secret. You see what you are not supposed to see. You are not in the room yourself, you are a voyeur who conceals himself outside. I think that this is the reason we think there is a secret.

LIBRETTO

So the opera is about Johannes Vermeer, or more precisely, about the three women who write letters to him. Greenaway starts from the few historical facts that we know about him. No letters have been preserved either from or to Vermeer; there are official documents from the church and the police force. We know when his children were born and that his wife had an peculiar brother who drank too much and was a bad lot. Greenaway read, just as I did, the two or three books on Vermeer which exist. Then he knew everything – and used his imagination.

Vermeer does not appear in the opera himself. The three women, on the other hand, are continually on the stage. His wife Catharina came from a Catholic bourgeois family (Vermeer's own background was Calvinist but for her sake he converted). Catharina was sung by Susan Narucki, a concert singer whom I knew from a concert of music by Earl Kim (a very good, not-so-well-known American composer – a bit like Webern). Earlier she had sung the role of Hadewijch (the second part of *De Materie*). She sings like an angel. It is always beautiful; she cannot produce an ugly sound.

Johannes Vermeer and his family lived in Delft with his mother-in-law, Maria Thins, who ran a hostelry next to the house. She is the second woman in the opera and the role is sung by Susan Bickley. Bickley is a real opera singer but, as rehearsals progressed, she came to a better understanding of what I wanted.

The third woman is the imaginary model, Saskia, named after Rembrandt's wife. She comes from Dordrecht. The ups and downs of her love-life provide the only narrative element in the opera. Her father in Dordrecht wants her to marry some business man or other whom she doesn't like. Moreover, she has a boyfriend in Delft. So she wants to go back to Delft and also to model again for Vermeer. There is a happy ending. The boyfriend comes to Dordrecht with friends in a large wagon to visit her and even hires a hotel room for a few hours. A good decision. Don't be embarrassed.

Because Saskia is not in Delft, Greenaway shows her for the first time on a large video screen. There are all sorts of film screens with pre-made films but Saskia, sung by Barbara Hannigan, appears live. It looks as though she is miming to her own voice. Because of the other film screens, you don't immediately realise that she is really there. It works very well.

Saskia is the young, light voice, Catharina the mature mezzo-soprano and, of course, the mother-in-law is the mezzo who schemes. I didn't want to allow them to sound like classical singers so – no vibrato and legatissimo. In *M is for Man, Music, Mozart* that is even more important. I wrote that for Astrid Seriese, a jazz singer who can read music excellently and who sings legato and non-vibrato beautifully. I have found a sort of new Astrid, the young Italian singer Cristina Zavalloni. She also has a jazz background. I like working with these people – jazz singers who can read music, who can count and who are also actresses. They immediately want to sing from memory, not from the music.

The libretto contains next to no dramatic development. That is rather exceptional for an opera libretto. The pithy summary of opera by George Bernard Shaw has not yet been surpassed: "Opera is about a tenor who wants to go to bed with a soprano, and a baritone who doesn't like it." The

narrative structure is essential. Things have to develop to a dramatic conclusion, through which some sort of catharsis takes place. And so you
become a better person, at least according to Aristotle.

The lack of a development makes the libretto quite difficult for a composer, but I found it rather an attractive aspect. This is precisely what I find
so good about Samuel Becketts's plays. *Waiting for Godot* is a milestone in
twentieth-century literature. The story of James Joyce's *Ulysses* is completely unimportant. The reason we all read it (if we are courageous enough),
is because of the structure of the book, the different levels and the different
styles.

A problem in *Writing to Vermeer* is the language. The medium of communication in Greenaway's Delft is, unfortunately, English. But there is
something to be said for that. It is the language of the librettist and, what's
more, there were plans early on to take the opera to New York and Aus-
tralia. I changed a lot, so that 'Dear John' became 'Dear Johannes' and by
so doing, hope it sounds as though a Dutch opera has been translated into
English. It has its easy side too – it is easier to compose 'I love you' than 'Ik
hou van je'. Some day I will write a Dutch version of it, I promise. In order
to do that, I would virtually have to compose the opera again from scratch
because my setting of the text is rather specific. It would be a lot of work,
but I'd like to do it if a performance possibility came up.

The relationship between the words and the notes is an interesting topic.
You have to be very flexible in the relationship between the emphases in
the words and the main beats in the music. It is only the bad composers
who always make them synchronic.

If you don't pay attention to this, it all becomes very rigid – I learnt this
from French composers. Francis Poulenc goes the furthest and I really
studied how he set his texts. Ravel and Debussy were also very definite
about the relationship between language and music. Honegger is under-
rated in general and also as far as this is concerned. You find the same
flexibility with good song writers and composers of musicals. When I heard
Vermeer recently, it struck me that certain melodic lines in the vocal part,
together with the harmony, remind me of the American musical more
than I had realised.

INTERRUPTIONS

As I have already said, Greenaway initially thought of *Vermeer* as a
chamber opera. To make the subject matter fitting for the large stage in
the Muziektheater, I suggested that we should interrupt the tranquil domestic scenes with fragments from the outside world, like the knife cuts in
Fontana's paintings.

The outside world was not in the least peaceful. There were constant fights between Catholics and Protestants, floods and war with the Spanish (and later with the French).

In the opera you see different events which took place in and around Delft at the time, the most horrifying of which was the murder of the De Witt brothers, two leading politicians. They were slaughtered by a furious mob. That was the end of the Golden Age in the Netherlands and a very painful moment in the opera. Another interruption comes from the explosion of a powder magazine in Delft. Towards the end of the opera, the French army invades the Netherlands. The Netherlanders resisted the French invasion by flooding large areas of the country. This is an odd way of defending yourself, but it worked well. The French had no idea how to cross the immense stretches of water. This flood concludes the opera.

Not all the interruptions are violent. In the first scene, for example, suddenly everything stands still and you hear the Sunday morning church bells. There is also an interruption concerning a domestic accident (one of the daughters drank varnish on her birthday, which is very bad for one's health).

I thought a lot about these interruptions. At the beginning I wanted to compose the interruptions myself with, for example, a wind orchestra or percussion backstage. In the end, I decided not to do it myself but to ask Michel van der Aa to do it. This young composer can manage electronics very well and that seemed to me to provide a good contrast to the orchestra. I think the sound tracks are really good. They differ greatly from one another; some effects are pure electronic music and in other pieces he uses parts of my music. Gradually, the interruptions become increasingly important.

JOHN CAGE: *SIX MELODIES*

The libretto which I received from Greenaway consisted of six scenes of about equal length. He had assembled six letters from all the women, eighteen letters in all, arranged like the prongs of a fork. They alternate with each other continually.

This form made me think of a piece by John Cage, the *Six Melodies* for violin and piano. The six pieces are of approximately equal length, mostly slow (some are slightly faster or even slower), with only eight or nine musical elements which constantly revolve around themselves without transpositions. Because they are precisely the right notes you feel, after a while, that it is a very well-considered and elegant musical situation. I really love these pieces.

A few weeks before I received the libretto I had heard a beautiful performance by an American violinist, Monica Germino, with a good friend of mine, Gerard Bouwhuis, at the piano. He had already played a lot of my music and later, he performed in *Vermeer*. I found all of this to be a good introduction to doing the same thing as I did in the last part of *Trilogy*: use an existing piece as a model. You put down your own markers, as it were, when you compose. The choice of *Six Melodies* was a good idea because the form fitted the libretto. Moreover, there was another important conformity between Cage and the text, namely that there was no dramatic development.

The peace, calm and serenity which Greenaway had in mind I also found in Cage. I took over his time scheme for the structure of the entire opera, but then I multiplied it by the number I needed to get the length that I wanted. At the end of the day, a composer is also a bit of a mathematician. This number was 8.4.

The *Six Melodies* for violin and piano were written in the late forties. In that period, Cage was still writing real notes and structures; some years later he composed with dice. It struck Cage that his aleatoric music closely resembled music which had been precisely counted out. What had begun as a technical question then became a philosophical problem: what is the relationship between the compositional system and the musical result? He corresponded at the time with Pierre Boulez (who was then writing strict serial music) about this.

This question can be compared with the complex relationship between intuition and calculation which has a long history in the business of composing. J. S. Bach, whom we need to study closely because he is important on all levels, used numbers constantly in his music. Klaus Eidam, an old East German musicologist, wrote a biography of Bach, *The True Life of J. S. Bach*. I believe it is worth reading. Eidam is strongly opposed to the fact that musicologists dealing with Bach always want to track down numbers. To a certain extent he is right because many hypotheses in this area are dubious – if you believe these, Bach would have known the date of his own death. Undeniably, Bach did count continually on all levels within his compositions, although this does not get us any further in explaining the quality of his music.

These days, there is a striking misapprehension amongst current composers that you must be able to hear in the music whether it is strictly organised, serially or otherwise. In practice, what this comes down to is that this music must sound like Schoenberg. I think this is a strange view. The amusing thing about music is that it can be very highly organised and yet can sound beautiful, tonal and even naive. On the other hand you can write completely intuitive 'strictly serial' music. For this reason it is important to think about John Cage who was in a position to bring the problem into the open. What's more, in the third scene of *Vermeer*, I used dice, just like Cage.

Paul Auster

all music is about another music

twenty years to demolish barriers between
different kinds of singing!

In doing one finds what one wants to do.

Thinking about the end before beginning the process.

FORM

It is very clear that Cage was doing a lot of counting when he was writing *Six Melodies*. All the note values are more or less based on series of numbers. He was very definite on the subject of the twelve pitches for the violin and even indicates on which string each note should be played. The piano part is, to an extent, like the violin part but does contain its own material. It is important that the six movements are played non-attacca. You cannot make one large movement out of it; that conflicts with the nature of the music. There is no curve which spans the six movements.

What interested me most, however, was the form. Now, form is a prob-lematic term because you can interpret it in many ways. My current theory is that form is, simply, length. When you say "this is sonata form", you are saying that you have used the sonata model for the structure. This says nothing about the form. This notion of musical form as a *model* is akin to the nineteenth-century idea of form. You write a minuet or a symphony and, in so doing you have, of course, complete freedom. In the last part of the *Trilogy* I did not choose the form itself (the scherzo) as a model but rather a specific scherzo, namely the *Danse Macabre* by Camille Saint-Saëns.

Form can also be *non-developing* (forma formata) or *formative* (forma formans).[111] You see the latter in, for example, improvisations and tocca-tas by Sweelinck. A toccata such as one of Sweelinck's is a forma formans, in contrast to a sonata, for example, which is a forma formata.

In the end, form is the same as length. If you have an idea of the propor-tionate lengths before you write larger works, then you've achieved a great deal. Number relationships create form. The numbers 1-2-3 produced a completely different form from 1-11-6.

In the *Six Melodies* you can also detect the idea that form is the same as duration. Cage tried to clarify his way of working in the score. His first sentence about form runs, very profoundly, as follows: "These melodies are written in the rhythmic structure 3½-3½-4-4-3-4." It is clear that he means the length of the pieces which, in my opinion, has nothing to do with rhythm.

I did, however, look for rhythmic elements which agreed with the above-mentioned number values; I counted crotchets, quavers and semiquavers and got nothing.

Because I don't like fractions, I took that so-called 'rhythmic structure' and multiplied it by two. Then you get the following sequence: 7-7-8-8-6-8.

So there are three different lengths. The two halves are symmetrical because the length of the first three parts is the same as that of the last

---

[111] See F. R. Noske, *Forma formans* (Amsterdam, 1969).

three. This brought me to the idea of placing a musical mirror in the middle of the opera. A mirror has associations not only with many musical elements but also, in the first place, with Vermeer's paintings. We have already seen the interesting reflection in *The music lesson*. Windows function as mirrors too, as in *Young woman reading letter by window*. But much more important than all the reflective objects in his work is another characteristic of all his paintings; they are moving and full of melancholy, but at the same time cold and distant when you compare them with paintings by Rembrandt and other of his contemporaries. It is as though there is a sheet of glass between you and the girl. Although, seen from the perspective art history, this may not be completely correct, I have always found Vermeer to be a good example of a Classicist. In the Classical conception of art it is not important that you, as an artist, express your own feelings but that you depict an object which is 'outside' you. People like the work, the object, better than its creator. Around 1800, with the emergence of Romanticism, the idea of individual expression becomes more important. This concept reached its high point in northern Europe after 1830. I have my doubts as to how important this is as regards music since 1840, with the exception of the geniuses. Don't tell me that Chopin is a Romantic composer. He is a Classicist.

The mirror was a way for me to structure the whole and to think about the non-developing music which I had resolved to write. I decided to do something which is in direct conflict with Cage's stasis. After the mirror (scenes 4-6), I did not only use reflected material from the first half but continually added new music. This related to the fragments reflecting the outside world which became increasingly violent in the second half.

I wanted to combine the non-developing form with a dramatic development in the music. You already hear this in the first scene. The music seems to be elegant and Ravel-like, but there is also a sense of melancholic tension. The facts which the women describe in their letters are not at all dramatic but I hoped, certainly in the second half, to make it clear in the music that they are not singing what they feel. They conceal their true feelings and you can hear it. They conceal that they are always afraid and are becoming more afraid, that misfortunes happen, that the children are thrown into the canal, that Vermeer won't come home because he is abducted on his journey, or is beaten up by Protestants and that something happens to Saskia. It is, of course, especially mothers who are afraid that something will happen to their children. This fear – of misfortune, of death – is the most important subject in the music, but it takes one hundred minutes before it becomes completely clear. I had this in mind when I began composing it and after my advice to Greenaway to interrupt the peaceful scenes harshly with the real violence of the real world in Vermeer's time.

Because this tension is already present in scene 1, I have the idea that the opera is one great arch. This is the most difficult thing to compose. I am a child of the sixties. We really enjoyed six-hour performances by Wilson and long films, but we also enjoyed the miniatures by Anton Webern. Dealing with very different lengths of timing was typical of my youth. I have no preferences as far as that is concerned – it is just interesting to think about it in different ways, especially in the theatre. In modern dance, you would call a fifty-five minute performance a whole evening.

MEMORY IN MUSIC

Memory in music has nothing to do with melodies in retrograde motion. It is a strange idea that you should recognise a series of notes in reverse order. This is not the case. The memory only works in the same direction, just like a photo. In the music of the Renaissance and of the Second Viennese School, melodies were often literally mirrored. The little melody

in Schoenberg and also in Josquin, turns into:

At the very most, you hear an indirect connection between the two melodies. The memory of the first melody sounds like this to me:

The mirror point in the opera, namely the transition from the third to the fourth scene, is almost literally in retrograde motion. Furthermore, in the second half of the opera, I use – after the mirror – literal quotations from the first half. If I had given this talk to composers in 1963, there would have been uproar. Something like this was strictly forbidden then. Happily, times have changed. We had to fight about the most stupid things.

What interested me was musical memory because a reflection in time and also in music is, in fact, a memory. It is a miraculous phenomenon in music, that a repeated fragment can sound completely different from the original fragment because the musical situation has changed. You can try (once) yourself to create a beautiful harmonic transition, followed by another wonderful harmonic transition and then come back with the first one. If you are a good composer, you can get the third one (which is a repeat of the first) to sound different from the first by means of what has happened in the middle. We all experience that when we play the piano or listen to music. A note is only right because of what went before it and because of the following note; the harmony only has to do with the harmony before and after it. That is what I am beginning to understand after a long life. As a composer, you must see that you get a grip on these sorts of problems.

SIXTEEN DANCES

The mirror made me think of another work by Cage, *Sixteen Dances* for chamber ensemble, which he wrote for his friend, the choreographer Merce Cunningham. Just like the *Six Melodies* it consists of a limited number of small musical elements which are varied and not transposed. It is music which revolves around itself. I advise you to listen to it – there is a very good recording by Ensemble Modern. They are sixteen small pieces, each lasting two or three minutes. I decided to use the work as a model for scenes 3 and 4 of *Vermeer*. The two central parts both consist of eight pieces each lasting two minutes which together reflect the relative lengths of the *Sixteen Dances*. Because I was very precise as regards the length, scenes 3 and 4 both last 16 minutes.

The *Sixteen Dances* had a great influence on two of Cage's friends, Earle Browne and Morton Feldman. I regard Feldman as a great composer of the second half of the twentieth century but, in this context, it is especially important that he, with John Cage, introduced a new approach to time in the fifties. Their music is non-developing and has few dramatic implications. They use musical motifs as sort of *objets trouvés*, following the example of Marcel Duchamps.

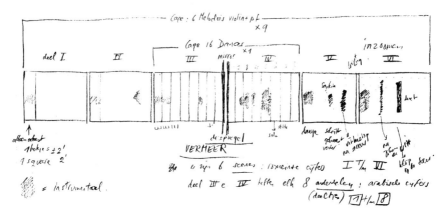

Many of Morton Feldman's later works have extremely long forms. I hope that you will be able to listen to his later pieces (some of which last several hours without much happening). He wants you, as the listener, to make your own choices and to wonder about things such as: "Do I have to enjoy myself?" He also permits you to leave the hall and come back later.

Conversely, I believe that, in *Sixteen Dances*, Cage was also influenced by Feldman, particularly by the manner in which Feldman used chromatic material. His music is inconceivable without the late works of Anton Webern. The chromatic material in *Vermeer* refers to this heritage. So Feldman's Webern gets into the opera via the *Sixteen Dances*.

Here, I treat the material and the form in which it was originally used as two independent elements. You mustn't be too academic about it. The two-minute pieces in scenes 3 and 4 often have a small mirror in the middle, as you frequently see in Webern's opus 20 to 30. Here, I do use the twelve-note retrograde motion; I turn the little motifs around note for note. The Cage stuff is not repeated after the mirror between scenes 3 and 4, but there are continual references to it.

I have given names to each of the individual two-minute pieces. The first two are called Cage and Feldman, and the sixth and seventh, for example, are called Berio and Scriabin. They are not in the least style quotations, but there is a distant relationship between the pieces and these two composers. I am constantly aware that I have relationships with other music. References are reflected too.

Cage used dice for *Sixteen Dances*. I decided not only to use the structure but also the method he used, with the consequence that, a bit later, I had to go to a toy shop to buy dice once more. I used the dice to get eight or nine little motifs and rests of varying lengths for the instrumental parts in scenes 3 and 4.

Unlike Cage, I allowed myself to use transpositions and also add rests, which are often forgotten – neglecting rests is one of a composer's pitfalls. Rests are much more important than the music.

Because I am no slave to bureaucracy, I naturally changed everything which I didn't think was good. But the length of each of the sixteen parts remained precisely two minutes. Meanwhile, the singing more or less went its own way.

The use of models is very hip and post-modern since Rauschenberg, and others, painted their own Velasquez's, but it has been happening for centuries. For me, models are not only important beacons in composition; music that I find good always refers to other music. Bach's Passions, which he composed for the Church of St. Thomas and the Church of St. Nicholas in Leipzig, are complicated combinations of different styles. Bach used the old Netherlands counterpoint; the chorales are deeply rooted in German

Protestant music and the arias are like Italian opera arias which, in the Germany of 1730, were completely avant-garde. In the book by Eidam which I mentioned previously, a rich lady is quoted. At the performance of the *St. Matthew Passion* in the Church of St. Thomas, she shouted out: "It's like being in the theatre!" This woman really understood the music. We just don't realise now that 'Blute nur' or 'Erbarme dich' were written in the style of Corelli (or another Italian composer). I like the fact that Bach did those sorts of things.

Bach's Passions are wonderful operas. They are very static. I do not believe that he follows the drama with the music. The first chorale is as moving as the last. There are indeed dramatic moments, like the arias I just mentioned, but he is not trying to tell a story. This is unrelated to the fact that it is a very dramatic story.

Each scene in *Vermeer* begins with an instrumental introduction which I call 'sinfonia' in imitation of Bach. These overtures last precisely three minutes, just like the beginning of his French overtures. There too, the ratio between the opening part (sinfonia) and the whole is approximately 1:5.

The more you steal, the better. It makes your life easier. Composing is already difficult enough.

Sweelinck

In addition to John Cage, I used yet another composer as a model – Jan Pieterszoon Sweelinck. In Vermeer's time, he was an organist, harpsichord-ist, composer and teacher in Amsterdam. He was contracted to the Oude Kerk [Old Church] and could tune a harpsichord in a quarter of an hour. Fortunately for me, he was indirectly (via Scheidemann and Reinken) Johann Sebastian Bach's teacher. So he was Bach's teacher's teacher's teacher. If you study north European keyboard music from 1620 to 1720 you can clearly follow the trail of developments. Important subjects at that time were tuning and the growth of non-vocal, instrumental music.

In Amsterdam you can still hear the old tuning daily. There are various big carillons, with easily forty or fifty bells, in Werckmeister's old mean tone temperament tuning. They were cast and hung at the time that Sweelinck was playing the organ in the Oude Kerk. The peals ring every quarter of an hour and the carilloneur gives recitals three or four times a week. I find these waves of sound over the city extraordinarily moving but people don't listen. They are already continually surrounded by sound and shut themselves off from it. But the bells don't care and carry on singing.

At first, I went on a hunt through Sweelinck's harpsichord music, which I have always found the best. His toccatas are famous. Around 1620 (and so before Vermeer's time) he also wrote variations on a sad and splendid German song, 'Mein junges Leben hat ein End'. I quickly decided to make this melody the central motif of the whole opera. In scene 4 of Greenaway's script, Saskia talks about 'Mein junges Leben'. Her mother bought sheet music at the flea-market but two pages are missing from Sweelinck's piece. This was a good reason to use it.

My life became a bit more complicated when someone gave me a copy of a BBC documentary on the techniques which Vermeer used. It was a good film and a well-known English film composer had written the music for it. To my horror he had done what I wanted to do: 'Mein junges Leben' was the most important motif in the film score.

I thought: "What can I do now to show that I am a better composer than you?" I went back to Sweelinck and chose another four melodies which he used for variations. 'Mein junges Leben' remained the most important motif (the *leitmotif*, as the Germans say). Scene 4 contains Sweelinck's harmonisation of that song but, in addition to this, each scene got its own old melody.

Many of these little songs can be found in the book which Adriaen Valerius published around 1630, the *Nederlandtsche Gedenck-clanck* [*Netherlands Memorial Music*]. Valerius was not a composer but an enthusiast who collected together all the songs which were sung by Protestants, – old folk songs and also revolutionary songs which were sung during the war against the Spanish, like the *Wilhelmus*.[†] Sweelinck must have been familiar with this collection of songs.

The beginning of 'Mein junges Leben' sounds like this:

There are no flats in the key signature. From this it is clear that it is not in F major, as the second bar suggests, but rather in the Dorian mode. The fourth bar suggests D major, but the minor third follows on the second beat. The Sweelinck in my opera is more modern than the virtuosic but formal organ composer that he essentially was. He wrote variations on 'Mein junges Leben' and, in the opera, I have made a song from it once again. In this way, it is an example of a monody. This style, a song with

[†] The Dutch national anthem.

accompaniment, was the beginning of tonality.

SWEELINCK MELODIES

I could play the Sweelinck melodies… with a bit of imagination you would certainly recognise them yourself. I have not used the most obvious ones and I had to change them quite a bit, because if you simply play them on the piano they sound as dull as ditchwater. I wanted to write something that we would like and, at the same time, that we would recognise as seventeenth-century music. In doing this, one has to remain critical. A good example of this is what happened with 'Malle Sijmen' ['Silly Simon'], which was originally not a song but a dance. I was busy arranging the melody for scene 5 and I used a sort of Neapolitan chord:

Then I shouted: "No, don't do that – that is Déodat de Sévérac."

Déodat de Sévérac is a French composer who has been completely forgotten, a contemporary of Franck, d'Indy and, to an extent, Debussy. I know the name because my father, who was pro-French, had some piano pieces of his. I hadn't heard a note of his, but I knew that Déodat de Sévérac would have used that chord if, in France in 1880, he had arranged a song like this for piano for small, bourgeois French children. This was a good reason not to use it. Eventually, I did use it because, in context, it was not so bad. I told this to a friend of mine who is also a composer and a teacher in The Hague, Diderik Wagenaar. A few days later he and his wife sent me *En Vacances. Petites pièces romantiques* for piano by Déodat de Sévérac. She had found it in her music collection. You won't believe it, but in a fast sort of menuet I found this:

Precisely the same chord in precisely the same key – E flat major in D minor, so I was very surprised. But it got worse. A bit further on in my song there was a small quasi-Spanish piece, because everything in music and society in Holland in the seventeenth century fought against Spain. There I used trills in the top notes with that E flat giving it a Phrygian feel.

One page further on in *En Vacances* I found a sort of *à l'espagnole*, with precisely the same trills and in D minor too:

When you compose, you also need to know what you *don't* want and, for that, you need to be an experienced listener.

'Malle Sijmen' is also the name of a popular recorder quartet in the Netherlands: four brilliant young recorder players. This has nothing to do with amateurs giving concerts at home – they are unbelievably good and look like the Spice Girls. They commission many new works for their quartet and also work with electronics. I really liked the idea of their having a place in the opera through my choice of this old Scottish dance.

BAROQUE AND BARTÓK

The role which music plays in society has diminished increasingly during the last century. Since the invention of television, the visual arts have taken over as the fashionable art form in daily life. Pop music is more a visual than a musical art.

In Vermeer's time, it was completely different. In order to hear music you had to play it yourself or ask someone very nicely if they would play something. We know a little about music in Delft around 1650. For me as a composer it was interesting not to guess, but to be very precise, about the music from that time. I refer to this in the opera in two ways. As I have just described, I used music which was played at that time. In the second place, in my choice of instruments, I have striven for a sound which resembles – or makes you think of – music from 1650.

To orientate myself, I first wrote a small piece of the overture and invited two good violinists to my house. I was thinking about a sort of cross between Baroque techniques and modern string playing techniques – let's say Bartók violin versus Baroque violin. One of the violinists, Monica Germino, had performed the *Six Melodies* before and in the main plays new music; the other, Lucy van Dael, is the leader of the Orchestra of the Eighteenth Century. This orchestra, conducted by Frans Brueggen, plays music up to early Beethoven (around 1810). They know how pre-1800 music should sound – elastic and animated (like hearing Mozart and Bach for the first time). We are always being told that Beethoven was a bad orchestrator but when this orchestra plays early Beethoven on original instruments, you can at last understand what a daring orchestrator he was. Hearing the sound of the natural horns, you realise why Beethoven wrote like that. In the third symphony he wanted an ugly growling sound in the horns – GGGRRRRGGGRRR. When a classical symphony orchestra is playing, you hear an untroubled pop-pop-pop-pop-pop-pop-pop-pop-pop at this point. Complete nonsense.

It is always said of Ravel (my beloved hero) that he is such a good orchestrator, but I think that is nonsense. The modernist, intellectual generation in Germany and France, from Boulez onwards, finds Ravel too simple, too vulgar, too popular – everything that is bad in art. But, they say then, he is a good orchestrator. I do not believe that he is a good orchestrator. I do not believe that orchestration can be separated from musical thinking. Never. Ravel is as good an orchestrator as the so-called bad orchestrator, Chopin. Don't listen to your teachers. When Chopin wrote his two piano concertos when he was twenty [someone in the hall whispered: "Nineteen!"] and only used the strings as a sort of synthesizer, he knew precisely what he was doing. He chose this curtain-like sound in the strings in order to allow the piano to flourish from the first to the last note. He didn't write the string parts like that because he didn't have a clue about orchestration. Nonsense – he was a genius. He liked the sound of sustained chords.

Bach also knew precisely what he was doing in the short aria 'Zerfliesse, mein Herz' from the *St. John Passion*. It is sung, after the Crucifixion, by a boy, accompanied by an oboe da caccia and a baroque flute. The baroque flute plays in F minor in the low register. Bach knew that all the notes would sound a bit out of tune, because the notes he chose are very difficult to play cleanly so low. Symphony orchestras use modern flutes which can play all notes easily and so then, you don't hear that the F minor aria essentially sounds painfully out of tune. Symphony orchestras are only well equipped for the repertoire from 1830-1880. And one more thing – I am sorry that I have to say negative things about it, but I believe it is very important for all composers – the performance of contemporary music by symphony orchestras is completely uninteresting. The musicians don't like playing it, the audiences don't like it, so I would say: stay out of the way of the symphony orchestra.

When I got the two violinists to play a fragment from the overture to scene 1, it became clear very quickly what the ideal sound for *Vermeer* was. I wanted to work with musicians with a new music background who could adopt the Baroque style of string playing (legatissimo with a lot of bow and little pressure), so that the sound and the pitch are the same at the beginning, middle and end of a note. In this way you achieve a sound on new instruments which makes you think of the old Baroque style of playing. At the Conservatoire, all violinists have learned to play Kreisler and Tchaikovsky, playing right into the string, with notes that have a 'paunch'. Every note is a small crescendo with a diminuendo. That is strictly forbidden in my music.

In *Vermeer* there is a chorus of a small string ensemble: 6 violins, 6 violas, 4 cellos and 2 double basses. It can't be much larger than this because it mustn't sound like a string orchestra but more a sort of Baroque orchestra.

The choice of the other instruments also refers to the Baroque. I wanted a line-up in which the strings themselves don't make the accents. You hear this predominantly in the first half. The wind here don't play a large role, the strings often being doubled by articulated beats on strings of other instruments. I think that these struck strings form the most important sound in the opera. In addition to two harps, two pianos, two classical guitars and a harpsichord there is also a cymbalom.

In Dutch, the cymbalom is called the 'hakkebord' (dulcimer) and this is a very fitting name. It consists of a piece of wood over which strings are stretched, and it is played with little sticks. It is scarcely played now in the Netherlands, but it certainly was in Vermeer's time. You also see it in paintings.

I love the cymbalom; it's like a strange piano. It is, in fact, the predecessor of the piano. Many people think that the piano developed from the harpsichord, but a harpsichord's strings are plucked, just like the harp. The piano system is a complicated version of the cymbalom – little hammers which hit the strings. One of the inventors of this hammer-mechanism was the German clavichord player Schröter. He had the idea when he heard

[†] Pantaleon Hebenstreit (1669-1750) was also involved in improvements to the dulcimer.

Pantaleon Hebenstreit[†] playing the cymbalom.

The cymbalom does not only refer back to Vermeer's time but also provides a beautiful link between the piano and the plucked strings in the orchestra, such as those of the harp, the guitars and the harpsichord.

In *Mausoleum*, which I wrote in the late seventies, I also used a cymbalom. That piece is a homage to two Russians – Igor Stravinsky and the philosopher of anarchism, Mikhail Bakunin. As far as I am concerned, anarchism is still the ideal way of thinking about society, society in which no one can have power over anyone else. In *Mausoleum*, two men yell out angry texts by Bakunin. The cymbalom in the piece is, in the first place, a metaphor for East European music and, in addition, it has a psychological and political function. In *Mausoleum*, I have used many hoquets, in which eight horns are divided into two groups. These sections are very difficult to play. To keep everyone together, I have added an important cymbalom part. You see this in the stage set-up; the horns are sitting on either side of the cymbalom.

The idea of letting the accents in the strings be articulated, doubled to a large extent by struck strings, is one of Stravinsky's original ideas for the orchestration of *Les Noces*. I must admit that I had forgotten. I had read about it in the late seventies, when I was working on a book on Stravinsky with Elmer Schönberger. I only remembered it once *Vermeer* was completed. Stravinsky also wanted to write a version of *Les Noces* for strings and piano and perhaps he also had cymbaloms in mind. He did use them in the unfinished 1919 version, with harmonium, pianola and percussion.

Because of the chosen instruments, the low notes in *Vermeer* are problematic. There are no low voices in the singing, but also scarcely any in the orchestra. There are two double basses, but no trombones, and no bass guitar which, in the last twenty years, have been practically unavoidable in my music. I don't like bassoons; I find them too strikingly classical – just like clarinets (and I'm not crazy about *them* either). They mix too well with other instruments – they are orchestral whores. The other whores of the orchestra, the horns, are good, I think. No-one should have to be completely against flexibility. So I have two horns. They have the same quality of being friends with everyone, but they can also be boring, like the untroubled pop-pop-pop I mentioned before. In addition to the double basses there are low clarinets – the bass, and especially the contrabass, varieties that don't sound like clarinets.

The wind instruments are actually the singers of the orchestra. They also use air to produce sound and they have to breathe.

SCENE 1

Writing to Vermeer begins with a direct reference to its source: Cage's *Six Melodies*:

The quotation with which the opera begins is much slower than the original, the tempo is a quarter of the original:

In addition to this, two things are important. I am very sensitive to good placing of bass notes. In this case I have added a pedal point, a long, held bass note, to the whole first piece. I am not completely sure I was aware of it while I was composing it, but this is a reference to the two great operas which begin with a pedal point: Bach's *St. John* and *St. Matthew Passions*. In general, I would advise against beginning works with a pedal point because you are constantly postponing the beginning. The pedal point is more appropriate for an 'imposing finale'. The bass note which, however, can also be found in the soprano, sweeps away every harmonic rhythm because all the harmonies become transitional chords fulfilling the same harmonic function. A famous example of an extremely successful sustained bass note at the beginning of a piece is the beginning of Mozart's Symphony in G minor. The bass note remains on G for two bars too long, before he follows the harmony of the melody to F sharp.

Bach, too, uses the sustained bass note very elegantly. He has all sorts of profound reasons for so doing. The sustained bass note suggests something like acquiescence when faced with an inevitable destiny.

After John Cage, we hear the following:

When I was a bit further on in the composition, I looked back at what I had done. I saw that I had already composed 'Mein junges Leben' without knowing it (see * in the musical example on the previous page). Then I thought: "If you just do your best, something good will come out of it."

Soon, the children appear on the stage. In Vermeer's household, ten to twelve children were running round and they also appear in the opera. There are two parts which are sung by four children's voices, so both parts are doubled. They were astonishing. The sound of children's voices fitted in very well.

I really like singers who sing like children. Classical singers (even in contemporary music) are generally much too articulated and much too 'beautiful'. Each note is eaten up and spat out again. You hear this in instrumental music too. I once heard some uninteresting music from about 1820 on a car radio. The way it was played was so delicate that it sounded like a real masterpiece. I quickly guessed what was going on; the piece was written by a famous master and so everyone immediately thinks that it is a masterpiece. All those famous composers wrote bad pieces too. Schubert is a special case, but Beethoven had many small commissions which paid well.

These children just *sing* – that's why I like it so much. The music is, I just hope, beautiful enough; you don't need to make it any more beautiful than it is.

If you go and listen to it soon,[†] you would do better to follow the libretto than the score. My music sounds better than it looks. Moreover, many of the musical details can only be explained from the libretto, especially in the second half.

Three words are very important: 'light', 'blue' and 'love' get a special, I would almost say, manneristic treatment. Each has its own motif and a harmonic transition which is, in general, prepared by a composed ritenuto. By this I mean that it is not the conductor who makes it slow down; it is already written into the music.

SCENE 2

The second scene is a sort of scherzo. The beat of the entire bar (3/8) is ♩. = 61, much slower than the first scene, which has a beat of ♩ = 92. With this short 3/8 bar you can write music which sounds fast but which has a slow beat. In the second scene, the harmonic rhythm is much quicker than in the first. Each bar has at least one harmonic change, in all sorts of different places. The semiquaver is the pulse for the second scene. It is introduced in the low instruments. In scene 2, the singing becomes slower. Then, after the introduction of the children, the singers sing notes that last the whole bar while the clarinets play six notes to a bar – so the pulse is six times as fast.

The appearance of the third main character, the young model, is very important in the second scene. She is accompanied by completely new material – high, repeated chords. She only appears after twelve minutes, a trick I learnt from classical and romantic opera. The hero or heroine can't appear immediately, but only after a time, so that you have high expectations. One of the reasons that I composed this character with pleasure is that I found a young Canadian singer who looked like a girl in a Vermeer painting – Barbara Hannigan. I met her by chance five or six years ago in Toronto. Someone went to a concert in which she appeared and I went along too. First we heard real modern music, with a Darmstadt ensemble, and then this amazing singer. Later, she came to the opera class in The Hague and now she has a career singing Mozart and stuff in Salzburg. She is very intelligent and has a lot of experience with new music. Luckily she was free at the time of *Vermeer*. She is young but almost world-famous,

---

[†] After this talk, a recording of the first scene of *Writing to Vermeer* was played.
[112] The famous 'Queen of the Night' aria, from Mozart's *The Magic Flute*, contains a few very high notes.

because she can sing the Queen of the Night[112] with the high F (which actually doesn't interest me very much).

My models of wonderful singing are Jacques Demy's sung films, the music for which is by Michel Legrand. I rate him just as highly as Ennio Morricone. In 1964 he wrote his first film score, *Les parapluies de Cherbourg* [*The Umbrellas of Cherbourg*]. The film featured film actors – it was one of Catherine Deneuve's first parts – but the score was recorded first, sung by people associated with the Swingle Singers who were still known as Les Double Six at that time. This way of singing stems much more from the text than from the music. They sing legato and non-vibrato very well, just like normal singers, and that has actually always been my model.

Saskia's melodies are completely different from those of the two other women in *Vermeer*. They are more tonal, you could say: childlike.

She is also a lot younger than the wife and the mother-in-law. I now realise that Saskia's material is much closer to the old folk songs because of its simplicity.

The end of the scene is important because here I make a transition from this to the following scene, so that the end of one scene is also the beginning of the next.

Scenes 3 and 4

As I have already said, John Cage's *Sixteen Dances* form the model for scenes 3 and 4. The musical entrée of the singers in the third scene is an interruption of the Cage processes in the orchestra, just like the tapes by Michel van der Aa. During scene 3, the orchestra becomes tense and the musical drama begins.

The first music which turns up then is a melody by my brother Jurriaan, from his *Magnificat*, a wonderful aria for soprano. Both of my brothers died approximately one year before I started on *Vermeer*. Jurriaan wrote this piece in the fifties, after he had returned from America. He had studied there from 1949 to 1951. When I went to Berio in Milan, I took it with me on tape. I really loved that piece and I listened to it and played it often. The wonderful melody in the soprano (very gentle in Jurriaan's piece), I let it flourish in *Vermeer*, very loudly, like a homage to him, and also to a particular aesthetic from my youth.

In the last part of the third scene, new material appears. The Cage material seems to fade away, but comes back in the fourth scene. The connection between the end of scene 3 and the beginning of scene 4 is important to me. This is where the mirror is which creates a link between the beginning and the end of the entire opera. As Machaut says in one of his Rondeaux: "Ma fin est mon commencement" ["My end is my beginning"]. About two-fifths of the second half of the opera consists of remembered material. The interruptions on tape become increasingly more important and violent. And so it becomes increasingly strange that the women in their letters do not react to the events in the interruptions.

Because of the mirror, scene 4 has no overture. In place of this, there is a long orchestral passage about half way through the scene. This tense music is especially important for what follows. It is not film music but it does suggest a lot of action. This immense amount of sound in the orchestra prepares you for the most important silence in the opera. This is an old law of composition: if you want to create a marvellous intimate moment, you must first make a lot of noise.

In this central moment in the opera, at the golden section, I had first thought that Saskia would sing and play 'Mein junges Leben hat ein End' on stage on the harpsichord in Sweelinck's setting without the orchestra. Barbara Hannigan plays the piano well, so she could have done it. But director Saskia Boddeke found this too 'naturalistic'. It didn't fit in with her 'concept'. Eventually, we had a harpsichord at the side of the stage; Barbara didn't play it herself. I can tell you in confidence that I have improved Sweelinck by changing a few notes in the accompaniment.

There follows, immediately afterwards, the most silent interruption in the opera. Here I wanted to have the sound of a Sunday morning in Delft in Vermeer's time – what you would hear when Saskia opens the window. You hear children's voices, the soft lapping of water around a rowing boat and a church clock chiming ten times. This 'silence' is actually more profound than no sound at all.

SCENES 5 AND 6

Just like scene 2, scene 5 is in a different tempo, with a quicker momentum in 3/8 time. This scene contains the melody 'Malle Sijmen', so here Déodat de Sévérac joins in. In the last scene, new material is again introduced. The music becomes more chromatic and uses more counterpoint. You might call it Expressionist. This brought me to Schoenberg, who found it necessary to indicate which was the principal musical voice ('Hauptstimme'). I have adopted the sign he used for this:

$\vdash$

He also introduced a sign for the second most important voice, the 'Nebenstimme':

At the beginning of scene 6 I adopted these two signs.

After the last interruption by Michel van der Aa's electronic music, Saskia comes back on stage as though she has no idea what's going on. She sings her 'naive' music from the second scene. Fairly soon afterwards you hear a new motif consisting of groups of repeated notes. I suspect that that is an old opera tradition – the Grim Reaper is knocking at the door. It is a sort of fate motif:

In the panic of the last few minutes, Catharina sings:

This is from *The Rite of Spring*. Shortly afterwards, the orchestra plays two bars from the last dance of *The Rite of Spring*. Now, you may say that this is therefore a quotation from the *Rite* too, but I regard it as a quotation from my previous opera *Rosa*, in which I already quoted this fragment. This double quoting is comparable with what Catharina sang in the preceding scene:

This is a melody from *Rosa*, but in *Rosa* it is a little Brahms waltz. Whilst I was composing this scene, *Rosa* was revived by De Nederlandse Opera, so I constantly had rehearsals for *Rosa*. It would have been very easy to keep it out of my new work, but I decided not to do that. We all have to deal with these sorts of amusing snippets which are running around in our heads. You must enjoy them and use them if it suits you.

The ending reminds you of the beginning of the opera, but here the music is much more dramatic. At the end of the opera, the whole stage is under water. This is one of the most effective things in the production. The water supply system in the Lincoln Center in New York was not sufficient for the amount of water that was needed for this. This was only one of the practical difficulties. Three pumps are needed to pump the water continually. Moreover, where do you put all that water on the stage? How do you get rid of it? How do you heat it, because there are people moving through it so it must be at body temperature. In New York, six or seven Netherlands engineers were kept busy changing the entire water supply system in the Lincoln Center.

At a particular moment in the score, the noise of the water drowns out the music. Because of the flooding, the last scene is one minute shorter than in my plan. The transition from the orchestra and the singing to Michel van der Aa's tape is flawless, because he started the tape with material from my music.

Irony

When I was your age, I did not believe anything that any teacher said. I did not want to be part of a group of people who listened to the same person. This deep feeling, not so much of individualism as anarchism, has never completely left me. I think that it springs from the thought that you always have to change everything. I don't want to listen to anyone else because I think that I have to do it better myself. But in order to do things well, you naturally have to keep your eyes and ears open. As a composer you listen to everything which is even slightly interesting.

This feeling of opposition to what your mother tells you to do, is still deeply embedded in me. For this reason I don't want to be a teacher who tells you what is better and what you must do, but in the meantime that is what I have constantly been doing.

Life is full of such contradictions. We all have to recognise a world which has all sorts of limitations. You must find an answer on all levels – personal, social, political. In different cultures, religion has for a long time helped to determine attitudes to such questions. Philosophy is related to this. The Greek philosophers already used a term that is central to my approach to life: irony.

This does not mean: make jokes. I never do that, even when I am making jokes. On the other hand, when I say something very serious, I am not always serious. Originally, irony was a technique used in rhetoric, namely, saying the opposite from what you mean to make it very clear what you *do* mean. This concept developed in literature. In the books on the dialectics of irony (I can heartily recommend the two by D. C. Muecke[113]) you constantly find Shakespeare's name. Irony reappeared in philosophy at the time of your beloved compatriot and fellow-composer Frédéric Chopin. Around 1800 young philosophers were considering the theories of people such as Kant. They introduced the word irony, not in the sense of making jokes or saying the opposite of what you mean, but anticipating the development of Hegel's dialectic theory. Hegel says that things always have an antithesis. From this, tension arises which brings a new thesis and a new antithesis and which ultimately, we hope, leads to a better world. People such as Schlegel and Fichte, deeply rooted in irony, make it much more complex. Hegel was mistaken in his positive approach to the future of the world. According to Schlegel and Fichte, it is much more painful because we can't understand things if we do not accept that everything is contradictory in itself. Schlegel said: "Mit der Ironie ist durchaus nicht zu scherzen." – you can't fool around with irony at all.[114] This is a good approach to the subject. The same man said: "We can't be certain of anything in the world, because everything in society can also be its own antithesis, except one thing: that we will die." As you become older you become interested in this subject because you then notice that life is much shorter than you thought. That is, I think, what Schlegel meant by dramatic irony and now I have ended up thinking about life and composing. That is not dramatic. It is more a liberating and open approach to the world and to life. It just makes me an optimistic person.

[113] D. C. Muecke, *The Compass of Irony* (London and New York: Methuen, 1969 / 1980) and *Irony*, The Critical Idiom Series, Vol. 13 (London: Methuen, 1970).
[114] Friedrich Schlegel, *Über die Unverständlichkeit* [*On the Incomprehensible*], (1801).

APPENDICES
& INDEX

Bibliography

Selected works that have *not* been included in this book

DE VOLKSKRANT

Louis Andriessen, Luigi Nono, *Intoleranza '60*, de Volkskrant 1961?

Louis Andriessen, ' "Lulu in La Scala". Alban Berg no match for Verdi. Italians know nothing but their *bel canto*', de Volkskrant, 2-3-1963

Louis Andriessen, 'Strange happenings at the ballet premiere', *de Volkskrant* 4-5-1963
    Festival of contemporary music in Venice: The Dancers' Workshop Company with the ballet *Esposizione* (music Luciano Berio, choreography Ann Halprin, texts Edoardo Sanguineti) (= *Laborintus II*)

Louis Andriessen, 'Opera with spoken chorus in "La piccola Scala". Luciano Berio in the company of Purcell', *de Volkskrant* 25-5-1963
    Henry Purcell, *Dido and Aeneas* and Luciano Berio, *Passaggio*

Louis Andriessen, 'Experimenting with film: sniffing the wind...', *de Volkskrant* 10-1-1964
    On the experimental film festival at Knokke

Louis Andriessen, 'Berlin: contemporary art', *de Volkskrant* 6-2-1965
    Modern Theatre on Small Stages, Living Theatre, Compagnie Jorge Lavelli with works by Kenneth Brown, Peter Weiss, Witold Gombrowicz, Vladimir Majakovski

DE GIDS

Louis Andriessen, 'Time in contradiction', *De Gids*, 1968 / 8 pp. 178-181
    On his piece *Contra Tempus*

WIDESPREAD ARTICLES

Louis Andriessen, 'Composing for "de maatregel"' In *te elfder ure 19, brecht en het leerstuk*, 1975, vol 22, no. 22, pp. 429-446. German translation:

Brechts Modell der Lehrstücke, Zeugnisse, Diskussion, Erfahrungen. Frankfurt, Suhrkamp, 1976, pp. 362-383

Louis Andriessen, 'A few observations on music theatre, with reference to "Matthew Passion"'. In *Raster 3*, 1977 on music theatre, pp. 110-116

Louis Andriessen / Elmer Schönberger, 'Composing: a lesson. Text of a television programme by Hans Hulscher on Louis Andriessen'. In *Muziek & Dans*, March 1979

Louis Andriessen, 'straight through culture'. In *Straight through culture.* Amsterdam, De Balie / Rijksakademie, 1990, pp. 57-64

Louis Andriessen, 'Reinbert, a little garden chair and the American connection'. In Peter Peters (ed.), *Searching for the as yet unheard. 20 years Schoenberg Ensemble.* Amsterdam, International Theatre & Film Books, 1995, pp. 108-114

BOOKS

Louis Andriessen / Elmer Schönberger, *The Apollonian Clockwork. On Stravinsky.* Amsterdam: De Bezige Bij, 1983

Frits van der Waa (compilation), *What makes Andriessen tick*, Amsterdam, De Bezige Bij, 1993. With contributions from J. Bernlef, Marinus Boezem, David Dramm, Peter Greenaway, Edward Harsh, Pay Uun Hiu, Steve Martland, Karin Melis, Willem Jan Otten, Elmer Schönberger, Johanneke van Slooten, Jacq Vogelaar, Frits van der Waa

Maija Trochimczyk (ed.), *The Music of Louis Andriessen.* Studies in Contemporary Music and Culture. New York: Routledge, 2002

VIDEOS

Louis Andriessen / Peter Greenaway, *M is for Man, Music, Mozart*, 1991. Artifax films for Avro, BBC TV and RM Associates

Louis Andriessen / Peter Greenaway, *Rosa – The Death of a Composer* (television adaptation), 1994. Kasander Film Company, Rotterdam

Frank Scheffer, *Tao – The Road*, 1998. Allegri Film, Amsterdam

Louis Andriessen / Hal Hartley, *The New Math(s)*, 2000. True Fiction for the BBC and Pipeline films in association with the NPS

List of musical examples

Index

Biographical information

Louis Andriessen (1939) is one of the most important composers alive today. As a teacher at the Royal Dutch Conservatoire at The Hague, he was, and continues to be, a mentor to many young composers, both in the Netherlands and abroad. Outside of the Netherlands he teaches at a number of academic institutions, including Yale and Princeton universities.

Mirjam Zegers (1965) has been following the music of Louis Andriessen since the early eighties, when she was studying Dutch at Nijmegen. She wrote articles, amongst others, on the opera *Rosa* for De Nederlandse Opera, was editor-in-chief of *Mens en Melodie* and now works with Donemus / Muziekgroep Nederland.

Clare Yates was born in London and was educated in Manchester and Pembroke College, Cambridge, where she obtained a degree in German and Dutch. After studying at the College of Law in York, she qualified as a solicitor and now works in London.